TELEVISION POLICIES OF THE LABOUR PARTY
1951–2001

D0139616

CASS SERIES: BRITISH POLITICS AND SOCIETY
Series Editor: Peter Catterall
ISSN: 1467-1441

Social change impacts not just upon voting behaviour and party identity but also upon the formulation of policy. But how do social changes and political developments interact? Which shapes which? Reflecting a belief that social and political structures cannot be understood either in isolation from each other or from the historical processes which form them, this series will examine the forces that have shaped British society. Cross-disciplinary approaches will be encouraged. In the process, the series will aim to make a contribution to existing fields, such as politics, sociology and media studies, as well as opening out new and hitherto-neglected fields.

Peter Catterall (ed.), *The Making of Channel 4*

Brock Millman, *Managing Domestic Dissent in First World War Britain*

Peter Catterall, Wolfram Kaiser and Ulrike Walton-Jordan (eds), *Reforming the Constitution: Debates in Twentieth-Century Britain*

Brock Millman, *Pessimism and British War Policy, 1916–1918*

Adrian Smith and Dilwyn Porter (eds), *Amateurs and Professionals in Post-war British Sport*

Archie Hunter, *A Life of Sir John Eldon Gorst: Disraeli's Awkward Disciple*

Harry Defries, *Conservative Party Attitudes to Jews, 1900–1950*

Virginia Berridge and Stuart Blume (eds), *Poor Health: Social Inequality before and after the Black Report*

Stuart Ball and Ian Holliday (eds), *Mass Conservatism: The Conservatives and the Public since the 1880s*

Rieko Karatani, *Defining British Citizenship: Empire, Commonwealth and Modern Britain*

Des Freedman, *Television Policies of the Labour Party, 1951–2001*

TELEVISION POLICIES
OF THE
LABOUR PARTY
1951–2001

HE
8700.9
G7F73
2003
VAN

DES FREEDMAN

Goldsmiths College, University of London

Foreword by
ANTHONY SMITH

FRANK CASS
LONDON · PORTLAND, OR

First published in 2003 in Great Britain by
FRANK CASS PUBLISHERS
Chase House, 47 Chase Side, Southgate
London N14 5BP

and in the United States of America by
FRANK CASS PUBLISHERS
c/o ISBS, 920 NE 58th Avenue, Suite 300
Portland, Oregon, 97213-3786

Website: www.frankcass.com

Copyright © 2003 D. Freedman

British Library Cataloguing in Publication Data

Freedman, Des
  Television policies of the Labour Party, 1951–2001. – (Cass series. British
politics and society)
  1. Labour Party (Great Britain) – Platforms 2. Television broadcasting
policy – Great Britain – History
  I. title
  384.5'5'0941

ISBN 0-7146-5455-8 (cloth)
ISBN 0-7146-8387-6 (paper)
ISSN 1467-1441

Library of Congress Cataloging-in-Publication Data

Freedman, Des, 1962–
  Television policies of the Labour Party, 1951–2001 / Des Freedman; with a
foreword by Anthony Smith.
    p.   cm. – (British politics and society)
  Includes bibliographical references and index.
  ISBN 0-7146-5455-8 (cloth) – ISBN 0-7146-8387-6 (paper)
  1. Television broadcasting policy – Great Britain. 2. Television –
Deregulation – Great Britain. 3. Labour Party (Great Britain) I. Title.
II. Series.
  HE8700.9.G7F73 2003
  384.55'4'094109045–dc21

2003043888

*All rights reserved. No part of this publication may be reproduced, stored in or introduced
into a retrieval system or transmitted in any form or by any means, electronic, mechanical,
photocopying, recording or otherwise, without the prior written permission of the publisher
of this book.*

Typeset by FiSH Books, London
Printed in Great Britain by MPG Books Ltd, Victoria Square, Bodmin, Cornwall

Contents

Foreword

Labour governments were in power for only 15 of the 50 years covered by this book and in those years enacted none of the historical measures which shaped the forms and impact of television during the two emergent generations of the medium. During those years no Labour government sought to overturn the measures of the administration which preceded it – though sometimes threatened to do so. Yet television, together with all of the other new communication industries, was the constant subject of policy discussion within the Labour Party, most of it instigated from outside, in trades unions, *ad hoc* industry groups, public pressure groups, sympathetic newspapers and by individuals.

Television seemed to present the Labour Party with a challenge to its basic tenets: it was not susceptible to nationalization in the classic manner; its workers generally benefited in levels of pay from the great profits of the principal employers; the licensing system of commercial television enabled people to rise from shop floor to employer status relatively easily. Labour governments even refrained from taxing it as enthusiastically as Conservative ones. Moreover, some of the wealthiest of television employers were ardent Labour and union supporters. The BBC, though arguably the exemplar of public corporations, its structures suffused with the genius of inter-war Labour, was the object of continual Labour distrust. Threatened and cajoled by Wilson, Crossman, Benn and other Labour ministers, it survived intact, together with the licence fee, its lifeblood funding mechanism, which Labour policy paper after Labour policy paper denounced as regressive and a 'poll tax'. Television induced a form of paranoia in Labour ministers, more seriously and more frequently than in Conservatives. But, taken over half a century, we see British television as having been subject, essentially, to bipartisan policy-making as it passed through all the stages from birth to maturity, from innovation to saturation.

None the less, it tended to be through the Labour Party and its surrounding movement that new issues were worked through and new ideas thrown up. All of Labour's historical ideology was put to the test – one might say tested to destruction – when confronting the circumstances of an expanding television medium. Nationalization, workers' participation in management, freedom of expression, institutional autonomy, the intellectual issues of objectivity and impartiality and their policing, and the underlying issues of access, accountability and control – all of these were dissected, 'resolved', hammered into programmes and policies and then generally, though not wholly, abandoned, in and around the Labour Party. Labour had surely something of historic importance to say, for instance, about reconciling the rights of television workers to control their working circumstances with the right of the wider public to enjoy the information and entertainment it wanted; yet the arguments of the 1970s about these matters leave us with no legislative heritage. Nothing *happened*.

History can point to only one actual institution that can be attributed to the actions of Labour and that is the Open University, much admired and imitated around the globe; but in the end it is an institution of education not of entertainment, and its television dimension, never crucial to its functioning, faded away as new and more effective media became available.

The technologies of mass communication have brought about great challenges to the political and intellectual left. The mass press, cinema, radio and television have been the products of capital but have been designed to be highly attractive to the mass working-class viewer or consumer. Ideologues of the left for a time constructed theories which tried to analogize the new mass culture to the more traditionally defined forms of exploitation. Cultural enthralment was seen as a substitute for, or an extension of, economic exploitation. Nye Bevan, after the Labour defeat of 1959, famously prophesied that Labour would return to power when enthralment by television had run its course. Much of the way in which left intellectuals rejected rather than espoused the mass media can be attributed to the work of the Frankfurt School in the 1930s, which argued rather disdainfully against the cultural influence of the cinema and the mass press. But by the time that the events recounted in this book began to unfold all the European parties of the left were having to confront the fact that the latest 'consumer' stage of capitalism was raising living standards and had in fact come to depend greatly upon television and other forms of advertising. Class consciousness was dissolving as the new images of the television medium began to flicker in every continental home, and it was possible to lay the blame on television but impossible to work out the precise line of causation. The influence of television was everywhere, though extremely difficult to calculate and to separate out from all of the other strands of change.

Perhaps it is the special and peculiar form that British pluralism has taken that explains the combination of Labour's intellectual ferment with its inactivity. For in Britain a mixed system was evolving – a Third Way, *avant la lettre*, between commercial and public systems: the BBC eschewed advertising, while ITV made unbelievably large commercial profits and Channel 4 advertised but without profits, receiving a proportion of ITV's advertising revenue. Each element had been founded on the basis of its own separate pot of money, avoiding neck-and-neck competition, each element of the system with its own cultural remit and its own way of addressing the audience.

Towards the end of this half-century of policy-making the pluralist consensus was broken up by deliberate government action. The 15 companies of the ITV system were openly encouraged to amalgamate – eventually perhaps into a single company – and a fifth terrestrial channel was opened up, to suit no particular cultural initiative, but rather to ensure direct competition for advertising between the (now three) commercial terrestrial channels. It was even made possible for foreign media concerns to enter the new competitive British media economy.

Meanwhile, of course, new means of delivery of images had arrived, cable and satellite, video and the internet, and a wholly new stage of globalized media culture appeared to have arrived. Appeared, one must still say, for despite the now abundant signals the main pillars of the pluralist system survive, unhappily forced into often uncomfortable and half-comprehended competition. And in the wake of these far-reaching changes we are told, with authority, that the pluralist solution that lasted from the 1970s until the 1990s cannot survive. There is renewed talk of forcing the BBC to take advertising and to share or abandon the compulsory licence fee. It is hard to tell whether this emanates from some form of historical necessity or merely out of the ideological triumphalism of the economic liberal right, whose vision has been adopted enthusiastically by the leaders of New Labour.

It is good that this book has been written, to help keep in mind the long evolution of the debate about television within the Labour Party. For in the era of New Labour (which lies mainly outside the compass of the book), policy has taken turns that would have been incomprehensible to most of the people who have argued and campaigned about the organization of television since the 1950s. The causes over which so many of my contemporaries wrangled now seem as hazy as the Corn Law agitation and the arguments as hard to reignite in one's mind. Such are the movements of political time.

Anthony Smith
President, Magdalen College, Oxford
February 2003

Series Editor's Preface

The first book in this series scrutinized the early years of Channel 4. Although established by a Conservative government, as is demonstrated here, Channel 4 grew out of a ferment of ideas, especially on the left, in the late 1960s and 1970s. The critique, as Des Freedman explains, was that powerful interests in the media duopoly of ITV and BBC at the time worked to screen out alternative voices from the airwaves. The need was for a mechanism to 'democratize' broadcasting.

Thirty years on, the duopoly is gone. Whether the 1970s radicals would feel much satisfaction with what has come in its stead is, however, very much open to doubt. More channels do not seem to have lead to dramatically more choice. Current affairs broadcasting in particular seems to have been marginalized and trivialized, as the example of *Panorama* testifies. Meanwhile, Channel 4 has scored its biggest success with a voyeuristic reality soap, ironically, given the hopes the channel initially inspired on the left, entitled *Big Brother*. This, in turn, spawned a wave of imitations. The changes of the past 30 years, in other words, do not conspicuously seem to have let a thousand flowers bloom as far as programming is concerned. What we have seen, driven perhaps as much by technology as by the policy preferences of either major political party, is not the promotion of alternative voices but the workings of a particular form of competition. Cheap formulae, such as game shows and the proliferation of the docu-soaps pioneered by Channel 4, have coincided with a search for ratings in an increasingly cut-throat marketplace.

In theory, of course, a more diversified range of suppliers ought to be offering an equally diversified range of products for the market. However, while the duopoly could carry specialist programmes for sections of that national market – indeed, the advent of Channel 4 in the early 1980s if anything initially extended the range of specialist programmes on offer – commercial pressures, of the kind radicals had once complained about, to aim for a homogenized national rather than segmented market seem to have increased rather than decreased with the growing number of channels. Even the BBC and Channel 4, theoretically insulated from these pressures by their relationship to the state, have not been immune.

While technology, especially the advent of cable and satellite, has made the proliferation of channels possible, European pressures have also had a material effect on the market for television in Britain. In 2000, it might be noted, the European Commission's *Competition Policy Newsletter* praised the UK for introducing competition from the start in the provision of digital television, though this turned out to have a less happy outcome when ITV Digital collapsed in 2002. Nevertheless, this makes the thrust of European policy clear: to encourage competition. Ultimately, despite the recognition that television markets, if only because of language barriers, remain essentially national throughout the European Union, this encouragement of competition is about building the Single Market. For instance, in 2000 the European Court of Justice found against the 'golden shares' introduced in Italy to try to curtail Burlesconi's dominance of the local market on the ground that they conflicted with the objective of securing free movement of capital within the Single Market, a ruling that no doubt had an (unacknowledged) impact on the subsequent framing of the Blair government's Communications Bill.

The literature on Labour's television policies up to this point has tended to portray them as timidly reactive to such pressures. Socialist critiques of the dominance of the television market by powerful interests were tempered, it was argued, long before the advent of European legislation in this area, by a desire on the part of the party leadership not to antagonize these interests. But this, as Des Freedman shows, is to simplify both the intra-party debate and the nature of those interests. It is not just that increasing competition has been seen at different times by both the left and right within the Labour Party as a way of advancing their goals. It is also that the right has, especially under New Labour, come to reject left-wing critiques of media interests as monopolistic and antagonistic, and sought instead, not just accommodation with them, but to structure them in their own interests. As Freedman shows, this process did not start with Blair, although he has arguably been more successful in pursuing it than Harold Wilson. Wilson had little alternative to the duopoly, whereas Blair has had a far more competitive environment with which to threaten media elites, while simultaneously promising them protection against the chill wind of full competition that might be ushered in by a resurgent Conservative Party. For though some competition was introduced in the 1980s, the basic contours of corporate control if anything narrowed through mergers within ITV. And the television industry remains very much a hybrid, with major players such as the BBC and Channel 4 still within the public sector. Such liberalization as is envisaged by the Blair government is unlikely to change that, or to allow a more diverse range of voices onto the airwaves. Until radicals of either right or left achieve a more substantial restructuring of the industry, the corporatist centre seems likely to hold.

Peter Catterall
London

Acknowledgements

This book could not have been written without the invaluable support, advice and choice of mineral water of Peter Goodwin.

I am grateful to all those individuals who took the time to speak to me although I would particularly like to thank James Curran, who is both a player in and a source of information for this story.

I benefited from the patience of all those who helped me in the National Museum of Labour History archive, the British Library of Political and Economic Science, the TUC Library, BBC Written Archives, the Public Record Office and, especially, the treasure trove that was the Independent Television Commission library.

My colleagues in the School of Social Sciences at the University of North London and in the Department of Media and Communications at Goldsmiths College provided me with a stimulating atmosphere in which to do the research. I would also like to thank everyone at New York University in London for providing me with a quiet space in which to finish the book. Peter Catterall was an excellent and highly knowledgeable series editor, to whom I am also grateful.

Most of all I would like to thank my close friends, my father and, above all, Kirstie, for arguing with me all the time. The point of a book like this is to refute the notion that nothing can ever change and to encourage readers to help to build different models – of broadcasting as well as of all other social structures.

Abbreviations

ABPC	Associated British Pictures Corporation
ABS	Association of Broadcasting Staff
ACT	Association of Cinematograph and Allied Technicians
ACTT	Association of Cinematograph, Television and Allied Technicians
AES	Alternative Economic Strategy
AEU	Amalgated Engineering Union
ATV	Anglia Television
BECTU	Broadcasting, Entertainment, Cinematograph, and Theatre Union
BETA	Broadcasting and Entertainment Trades Alliance
BSkyB	British Sky Broadcasting
BT	British Telecom
CBF	*Communicating Britain's Future*
CND	Campaign for Nuclear Disarmament
CPBF	Campaign for Press and Broadcasting Freedom
CQT	Campaign for Quality Television
DCMS	Department of Culture, Media and Sport
DG	director-general
DNH	Department of National Heritage
DTI	Department of Trade and Industry
DTT	digital terrestrial television
EEC	European Economic Community
FCG	Free Communications Group
GLC	Greater London Council
GLEB	Greater London Enterprise Board
GUMG	Glasgow University Media Group
HPC	Home Policy Committee

IBA	Independent Broadcasting Authority
IMF	International Monetary Fund
IPPR	Institute of Public Policy Research
ITA	Independent Television Authority
ITC	Independent Television Commission
ITV	Independent Television
NATKE	National Association of Theatrical, Television and Kine Employees
NATSOPA	National Society of Operative Printers and Assistants
NEC	National Executive Committee
NTC	National Television Council
NTF	National Television Foundation
NVLA	National Viewers and Listeners Association
OBA	Open Broadcasting Authority
OFT	Office of Fair Trading
OU	Open University
PBC	Public Broadcasting Commission
PLP	Parliamentary Labour Party
PMG	postmaster general
POEU	Post Office Engineering Union
PSBC	Public Service Broadcasting Campaign
RPI	Retail Price Index
SCoB	Standing Conference on Broadcasting
SDP	Social Democratic Party
TGWU	Transport and General Workers' Union
TPATM	*The People and the Media*
TUC	Trades Union Congress
TW3	*That Was the Week that Was*
UCS	Upper Clyde Shipbuilders
3G	third-generation

— 1 —

Introduction:
The 'Non-Issue' of Television

For too long the UK's media have been over-regulated and over-protected from competition. Despite this, the last ten years have seen a dramatic increase in the range of voices in the market place. The draft Bill we have published today will liberalise the market, so removing unnecessary regulatory burdens and cutting red tape, but at the same time retain some key safeguards that will protect the diversity and plurality of our media.[1]

These are the words of New Labour culture secretary Tessa Jowell when unveiling the government's draft communications bill in May 2002. The legislation that follows from this will determine the environment in which British television operates for the foreseeable future. It is a future where any remaining commitment to diversity and pluralism is to be facilitated by structures that privilege principles of efficiency, competition and market value. It is a conception of media policy that is likely to transform British broadcasting into an overwhelmingly commercial proposition in the next few years. Since it was first elected in May 1997, the New Labour government has embraced the possibilities of digital and broadband technologies for use by business, education, government and consumers; it is determined to modernize the UK's regulatory framework to adapt to and facilitate the convergence of broadcasting, IT and telecommunications.

This activity appears to stand in stark contrast to both the Labour Party's former opposition to a commercial television system and its indifference or hostility towards innovations in the field of electronic media. With the exception of the Open University, the party has not been *directly* associated with any of the major developments in communications – the launch of ITV, BBC2 and Channels 4 and 5, the development of commercial radio and the go-ahead for cable, satellite and digital systems – all of which have occurred under Conservative administrations.

This is partly due to the fact that the Conservatives have been in government for 35 of the last 50 years but it has also been argued that Labour has traditionally been less interested in transforming the institutions of the British media. Back in 1968, a *Guardian* editorial reflected on the lack of debate on communications policy at Labour's annual conference: 'The subject [of communications] is one on which the Government has no ideas and the party only wishful thoughts.'[2] The trade unionist and future Labour MP, Denis MacShane, wrote in 1987 that, although the party did by now have resolutions routinely passed at conference, 'the Labour Party still has no agreed policy on the media'.[3] In the influential history of UK media by James Curran and Jean Seaton, Curran argues that Labour's instinct is 'to slap a preservation order on the broadcasting system as it now is even on the eve of digital TV. In this sense, it is more conservative with a small "c" than the Conservative Party.'[4]

While these quotes are, of course, highly selective, they never-theless express a widely held view that Labour has tended to defend the status quo when it comes to communications policy. Labour supporters have provided a number of explanations for their party's apparent lack of innovative or proactive policy on the media. Mulgan and Worpole attribute it to the economism of its trade union supporters and argue that 'Labour Party puritanism has failed to understand exactly how liberating ... some patterns of consumer spending [on media] have been'.[5] MacShane blames the influence of Labour-supporting media trade unionists who have consistently prioritized defence of their pay and conditions above programmes for broadcasting reform.[6] Collins and Murroni can find just two official Labour policy statements on the media and explain this in terms of the party's traditional hostility to private ownership and competition which, they argue, is 'fundamentally flawed'.[7]

As this volumes demonstrates, these arguments seriously under-estimate the amount of discussion on the media that has taken place at all levels of the Labour Party. Instead of bemoaning the lack of attention that the party has paid to communications policy, the book seeks to highlight and to analyse the wide-ranging debates that *have* occurred and the numerous policies that have been developed in the past 50 years. What is interesting is not the absence of debate about media policy among Labour supporters but the way in which the many debates on this subject have connected to wider questions about the political aims and objectives of the Labour Party. Communications has never been the most important area of interest for Labour (or indeed Conservative) policymakers but it has illuminated many of the tensions – between left and right, between consolidationists and revisionists, between traditionalists and modernizers and between Old and New Labour – that have proved to be so decisive in the fortunes of the Labour Party.

The object of this volume is not 'mass media' or 'mass communications' policy as a whole but British television policy in particular. The omission of press policy should in no way imply that it lacked importance for the Labour Party. The role of the press has absorbed the minds of party leaders and ordinary members for many years, from concerns about monopolization and anti-Labour bias to proposals for a sympathetic or in-house daily newspaper. Labour governments have initiated two Royal Commissions on the press and the need for press reform has long been discussed at party conferences.[8] This book focuses on broadcasting because it is increasingly seen as the most dominant cultural institution; and on television, as opposed to radio, because the two media have traditionally operated under different policy dynamics with television assuming a much more visible place in public policy debates over the past 50 years.

While there is a rich body of literature on British broadcasting history and policy (most notably Asa Briggs' five-volume history of the BBC quoted throughout this book), there is very little that deals specifically with the impact of political parties on television policy. Existing literature in this area tends to deal either with the relationship between parties and the directly political communications *process*[9] or with a conception of television policy in which party political actors are simply one feature of the general policy environment.[10] While these studies seek to provide an admirably holistic view of the development of television in the UK, they are clearly not written with the singular purpose of identifying the dynamics of specific political actors in their approach to television policy. I therefore apologize in advance for the limited scope of this study, in that Labour's attitude towards particular television programmes, spin doctors, political broadcasts, election campaigning, freedom of information and censorship are almost entirely absent.

E. P. Thompson contends that the historian's task consists of 'the close interrogation of texts and contexts'.[11] In each chapter, I frame the analysis of specific Labour television policies with a brief consideration of the key political, economic or social conflicts of the particular period. It would be extremely short-sighted to consider Labour's approach to television in the 1950s without a discussion of revisionism and the 'embourgoisement' thesis. It would also paint an incomplete picture to examine the 1960s without acknowledging the importance of the balance-of-payments crisis, the 1970s without tackling the general political shift to the left, or the 1980s and 1990s without focusing on the increasing hegemony of pro-market arguments inside the Labour leadership. There are additionally some general themes and questions on which the book seeks to reflect, for example:

• To what extent has the Labour Party pursued a coherent and consistent approach to television policy since 1951?
• In what ways have Labour's television policies differed from those of the Conservatives?
• To what extent has communications policy been used as a means of 'rebranding' and 'repositioning' the party since 1951?
• Which constituencies of interest (i.e. trade unions, parliamentary leadership, intellectuals, the 'left' or the 'right') have been most influential on the development of the party's television policies?
• To what extent have Labour's television policies been conditioned by the party's relationship with media entrepreneurs?
• To what extent has the Labour Party acted as a vehicle for the transformation of broadcasting institutions and structures?

This book attempts to evaluate the Labour Party's approach to television policy-making through reflecting on the project of 'Labourism' over the last 50 years and, as such, is intended to contribute to an understanding of both British broadcasting and of the possibilities and limitations of the Labour Party. It highlights the possibilities of imaginative, socialist approaches to television policy that have been proposed by sections of the Labour Party and the ultimate undoing and neutralization of these approaches. My aim, as a socialist outside the Labour Party, is not at all to pour scorn on the attempts by socialists inside the party to reform and democratize television, but to begin to explain why these valiant attempts have met with such resistance and, in the end, with such little success in implementing radical policies for television. At a time when a Labour government is determined to deploy market forces to shape our social and cultural environment, it is a debate worth having.

NOTES

1.   T. Jowell, quoted in Department of Trade and Industry press release, 'Draft Bill Overhauls Legal Framework for Communications Industry', 7 May 2002, P/2002/274.

2.   *Guardian*, editorial on Labour Party conference, 3 October 1968.
3.   D. MacShane, 'Media Policy and the Left', in J. Seaton and B. Pimlott (eds), *The Media in British Politics* (Aldershot: Avebury, 1987), p. 218.
4.   J. Curran and J. Seaton, *Power Without Responsibility*, 5th edn (London: Routledge, 1997), p. 355.
5.   G. Mulgan and K. Worpole, *Saturday Night or Sunday Morning: From Arts to Industry – New Forms of Cultural Policy* (London: Comedia, 1986), p. 12.
6.   MacShane, 'Media Policy and the Left', p. 226.
7.   R. Collins and C. Murroni, *New Media, New Policies* (Cambridge: Polity, 1996), p. 5.
8.   See, for example, J. Curran (ed.), *The British Press: A Manifesto* (London: Macmillan, 1978) and T. Baistow, *Fourth-Rate Estate* (London: Comedia, 1985) for critiques of and proposals for press reform from within the labour movement.
9.   Texts on party political communications in the UK include P. Hennessy, D. Walker and M. Cockerell, *Sources Close to the Prime Minister* (London: Macmillan, 1985), M. Cockerell, *Live from Number 10: The Inside Story of Prime Ministers and Television* (London: Faber & Faber, 1989) and M. Scammell, *Designer Politics* (London: Macmillan, 1995).
10. See A. Briggs, *Sound and Vision:* vol. IV of *The History of Broadcasting in the United Kingdom* (Oxford: Oxford University Press, 1979), A. Briggs, *Competition, 1955–1974:* vol. V of *The History of Broadcasting in the United Kingdom* (Oxford: Oxford University Press, 1995), Curran and Seaton, *Power Without Responsibility* and A. Crisell, *An Introductory History of British Broadcasting* (London: Routledge, 1997) for general histories of UK broadcasting.
11. E. P. Thompson, *Customs in Common* (Harmondsworth: Penguin, 1993), p. 431.

2

Labour and the Post-War Boom, 1951–64

LABOUR IN OPPOSITION, 1951–55

The Labour Party entered a long period of opposition that was marked by growing internal division. Labour leaders like Clement Attlee and Herbert Morrison were determined to downplay the importance of public ownership and 'attempted to throw off their commitments to further nationalisation as gracefully as they were able'.[1] The call for further nationalization would simply be a barrier to the urgent task of repositioning Labour as a national, and not a class, party and undermine its embracing of a mixed economy and social and political consensus.

These views were nourished and developed by writers organized around the journal *Socialist Commentary* in the late 1940s. Drawn from the right of the party and influenced by Labour figures like Evan Durbin and Douglas Jay, the journal presented an early example of 'revisionist' ideas which came to fruition in the booming economic conditions of the 1950s. One of the first influential pieces of revisionist writing was the Labour MP Anthony Crosland's contribution to *New Fabian Essays*, a compilation of articles published in 1952 to provoke debate about Labour's ideological mission and political strategy. Crosland argued that increases in national and personal income had confounded the Marxist prediction of economic crisis and that we had entered a new kind of 'pluralist' society in which '[i]ndividual property rights no longer constitute the essential basis of economic and social power'. Furthermore, as pure laissez-faire capitalism is challenged by state intervention and political and economic power is diffused, the rise of a technical and professional state has fragmented the existing class structure.[2]

The consequence for Crosland was that Labour's socialism should no longer concern itself with questions of redistribution along class lines but with equality and common interest. In place of extending welfare and nationalization, Crosland called for battles to increase a sense of participation and belonging in society: for example, more consultation in industry, more worker representation on boards, and agreements requiring companies to act responsibly towards their workers and communities. Crosland intended this as an attack on what he saw as the conservatism of the Labour leadership. The new 'pluralist society' required an urgent reconsideration of Labour's approach to questions of profit, public ownership, equality and the role of the state. 'The revisionists', according to Geoffrey Foote, 'were in revolt against Corporate Socialism and wished to release the radical energies locked up in the Labour Party by an outmoded class outlook'.[3] In the figure of Hugh Gaitskell, later to become Labour leader, the revisionists were to have a crucial influence on the party for the rest of its years in opposition.

From the left of the party, another group of MPs and activists were in revolt against the conservatism of the leaders and sought to protect the existing links of the party with the working-class movement and social ownership. The 'Bevanites', as those around Nye Bevan (the minister of health in the 1945 government) were dubbed by the press, provided the most serious and public opposition to the Labour leadership in the 1950s. Bevan attacked the boards of nationalized industries and called for an extension of the principle of industrial democracy. However, while the Bevanites sought a more favourable role for public ownership than that envisaged by either Morrison and the Labour leadership or the growing number of revisionists, they were wedded to parliamentary methods and focused, above all, on internal party reform. 'This was a movement of the ranks to take hold of its executive bodies and organisations to effect a return to radical policies.'[4]

The Bevanites were backed by the *Tribune* newspaper and commanded substantial influence in the constituency Labour parties as well as the trade unions. Their influence peaked at Labour's 1952 conference when Bevanite candidates won six out of the seven constituency seats on the National Executive Committee (NEC) and successfully proposed a resolution extending the range of industries to be nationalized. Throughout the early 1950s, the Bevanites were presented as an organized opposition to the leadership, blocking all attempts to 'modernize' the party and mobilizing the power of the grassroots to defend social ownership.

The reality is somewhat more complex. Resistance took place in the parliamentary arena and rarely spilled over into extra-parliamentary action. Furthermore, the clearest disagreements occurred over foreign and defence issues, particularly over German rearmament and relations with the USA. Ben Pimlott argues that it is 'hard to see fundamental differences between the two sides: Bevan and Crosland shared many opinions. Most of the conflicts were not of principle but of degree'.[5]

Labour failed to shrug off its ideological and organizational problems by the time it lost the 1955 general election. Throughout those early years of opposition, the party demonstrated a range of conflicting attitudes towards the USA, public ownership and private profit, state intervention and the free market. There was consensus on the need for a mixed economy, but the right of the party urged that the ties with the organized working class be loosened while the left argued to maintain these links. Bogdanor attributes Labour's 'years of wilderness' to the contradictions of the party's different constituencies:

> The Left failed to make a coherent and relevant case for nationalisation. The Revisionists failed to wean the party away from its traditional commitments. And those whose primary concern was to make the Labour Party an efficient and radical governing party failed to alter its doctrinal nature.[6]

The result was a programme that failed to inspire any constituency. According to Stephen Haseler, 'the lack of adventure in Labour's proposals was stultifying the Party and frustrating its true radicals on the Right as well as on the Left'.[7] All these positions and problems were played out in Labour's approaches to the debates on the introduction of commercial television to which we now turn.

LABOUR AND THE BATTLE FOR COMMERCIAL TELEVISION

The one million TV sets in use in 1951 were tuned into a single BBC channel. This monopoly was deemed unacceptable by a minority in the ruling Conservative Party who set about 'liberating' British broadcasting through the introduction of competition into television. The broadcasting historian Asa Briggs confirms that 'social change became associated, in consequence, between 1951 and 1955 … with the Conservative Party's policy of "setting the people free"'.[8] Despite an initial reluctance to sanction sponsored or advertising-funded television, most Tory MPs were even more reluctant to sustain a broadcasting monopoly and backed the introduction of a commercial television service in 1955.

The Conservatives were able to break the BBC's television monopoly and introduce commercial television for a number of reasons. H. H. Wilson argues that 'independent television' (ITV) was the product of a well-organized business lobby to unleash commercial forces inside broadcasting.[9] Whale claims that commercial television provided a convenient battleground for a group of Tory MPs desperate to undermine the monopoly principle in British industry and to extend the free market.[10] Seaton suggests that Winston Churchill was reluctant to defend the BBC, having harboured a grudge against the organization since the 1926 General Strike.[11] Briggs, however, emphasizes the compromises made during the passage of the legislation and notes how the eventual structure of commercial television was closely modelled on the BBC in terms of the role of governors and a public-service remit. He criticizes Wilson for undervaluing the parliamentary manoeuvrings with 'their many interesting undercurrents and the ultimate compromises on many points which ensured that even after the end of the BBC's monopoly Britain would still retain within a dual system provision for a single basic approach to the regulation and control of broadcasting'.[12]

The Labour Party was a key part of the broad movement – including religious figures, leading Tories, university vice-chancellors, newspaper editors and Lord Reith, the founder of the BBC – which set out to oppose and compromise commercial television. Labour MPs suggested an all-party conference on broadcasting, argued for a free vote in the legislation and tabled dozens of amendments – all of which were ignored by the Tories. Wilson's account of Labour's involvement, however, stresses the futility of its opposition, because

> it is conceivable that nothing done by either the [previous 1945–51] Labour Government or the proponents of public service broadcasting could have done more than delay the aspirations of those working within the Conservative coalition who consider broadcasting to be primarily a commercial instrument.[13]

Such a simple story fails to do justice to the myriad of positions held, principles argued and compromises negotiated by those around the Labour Party concerning the breaking of the monopoly. Television was not one of the key questions facing the party at the time but the events nevertheless reveal much about the priorities of and tensions between different elements of the party as it attempted to relate to the new economic developments and changing expectations of the early 1950s.

Firstly, it is worth noting that Labour leaders of the time considered television policy in general to be less important than either press policy or political broadcasting. Tony Benn complained in 1953 that the NEC was 'hardly concerned with broadcasting in between elections'.[14] Nye Bevan, according to one of his biographers, 'loathed television, believing that it turned politicians into "pure salesmen – like American politicians", and had never taken the trouble to master its techniques'[15] while Clement Attlee also 'took very little interest in the media'.[16]

This analysis gives a rather false impression of the then Labour leadership's ignorance about media matters given that Attlee and Morrison set up both the 1949 Royal Commission on the Press[17] and the 1951 Beveridge Report on Broadcasting. Yet it was press policy above all which captured the attention of party leaders who were irritated by the fierce criticisms of Conservative-supporting newspapers and worried about the future of a Labour press. At the height of debates over the introduction of commercial television, Labour leaders were still paying particular attention to the importance of newspapers. In 1954, for example, the future Labour leader Hugh Gaitskell tried to persuade Cecil King, proprietor of the *Daily Mirror*, to set up a new right-wing Labour newspaper to counter the influence of *Tribune* and the *New Statesman* in the Labour movement.[18]

The leadership was also interested in taking advantage of new developments in broadcasting for electoral purposes and moved quickly to draw up a policy over political broadcasting and the production of election broadcasts. In May 1950, Morrison set up a confidential Technical Committee on Broadcasting involving ex-journalists like Tony Benn and George Darling to advise on scripts and to prepare Labour leaders for broadcasting appearances.[19] In 1953, Tony Benn prepared a report for the NEC recommending the creation of a 'Joint Broadcasting Committee' to maximize the potential of television appearances by Labour politicians. Benn argued that the party 'should recognize the increased importance of broadcasting and Television and should seek to improve and extend existing techniques'.[20] This emphasis on political broadcasting as opposed to broadcasting policy was reflected in the weight attached to the former and the almost total exclusion of the latter in NEC meetings. The *only* time the NEC discussed its attitude towards commercial television between 1951 and 1955 was in September 1954, when it was forced to consider whether a resolution on the subject could go forward to annual conference. The NEC voted 13–9 to accept the resolution which criticized the Conservatives for introducing commercial television without a mandate from the British public and supported restoring broadcasting to public control with an additional channel. When it reached conference, the resolution was remitted and not commented upon further. The introduction of commercial television was thus never debated by a Labour conference.

However, the NEC had previously discussed policy when approving the party's evidence to the Beveridge Committee on Broadcasting, which the then Labour government had set up in 1949 to make recommendations on the future of the BBC. Labour's evidence was largely uncritical of the BBC and praised its 'tradition of fair comment and the presentation of all opinions on controversial subjects'.[21] It expressed a clear opposition to 'sponsored radio' as being desired only by advertisers, suggested a degree of regional decentralization for radio and opposed a separate corporation for television. This conflicted with the advice supplied to the NEC by George Darling MP, who warned that, given the experience of the BBC, 'a single-monopoly tends to become hide-bound, to work to rigid formulae, stifling initiative and accepting mediocrity as an easy substitute for enterprise'.[22] Labour's evidence did complain, however, of an 'anti-Labour bias' in news programmes 'as a matter of course'[23] and proposed that the BBC deal with this by broadening the field of recruitment to allow for the inclusion of more working-class viewpoints. Substantial reform, it felt, was unnecessary.

Tribune also came to the aid of the BBC. The BBC, it argued, was nothing like major private manufacturing monopolies and cartels where restrictive practices ought to be broken up. 'It is not an irresponsible dictatorship. Its affairs are under constant scrutiny in the press, and are supervised by public servants: that fabled despot, the D-G [director-general] , is not a free agent, but is responsible to the Governors'.[24] What was needed was devolution from London control and increased accountability and democracy in the organization. Both George Darling and Tony Benn suggested internal restructuring to iron out the problems arising from monopoly. Darling proposed four separate broadcasting corporations, 'efficiently manageable units',[25] but saw no need for an overall change in broadcasting policy. Benn's idea to set up four separate boards of management to deal with the 'legitimate objections'[26] to monopoly held by Tory MPs was even praised, though subsequently ignored, by Ness Edwards, the Labour postmaster general (PMG).

Labour's discussions on broadcasting policy in the early 1950s were therefore characterized both by a growing concern with the existence of an organization which held a monopoly of the airwaves but also by a firm defence of that institution. The key problems were identified as administrative and organizational; how to fix what Darling called an 'overgrown machine'.[27] There was little discussion about the political role of the BBC such as the make-up of its governors, its attitude towards the trade union movement, its interpretation of 'cultural unity' and, apart from occasional complaints to the general secretary, the extent of its impartiality.

Beveridge himself expressed harsh criticisms of the BBC's 'Londonization' and elitism, but nevertheless recommended the renewal of the BBC's licence as the most favourable option. Labour was voted out of office before it could pass the legislation, allowing the Conservatives to seize the opportunity for 'reform' and produce a white paper in May 1952 that included one clause relating to the possibility of allowing competition in broadcasting. It was from this time that the battle started and the features of Labour's opposition to commercial television emerged.

The key opponent of the proposed changes was the National Television Council (NTC), established by the Labour MP Christopher Mayhew in June 1953. This was a cross-party campaign whose organizing committee included an impressive array of lords, reverends, entertainment entrepreneurs, two viscounts and a media trade union leader – all united in defence of public service broadcasting. The combined forces of the representatives of entertainment workers and employers, religious and secular bodies, government and opposition made for a high-profile campaign but one in which there were very fragile common interests. For example, leading figures from theatrical producers Prince Littler Productions and the film producers Associated British Pictures Corporation, both of which came to be active in the early years of ITV, were involved in the NTC. Trade union concerns about the impact of commercial television on film technicians' jobs coincided with worries about the moral health of the nation.

The NTC argued that commercial television would not be in the 'national' interest. It avoided all criticisms of the BBC and conducted its campaign around the issues of protecting standards and values. A commercial network was being sought by a minority of 'interested parties' in Parliament and, furthermore, was not even desired by the general public. The NTC's pamphlet, *Britain Unites against Commercial TV*, highlighted a recent Gallup Poll, which showed that 'if the BBC were permitted to provide alternative TV Programmes only ONE IN FIVE British people would want Commercial TV'.[28] Mayhew was particularly concerned not by the commercialization of television per se, but by the increasing 'Americanization' of culture which commercial television would institutionalize. The scale of the American market, he argued, was such that not only would British networks be flooded by vulgar American imports but British commercial programmes would be tailored for export to the American market: 'The danger of this is obvious, not only to our television standards, but to our whole national culture and way of life'.[29]

Labour's public and parliamentary campaign against commercial television echoed many of these strands. Anti-Americanism, an important source of division inside the Labour Party at the time, was virulent. Labour MP Charles Hobson argued that the legislation for ITV 'absolutely stinks of Americanism and American business methods ... hon. Gentlemen will realise that their attitude was entirely wrong for British political standards'.[30] Mayhew claimed that the legislation was a Trojan horse for American business practices and warned that 'we all still underestimate the menace of the impact of Americanism which will come through this Bill'.[31] According to senior Labour MP Herbert Morrison, commercial broadcasting was 'totally against the British temperament, the British way of life and the best or even reasonably good British traditions'.[32]

Labour's central office issued a series of leaflets in 1953 in opposition to commercial television which pursued this twin-track approach of defending national cultural standards and attacking the commercialization of broadcasting. 'Not Fit For Children' screamed the headline of the first and claimed that '[t]his latest proposal is a menace to all our home standards and to the impressionable young minds of our children'. It criticized the 'Conservative TV (too vulgar) policy' and appealed to 'KEEP OUR TV AND RADIO STANDARDS'.[33] The next pamphlet called the Archbishop of York and the Bishop of Coventry as witnesses to the effects of commercial television and promised that '[w]e will resolutely oppose the introduction of commercial TV. This service which is bound to exercise a growing influence on our national life must serve values and purposes which the nation approves – not those which advertising agencies force upon us'.[34]

Labour's exhortation to defend the British way of life was matched by a warning that commercial television would unleash market forces and lower programme quality. The Tory proposal 'means that Big Business will be able to move right into your house to sell their products. The standard of programmes will slump when the commercialisers get busy on the TV screen'.[35] For one Labour MP, Malcolm MacPherson, this was a secondary concern: 'When people talk about the lowering of standards, what really matters is not primarily the standard of the programmes but the standard of our national life which will undoubtedly become debased if we increase the number of avenues by which money power can affect it'.[36] The Trades Union Congress (TUC) adopted a similar anti-commercial approach and issued a statement opposing 'Sponsored Television': 'The potential influence of television on the lives of the people … requires that in the public interest programmes should be controlled by a public authority which can give due weight to considerations of a non-commercial nature'.[37]

Both the TUC and Labour's official opposition to commercial television was marked by a firm defence of the status quo. According to H. H. Wilson this was no different to the position in 1946 when 'most of the critical opinion of the BBC seemed to centre in the ranks of the Labour Party, though the Party Leaders were then, as later, its staunch, unquestioning defenders'.[38] Nevertheless, Labour leaders made important points that the Conservatives' plans were driven by the naked self-interest of the commercial lobby and that a public monopoly was to be merely supplanted by a private monopoly. In December 1953, Morrison and other Labour MPs proposed an all-party conference on the future of broadcasting that was brushed aside by the Tories. Labour tabled a series of amendments that were all rejected by the government, and then attempted, unsuccessfully, to block the legislation.

If the Labour Party was opposed to the commercialization of broadcasting, what was it actually in favour of? Labour leaders displayed a very ambivalent attitude towards change. If the BBC's services 'are probably the best to be found anywhere in the world' as Morrison had argued in 1952,[39] then why bother to change the system? Indeed, although Morrison praised both the achievements of the BBC and the possibilities of television in general, he also argued that 'we must remember about television that we can have too much of it'.[40] Too many hours of television viewing, he continued, would put people off reading books and restrict their education. When Morrison came to admit, fairly reluctantly, that a second channel was inevitable, he insisted that the 'most economical and most public-spirited way of promoting competition and viewers' choice' would be to hand it over to the BBC because it was already running a 'responsible public service'.[41]

Labour leaders were desperately keen to be seen to be distancing themselves from the general principle of monopolies except in the specific case of the BBC. Anxious to appeal to what they perceived as the increasingly consumerist habits of workers, they were equally concerned to condemn the Tories as the stooges of American capital and champion Labour as the guardian of reliable British values. Labour's official policy simultaneously lined it up with the voice of the 'establishment' and failed to articulate its supporters' desire for increased choice after years of austerity.

The temperature was raised by Attlee's promise at a miners' rally in June 1953 that if the Tories 'handed over television to private enterprise' then Labour would 'have to alter it when we get back to power'.[42] This threat, repeated by Gordon Walker and Morrison during 1954,[43] had the effect, according to Briggs, of polarizing the issue along party lines. This position was also criticized by some on the left of the party who were unhappy with the trap the leadership was creating for itself. The *New Statesman* identified two problems with Labour's continuing hostility to commercial television. First, the promise to repeal the legislation would most probably be an empty threat because several polls demonstrated commercial television's likely popularity.[44] Second, 'Labour leaders may get led into an obscurantist and restrictive approach towards television in general. Nothing could be more deadly to the Party's chances of making an impact on the "unpolitical" voter'.[45]

The left of the party had already begun to show some inclination to change the broadcasting status quo. For example, the *New Statesman* displayed an early interest in the question of the structures of television. In 1952, an article advocated the creation of a series of local television stations accountable to elected councillors which would 'help refurbish the rich local cultural patterns of this country'. These competitive public local stations would provide an alternative to the BBC and safeguard against 'monopoly, bureaucracy and over-centralisation'.[46] A more detailed plan for broadcasting reform was suggested by the Bevanite *Tribune* newspaper with the following headline: 'Break up the BBC – But No Mr Muggs' (in relation to the notorious chimpanzee who entertained American viewers in the commercial breaks during coverage of the Coronation). *Tribune* moved away from its earlier defence of the BBC and attacked opponents of commercial television for pretending that 'the present public monopoly is perfect' and for abandoning 'the idea of any competition in television or radio services'.[47] It proposed an increase in the license fee to pay for new television services, the creation of separate public corporations for television and the devolution of the BBC into independent regional corporations. 'This is the way', the newspaper argued, 'to remove the evils of monopoly without placing television and radio at the mercy of commercial interests'.[48]

The revisionist *Socialist Commentary* immediately hit back at these suggestions and attacked *Tribune* for complicating the job of the Labour leadership, presumably for associating Labour with a tax increase. It urged a policy of pragmatism: 'It is attractive to ponder on the possibility of two or more corporations competing with equal resources and equal access to performers and public. The problem is one of finance.'[49] The call for pragmatism was echoed in the unions. The Labour-affiliated Association of Cinematograph and Allied Technicians (ACT) declared its 'unalterable opposition to the introduction of commercial television' but then faced two motions at its 1954 conference recommending the adoption of 'a more realistic attitude toward Commercial Television. If the Bill before the House is passed, which seems inevitable, then the ACT should do everything in its power to ensure that ACT technicians be employed.'[50] The BBC Staff Association (ABS), which was not affiliated to Labour, opted for an even more flexible line. It condemned the government's decision and declared in 1954 that 'it will in the national interest take every step in its power to maintain the existing high quality of broadcasting with a view to counteracting any deterioration of standards which may follow intrusion of the profit motive'.[51] When the subject reappeared the following year, the NEC decided that, 'while in no way relaxing our vigilance in regard to service standards, it would be inconsistent with our role as the representative of staff in commercial broadcasting undertakings to give any further publicity to this resolution'.[52]

Given that ITV would soon become a reality, the 14 unions in the entertainment industry collectively called for a quota of British material to be no less than 80 per cent. This resolution was remitted at the 1954 TUC conference on the basis that the television bill was not law but the broadcasting unions received an assurance from the General Council that '[w]e are anxious that this new commercial television system shall reflect, as the Bill originally said it should, programmes which are predominantly British in tone and style'.[53]

It was not only the unions who had conflicting interests over commercial television. Sidney Bernstein, the chair of Granada Theatres, was a long-term Labour supporter who, according to his biographer, was personally opposed to commercial television. This did not prevent him from writing to Morrison in 1953 informing him that Granada had already applied for a licence:

> This does not indicate any change of feelings about commercial or sponsored television; I still think the country would be better off without it. However, if there is to be commercial television in

this country, we think we should be in, and this may very well be useful one day.[54]

Eric Fletcher, the Labour MP for Islington and a vice-president of Associated British Pictures Corporation (ABPC), was also against commercial broadcasting, believing it to be a 'national mistake' that would force the BBC to lower its standards.[55] As a politician, he was involved with Mayhew's NTC and, according to H. H. Wilson, offered ABPC's services in the campaign.[56] However, as an entrepreneur Fletcher went along with the enthusiasm for commercial television shown by his shareholders. Despite opposing the bill:

> as a member of the Board I co-operated with the decision of the majority that an application should be made for a Television contract. Thereafter, I took a great interest in the activities of the new company, ABC Television … and I became Deputy-Chairman.[57]

Cecil King, the proprietor of the Labour-supporting *Daily Mirror* had been in favour of commercial television 'from the start as the only way of putting some life into BBC television'.[58] When approached by the Conservative PMG in 1954 to apply for a licence, King declined because 'fantastic restrictions had been introduced … which hacked the original TV Bill to shreds'. He made it clear that he was simply biding his time: 'I told my people we would come in after the second bankruptcy as I foresaw a large expenditure before any possible return.'[59] True to his word, in 1956 King stepped in with £750,000 to help ATV's finances and Hugh Cudlipp, the *Mirror*'s editor, joined the board of ATV. According to Sendall, '[t]here was indeed no opposition to the *Mirror* joining ATV: *not from any quarter*'.[60]

So, despite the official position of the Labour Party and the TUC of complete opposition to commercial television, by early 1956 Labour supporters were playing key roles in three of the four ITV companies.[61] This was not as surprising as it seems because, privately, not all Labour MPs were hostile to the idea of ITV. Indeed David Hardman, a former parliamentary secretary to the Ministry of Education in the 1945 government, associated himself with the Popular Television Association, the lobby group *in favour of* ITV. Richard Crossman, the editor of *New Fabian Essays* and a leading Bevanite, declared that, although he was against the government's plans to set up a 'mixed' broadcasting system, 'I do not feel as passionately as most of the Party against the principle of sponsoring'. He further proposed that the government retain the BBC's monopoly but also allow two hours of sponsored programmes every evening.[62] More importantly, Hugh Gaitskell, the shadow chancellor and future leader of the Labour Party, was never convinced by the opposition to commercial television. His biographer, drawing on unpublished comments from Gaitskell's diary, confirms:

> As a politician he knew that independent television was popular, and he would never join the Establishment's cultural crusade against it. As early as 1953 he told Crossman, who had asked if the next Labour government would reverse the newly proposed policy: 'No, and anyway, it's a pity we didn't encourage the BBC to lease out time to commercial companies'.[63]

Gaitskell does not figure in any of the public debates or statements concerning television, but his views about the need for Labour to relate to the changing expectations of the 1950s were clear. In a post-1955 election analysis in *Socialist Commentary*, which prefigured many of the debates of the rest of the decade, he emphasized the importance of connecting the party to the desire for material advancement:

> No doubt it has been stimulated by the end of post-war austerity, TV, new gadgets like refrigerators and washing machines, the glossy magazines with their special appeal to women, and even the flood of new cars on the home markets. Call it if you like a growing Americanization of outlook. I believe it's there and it's no good moaning about it … We must talk in terms that appeal to the ordinary citizen.'[64]

Labour's opposition to commercial television, therefore, was far from united and consistent. The party demonstrated a tactical flexibility in its attitudes towards the television bill that demonstrated a commitment more to electoral success than the defence of firm principles. Pressed in 1952 by the Tories on whether Labour would repeal the legislation, the former PMG Ness Edwards asserted that 'when we are returned to power our position will be completely reserved. This Government do not determine what the next Government are going to do.'[65] After Attlee's rather rash promise in 1953 to scrap commercial television, Morrison argued the following year in Parliament that Labour's position was highly contingent on the specific circumstances of the time:

> I must make it clear that the whole of this scheme is highly objectionable, and there is already substantial evidence that it may prove to be unworkable. In that case we … must reserve the right to modify or, indeed, abandon the entire scheme, and this may well include the complete elimination of the proposals for advertising.[66]

The position was finally thrashed out in January 1955 when a short-lived Joint Committee on the Future of TV was convened to sort out a party policy on television for the impending general election. The group included representatives from all sides of the party, from Tom Driberg on the Bevanite left to the Gaitskellite Patrick Gordon Walker. The minutes indicate a stormy meeting in which Morrison suggested 'an unconditional declaration' against advertising while another member proposed that the new corporation, the Independent Television Authority (ITA), be 'kept in existence and allowed to prepare its own programmes' with all advertising restricted to one hour each day.[67] It was agreed that 'although expensive, two programmes [channels] were needed' and that the BBC was best placed to deliver both, although there was no consensus on whether to increase the licence fee. Finally, a resolution was agreed that 'the Labour Party should declare itself opposed to advertising on TV, and in favour of the public service principle'.[68] This important statement laid the basis for the party's eventual manifesto declaration that '[t]elevision is a growing influence for good or ill. Labour will establish an alternative public television service, free from advertising.'[69] Commitments to repeal the legislation, to abolish the Independent Television Authority or to revoke the licenses of commercial television companies were all, however, noticeably absent.

Opposition to the Conservatives' plans for commercial television was not completely in vain. The NTC's high-profile campaign helped to convince the government to drop US-style sponsorship in favour of regulated advertising as the source of revenue for the new system. Furthermore, the NTC's influence, according to Wilson, was also 'important in the eventual creation of a public authority to own the transmitting facilities and license the programme companies'.[70] It is also likely that, although no Labour amendments were accepted by the government, its constant pressure was effective in securing the inclusion of various safeguards concerning programme range, editorial impartiality and limits on advertising time in the final legislation.[71] However, it is far from proven that it was vigorous parliamentary opposition that limited the total victory of free marketeers inside the Tory Party. According to Bernard Sendall, the historian of commercial television,

> since, as all parties to the debates seemed to accept, television broadcasting was a uniquely powerful means of influencing minds, then any person or persons granted the privilege of using that power should, in the public interest, be made subject to proper restraints. Thus in the debates that followed, Government

spokesmen repeatedly asserted a willingness – provided the two prerequisites of competition and advertising finance, stayed untouched – to consider, possibly to adopt, any reasonable measures to dissipate whatever grounds or justification there might be for the fears of the Bill's opponents.'[72]

In the end, Labour's resistance to the introduction of commercial television was undermined by a combination of factors. Television policy was not a central concern for the leadership and, given the likely popularity of commercial television among Labour supporters,[73] it was not prepared to antagonize its electorate. Labour leaders were firm defenders of the broadcasting status quo and, as Wilson argued, 'never fully comprehended the stakes involved in maintaining public service broadcasting'[74] seen by many as patronizing and distant. Labour's opposition was further compromised by the inclusion in or association with the party of those who were set to gain financially from commercial television. Having accepted the principle of a mixed economy, sections of the leadership reserved their criticism not for the pursuit of profit but for the spreading of 'foreign' values and the domination of US capital; others welcomed 'Americanization' and urged the party to embrace the consumer revolution.

The left, also wedded to the idea of a mixed economy, intervened only occasionally in the debates because its real interest lay elsewhere – in foreign and defence issues. Apart from the *Tribune* article previously mentioned, the closest the Bevanites came to tackling popular culture was Ian Mikardo's pamphlet on the Royal Commission on Betting and Gaming, *It's a Mug's Game*.[75] The ground was left clear, therefore, for the growing revisionist wing of the Labour Party to articulate an approach to culture in general, and television in particular, that sought to connect with rising expectations and living standards in the 1950s. Attlee's defeat in the general election of May 1955, the launch of commercial television in September of that year and the election of Hugh Gaitskell as leader of the Labour Party in December 1955 provided the conditions that allowed this approach to evolve.

REVISIONISM AND THE 'AGE OF PARTICIPATION'

In March 1955, T. R. Fyvel wrote an article for the revisionist journal *Socialist Commentary* which analysed the changing nature of British society and claimed that Britain had entered the 'Age of Participation'. In a buoyant economy, there is to-day an ever growing middle section of the population which can – and does – participate in the material good life of to-day which is based on the possession of cars, motor-cycles, radio and television sets, on super-cinemas, chain stores and organized holidays, on the Pools, the dogs, the mass circulation magazine, and the rest.[76]

He went on to argue that the Labour Party needed to recognize that this was a more dynamic and efficient form of capitalism where simply pledging to defend living standards would not be enough to appeal to the average voter. Labour's task was not to transform capitalism but to 'humanize' it, to increase access to the wonderful opportunities of the new classless, consumer society. The key to unlocking electoral success was to champion equality of opportunity and to distance the party from 'vague' economic questions such as the defence of living standards.

This analysis was amplified in Anthony Crosland's 'bible' of revisionism, *The Future of Socialism*, published in 1956. Crosland developed the arguments from his contribution to *New Fabian Essays* into a fully fledged statement that 'capitalism' was no longer an adequate way of describing British society in the 1950s and that the Labour Party would have to redefine its socialism to meet this change. It was an approach that provided an important intellectual justification for the Labour leadership's determination to reposition the party away from the trade unions and towards cross-class organization.

Crosland argued that British industry had become more specialized and complex in the previous decade and that the domination by entrepreneurial owners was being challenged by the rise of salaried managers. Companies were more likely to reinvest profits and not to turn to 'outside' capital to finance expansion. Indeed, profits were no longer the sole point of business as latter-day industrialists also sought the respect of their peers, intellectual prestige and a civic reputation, none of which could be guaranteed by capital alone. This did not mean, according to Crosland, that 'the profit-motive has disappeared' but that it was universal:

> It is a mistake to think that profit, in the sense of a surplus over cost, has any special or unique connection with capitalism. On the contrary, it must be the rationale of business activity in any society, whether capitalist or socialist, which is growing and dynamic.[77]

With the decline of 'traditional capitalist ruthlessness' in pursuit of profit, Crosland believed that private industry, to use Fyvel's term, 'is at last becoming humanised'.[78] All the features of capitalism that Marx had identified in the previous century had been superseded: laissez-faire had given way to state intervention, managerialism had replaced entrepreneurialism, 'the distribution of personal income has become significantly more equal',[79] private property had lost its ideological allure and, finally, class struggle was no longer in evidence. Given 'The Growing Irrelevance of the Ownership of the Means of Production',[80] as one chapter was headed, it was no surprise to learn that in answer to the question, 'Is this still Capitalism?', Crosland responded with a firm 'No.'[81]

While the theorizing of the decline of entrepreneurialism and aggressive profiteering is especially curious when applied to the cash-rich experience of commercial television in the subsequent years, Crosland's account of the withering away of capitalism had an immediate impact. He helped to write the party's *Industry and Society* document, passed at the 1957 annual conference, which signalled a further attack on Labour's commitment to public ownership, and attempted to provide Labour with a strategy with which it could realign itself as the party of social equality as distinct to social ownership.

There are two aspects of this strategy which are particularly relevant to the political status of television and culture in the late 1950s. First, Crosland argued that it was essential to raise the level of average income because

> the higher the level of average income, the more equal is the visible pattern of consumption, and the stronger the *subjective* feeling of equal living standards … the richer a country grows, the more equal the distribution of these particular forms of consumption becomes, almost regardless of the distribution of total income.[82]

Crosland's evidence of this was the polarization of wealth in developing countries in contrast to the more egalitarian situation in the USA with a much higher average income. Crosland argued that inequality was bound to fall in the 'modern mass-production economy'[83] because, as long as there is a limit to the consumption of the rich, the poor will be able to close the gap. What is more revealing is his emphasis on the *perception* of equal living standards and the call for increased consumerism, as opposed to any material redistribution of wealth. For the plan to work, however, the correct sort of consumption was needed if there was to be an 'atmosphere of greater equality'.[84] The problem in Britain, according to Crosland, was that increased consumption usually centred on 'low-status' goods peculiar to working-class interests, like magazines, cinema tickets, tabloid newspapers, alcohol and tobacco. Ordinary people, Crosland argued, had to shift their expenditure on to 'high-status' goods like television sets and car ownership. 'There are clear political implications here for the Labour Party, which would be ill-advised to continue making a largely proletarian class appeal when a majority of the population is gradually attaining a middle-class standard of life, and distinct symptoms even of a middle-class psychology.'[85]

The second task for Labour in the pursuit of social equality, according to Crosland, was to campaign over moral and cultural issues like sexuality, censorship and divorce. This required Labour to reject its previous economistic and puritanical attitudes and to 'turn our attention increasingly to other, and in the long run more important spheres'.[86] In a celebrated passage, Crosland explained that this meant:

> We need not only higher exports and old-age pensions, but more open-air cafes, brighter and gayer streets at night, later closing-hours for public houses, more local repertory theatres, better and more hospitable hoteliers and restauranteurs, brighter and cleaner eating houses, more riverside cafes ... and so on *ad infinitum*.[87]

While it is easy to criticize Crosland's idealism and necessary to point out that the adoption of such ideas did nothing to rescue Labour in the 1959 general election, it was at least an attempt to come to terms with changing circumstances. The Bevanite left, on the other hand, offered scarce intellectual challenge to revisionist ideas in the period between 1955 and 1959:

> While the revisionists wandered around the new post-capitalist Wonderland, the Bevanites, like the doormouse at the Mad Hatter's tea party, kept their eyes tight shut. They tried simply to deny the boom would last, saying that mass unemployment was only just around the corner. But facts are stubborn things.[88]

The facts were that, despite a few hiccups, the boom was continuing and the Tories once again benefited from rising living standards and won the 1959 'You've Never Had It So Good' election. The reaction to defeat was swift as the right argued that Labour was being severely compromised by its continuing association with working-class interests while the left argued the party had shifted too far away from nationalization and socialist principles. According to

Ralph Miliband, both were wrong: 'By 1959, Labour's image was much too blurred to give either defeat or victory so precise a political or ideological meaning.'[89] Nevertheless, the revisionists felt they were vindicated by the publication in 1960 of *Must Labour Lose?*, a short book which set out to examine Labour's role in the age of 'embourgeoisiement'. According to *Socialist Commentary's* Rita Hinden, Labour was destined to keep losing as long as it was perceived as being based on a class that was shrinking, and continued to identify with unpopular notions of solidarity and nationalization.[90] In reality, the survey on which the book was based found 'no homogeneous blanket attitude towards public ownership'[91] and provided no evidence that material advancement corresponded to voting Conservative. The sample of 724 people revealed that 'at least half the working class acquired durable consumer goods on at least as lavish a scale as their neighbours – but continued to vote Labour'.[92]

For some theorists, the rash of 'affluent worker' studies in the early 1960s that spoke of increased political apathy and a weak, functional attachment to Labour proved not that the working class had disappeared as a social force but that Labour had failed to link material expectations to a programme of structural reform. As one commentator wrote:

> Developments since 1950 have had the effect, not of decomposing the class or making it selfish or into a poor copy of its betters, but of allowing working people greater access to the opportunities and goods produced by an expanding economy.[93]

The result was a less instinctive loyalty to the Labour Party but hardly a sign of middle-class consciousness.

The most trenchant criticism of the revisionists was provided by a group with only indirect links to the Labour Party. The New Left grew out of the dissatisfaction with both Stalinism and Bevanism and was composed of former members of the Communist Party, individuals from the Labour left, peace campaigners and radical students. It sought to keep alive a genuinely radical anti-capitalist tradition and to build a democratic culture in opposition to the intellectual stagnation of the Bevanites and Stalinists. Focusing on the anti-nuclear struggle of the Campaign for Nuclear Disarmament (CND), the New Left made its impact with a 100,000-strong demonstration at Easter 1960 and the adoption of a unilateralist position at that year's Labour Party conference (albeit one that was reversed the following year).

In the pages of the new journals, *The New Reasoner* and *Universities and Left Review*, activists and commentators stressed the importance of collective struggle and democratic organization to change both economic and cultural circumstances. E. P. Thompson's account of the New Left railed against the intellectual conformity of the Labour Party and argued that 'the Fabian prescription of a competitive Equality of Opportunity is giving way, among socialists, before the rediscovery of William Morris' vision of a Society of Equals'.[94] For Thompson, cultural questions were not secondary to what the Bevanite left called 'bread-and-butter' issues but were intrinsic to debates on political power. While echoing the concerns of the revisionists to engage with questions of consumption, the New Left had different solutions: 'it becomes ever more clear that the fight to control and break-up the mass media, and to preserve and extend the minority media, is as central in political significance as, for example, the fight against the Taxes on Knowledge in the 1830s'.[95] Aware that the revisionists were attempting to monopolize debates on the consumer society, the New Left sought to win back for the left the idea of a democratic culture.

In doing so, the New Left was influenced by two critics of the effects of the commercialization of culture on working-class life. Richard Hoggart argued in *The Uses of Literacy*, first published in 1957, that the new cultural forms of popular music, sensationalist magazines and American television were usurping traditional working-class values. 'Everything has gone vicarious: this is puff-pastry literature, with nothing inside the pastry, the ceaseless exploitation of a hollow brightness.'[96] Hoggart and then Raymond Williams in *The Long Revolution*[97] counterposed the vision of an organic common culture which celebrated working-class life and institutions to the inauthentic commercial mass culture of contemporary Britain. Hoggart and Williams, according to Dennis Dworkin, 'were two of the most important influences on New Left efforts at reframing socialist priorities, and they were instrumental in establishing the parameters of the debate on working-class culture'.[98] Their ideas were to be particularly important for socialists involved in the debates around television in the early 1960s.

In the end, it was neither the traditional Labour left nor the New 'cultural' Left which weakened the grip of revisionism but a very old-fashioned phenomenon: the return of economic crisis. The slowing down of economic growth meant that '[r]evisionism took a new form. Hope of bright cafes, fashions and murals evaporated, along with major social reform and redistribution of wealth and income.'[99] Nevertheless, Croslandite revisionism provided the main backdrop for Labour's television policy from 1955 until the election of Harold Wilson and a new Labour government in 1964.

THE THIRD CHANNEL, ITV PROFITS AND THE PILKINGTON REPORT

Once the 1955 election had passed and commercial television had started, Labour showed little inclination to discuss television policy. Preoccupied with the Suez crisis, it was once again the question of political broadcasting which took centre-stage. Live broadcasts about the Suez situation by Prime Minister Eden and an Opposition reply by Gaitskell in November 1956 preceded the trial suspension of the Fourteen-Day Rule the following month.[100]

However, in November 1957, stimulated by rumours that the government was soon to decide on the status of a third television channel, the Labour Party Public Information Group met to consider the party's attitude towards television. Tony Benn had, in that same month, advocated the creation of a competitive broadcasting system consisting of two public radio corporations and two public television corporations (including the ITA), all allowed to carry advertising.[101] Benn opened the discussion at the meeting and noted that '[t]he reception was fairly frosty. Mayhew, who followed, wants to nationalise the commercial programme companies. He is a little better than Scholefield Allen [Labour MP for Crewe], who does not even have a television set.'[102]

Seven months later in July 1958, convinced that the Tories were about to decide on the future of the new channel (now called the 'Third Programme'), Labour's Home Policy Committee (HPC) set up a sub-committee on television and radio to advise on broadcasting policy. The sub-committee, which included Tom Driberg, Patrick Gordon Walker, George Brown and Richard Crossman, agreed that if an election statement was required on the subject it should say: 'The Labour Party is in favour of maintaining competition in the field of television.'[103] The committee further decided to prepare papers on the short-term and long-term problems of broadcasting. Four months later the committee reconvened with a paper that addressed two issues concerning television: the technical arguments for moving to 625 lines of transmission and the nature of the Third Programme.

Curiously, after years of uncritically defending the BBC, 'the case today for giving the Third Programme to the BBC is far less plain'.[104] The paper sketched out three objections to the BBC running a new network. First, ITV was more popular and 'if popularity is the test – and it cannot be dismissed as of no consequence – the BBC's claim is weak'.[105] Second, competition had been good for television in general and the BBC in particular: 'the ITA has in three years blown away much of the stuffiness, timidity and paternalism that characterised British broadcasting'.[106] Finally, the BBC was short of money and would require an increase in the licence fee if it was to operate a new channel.

With the exception of eternal worries about a rise in the licence fee, these were very new arguments for the Labour leadership. It had never before *publicly* accused the BBC of being stuffy, timid or paternalistic and it had certainly not claimed that popularity was the key test of public service in the debates in the early 1950s. The document went on to argue that 'the most powerful claimant to the Third Programme is the ITA'[107] because its programmes were more popular, it would introduce more competition into broadcasting and, crucially, it had no financial problems. Although there were some concerns with programme quality and origin and media concentration, 'the reality [of commercial television] has been far less awful than was anticipated. ITA has played its cards with skill.'[108] The key problem for sanctioning a second commercial network was that 'we have not yet had any experience of *competitive commercial television*' and that, if it was allowed, 'the Queensbury Rules of the past three years may quickly be abandoned'.[109]

Perhaps such a positive assessment of the first years of commercial television was to be expected given the political realignment taking place in the Labour Party and the undoubted popularity of the service. But the party was also reluctant to identify itself too closely with a system which, after all, was characterized by Roy Thomson's comment in 1957 that controlling an ITV franchise was 'just like having a licence to print your own money'.[110] Instead the sub-committee proposed a new independent, competitive public service organization: 'The Third Programme should aim to entertain and inform a wide public. Like the BBC its output would include programmes of minority appeal, but it would not generally, let alone exclusively, cater for high-brow or specialist groups.'[111] The network would differ from commercial television 'in that the new corporation would have the obligation to plan its own programmes' and would differ from the BBC 'in that its revenues would come in part from advertising' and in part from licence revenue.[112] It appeared that the committee was aiming to please a range of different constituencies because viewers would have more choice, advertisers would have more outlets, broadcasters would have an expanding and competitive system and government would not have to risk unpopularity by increasing the licence fee. The paper promised that, if the principle was accepted, a more complete financial account of the new channel would be prepared.

A new independent television corporation was both a convenient compromise for Labour and yet also an intriguing proposition that prefigured the discussions some 15 years later concerning an Open Broadcasting Authority running a fourth television channel. The Association of Cinematograph, Television and Allied Technicians (ACTT) broadly supported the sub-committee's plan for a more diverse channel and advocated a 'Television Foundation', the same phrase used by Anthony Smith 13 years later in his call for a 'National Television Foundation'. This was to be based on a 'new, independent, lively and modern approach which will command the respect of the viewers both for its integrity and its awareness of contemporary thought and issues'.[113] In fact there was a fairly broad consensus that, in order to increase programme diversity, neither the ITA nor the BBC should be given a new channel. Mayhew,[114] Greenwood,[115] *Tribune*[116] and Crosland[117] all supported the idea while Richard Hoggart,[118] although certain that commercial television should not get another channel, was not sure if the BBC could rise to the challenge. In a substantial poll before the 1959 general election, the ACTT polled candidates about whether they supported the idea of a new public corporation to run the third channel. Of Labour candidates who were elected, 79 per cent were in favour with only 2 per cent against; of those were not elected, 94 per cent were in favour with none against.[119] The demand for a new channel independent of both the BBC and ITV was evidently popular inside the Labour Party.

The television sub-committee met again in February 1959 to consider a paper outlining the financial plans for the Third Programme. The original proposal had suggested that the new corporation would be funded by both licence and advertising revenue. Accordingly, the paper argued that the new channel could be launched with the money returned to the Treasury from the excise on television licences as well as the Treasury deduction of 12.5 per cent from the licence fee itself. This would total around £16m in 1961 (compared to some £31m for the BBC as a whole) of which £2m could be given to the BBC in order to finance its extension of broadcasting hours, leaving £14m for the new channel. This would be supplemented by revenue from commercial television and the key question for the committee was 'how to obtain money from the programme companies'.[120]

Two methods were considered: either a special tax on the ITV companies' profits or an increase in the rents charged by the ITA. The former suggestion 'appears to be justified because the programme companies are, to a large extent, monopolies, and are therefore making monopoly profits'.[121] However, the paper then presented four arguments against this proposal. Firstly, '[a]s all taxes are unpopular, the programme companies might well be able to wage a powerful campaign against it'. Second, it might be seen as unfair to introduce this kind of windfall levy against only one type of monopoly profit. Third, 'it would be difficult to explain the nature of monopoly profits to the electorate ... What, the television companies might ask, is freer than air?' Finally, and perhaps most coherently, the Inland Revenue 'would find it difficult to distinguish television profits from those the programme companies make elsewhere'.[122]

The committee's reluctance to impose a tax on ITV profits was justified by the electorate's apparent inability to understand why the ITV companies were starting to make vast amounts of money. The committee's decision, however, also revealed the party leadership's lack of commitment to intervene in private business matters and a desire not to attack private profits per se. The document provides no detail as to why the population would be so baffled by the need to introduce a special tax on entrepreneurs with very lucrative monopolies on advertising, nor why legislation could not be introduced to force the ITV companies to be more transparent in their accounting practices. Perhaps it was the case that, as Labour leaders were busy theorizing the decline of entrepreneurial capitalism and the emergence of a new consensual relationship between the state and private business, this was a problem that simply could not be allowed to exist.

The paper rejected the imposition of a special tax and opted for the second suggestion: an increase in the rents charged by the ITA (delayed until 1964) that would amount to about £5m a year. The committee accepted the proposal and, in the knowledge that an election was due that year, prepared two statements. One was a detailed outline of Labour's proposals for the Third Programme in response to any government policy on the matter; the second was a more general account of party policy on television for use in the 1959 election campaign. This confirmed that the 'Labour Party is in favour of maintaining competition in the field of television', promised to enforce the safeguards on ITV more stringently, looked forward to a 'further expansion of television services' and publicly stated that the 'Labour Party believes that the Third Programme should go neither to ITA nor to the BBC but to a new, independent and non-commercial organisation'.[123] These pledges found their way into Labour's 1959 election manifesto, which repeated the party's promise not to abolish commercial television and recognized the strong case for giving the third television channel to a new public corporation.[124]

In March 1959, one month after Labour's decision not to impose a special tax on the programme companies, the question of ITV's profits became a public scandal. Robert Fraser, the ITA's director general, was hauled before the Public Accounts Committee of the House of Commons and forced to explain how £6 out of every £10 of income was kept as profit by the programme companies. By 1960, Fraser was arguing that 'public opinion would come to regard such profit levels as insupportable' and suggested some form of 'discriminatory taxation of television programme companies'.[125] 'Why should you pay to make these men rich?' screamed the *Sunday Express*, pointing out that 'never before in British history, not even in the railway mania of last century, have profits been made so fast as they have from the commercial TV boom'.[126] Even a Conservative-supporting newspaper like the *Sunday Express* (albeit one with no financial stakes in ITV) suggested forcing the ITV companies to contribute £2 towards every television licence, a 'tax' of £16m in 1959. Given this widespread criticism of ITV's avarice, the £5m increase on ITV rents that the Labour sub-committee had recommended to take place in 1964 pales into insignificance with the £21.5m that the companies actually paid as a result of Tory-inspired legislation. Labour's commitment to the broadcasting status quo and its desire not to antagonize ITV viewers undermined any attempts to tackle the question of ITV profits.

Discussions about the Third Programme and ITV finances became more urgent when the Conservative government set up the Pilkington Committee in July 1960 to report on the future of broadcasting. Labour was, at the time, in the middle of producing a new policy document and a 3,000-word draft had emerged in November that appeared to share the New Left's concern with the commercialization of the mass media. One passage, leaked to the *New Left Review*, argued that where 'money is king there is little room for any other values ... Commercial television is primarily an organ for selling, and public service broadcasting is starved of resources.'[127] The second draft, produced in March 1961, included the sub-committee's proposal for an independent third channel and a further attack on commercial forces in the media. 'If we want a wide choice of programmes and papers, if we want entertainment and information for their own sake rather than as a by-product of commercial advertising, then the community must be ready to act to get them.'[128]

When the draft was discussed at a full meeting of the HPC in May, its chair Harold Wilson initiated a discussion which concluded that the draft was too long, that 'it ought to be written more as propaganda and less like an election manifesto' and that '[c]ertain of the priorities were wrong'.[129] The committee agreed to focus on only four areas – the economy, education, social services and land – and to publish the document as *Signposts for the Sixties*[130] for that year's party conference. The result, according to the *New Left Review*, 'was inevitable. In the final version ... nothing at all is left of the cultural and libertarian ideas so reminiscent of dozens of New Left articles and discussions'.[131] All references to the need to challenge media monopolies, to the dangers of advertising and to proposals for a new independent television channel were dropped as the party leadership de-prioritized media issues that had been increasingly highlighted by the radical left. In the end, despite the activities of the sub-committee on television and its proposals for a third channel, the party failed to make a formal submission to the Pilkington Committee.[132]

The Pilkington Report was published in June 1962 and, according to Jean Seaton,

> was the product of two contemporary concerns: that the working class was being absorbed into the middle class, and that working-class culture was decaying because of the industrialization of leisure ... The committee had been asked to review the development of television. In fact they did much more, producing a report which judged the nation's culture.[133]

Influenced by the presence of Richard Hoggart, the Pilkington Committee reserved its venom for the effects of advertising and the obsession with popular entertainment which it felt was demeaning British cultural life. Using language similar to that in Hoggart's *The Uses of Literacy*, the report argued that '[p]rogrammes which exemplified emotional tawdriness and mental timidity helped to cheapen both emotional and intellectual values. Plays or serials might not deal with real human problems, but present a candy-floss world.'[134] The consumer culture represented by commercial television may have been popular but it failed to embody the breadth and depth of public life distinctive of 'good' broadcasting. Additionally, the advertisements on ITV were creating 'false needs' at the same time as the majority of its programmes were failing to meet the 'real' cultural and educational needs of viewers. The committee, therefore, recommended root-and-branch reform of commercial television, proposing that the ITA plan programming and sell advertising, leaving the ITV companies the job of simply making the programmes. The committee was much more sympathetic to the BBC and, although critical of the creeping triviality of its output, backed the corporation's bid to manage the Third Programme.[135]

Labour's reaction to the Pilkington Report demonstrated all the tensions and differences that underlay the party's attitude to television. Labour was, frankly, split over the issue, as observed by the BBC's political correspondent Hardiman Scott: 'the Party was about equally divided between those who broadly accepted the whole of Pilkington and those who did not'.[136] On the left, *Tribune* gushed that the 'strength of the Report lies in its brilliant diagnosis of the diseases of television and in the picture it paints of the medium in perfect health'.[137] It disagreed with just two of its recommendations. Giving the ITA more power and the BBC another channel would 'achieve the very opposite of what is intended', of extending the range of voices, subjects and debates on television. Instead, *Tribune* suggested granting individual ITV companies 'fixed incomes but autonomy in matters of taste' and supported the case for a new independent public corporation for the Third Programme.[138]

The Labour Party and TUC conferences both passed motions welcoming the Pilkington Report. The TUC resolution urged the government to 'adopt its recommendations which are designed to ensure that these most potent social, moral and cultural influences are used to bring enrichment and a high quality service to ordinary people rather than to further commercial interests'.[139] The Labour resolution supported Pilkington's proposals for the restructuring of commercial television and for the third channel to be awarded to the BBC,[140] rather than endorsing the party sub-committee's argument that a new public corporation was needed. Fred Mulley, speaking for the NEC, argued that the report was a 'slap in the face to the Tory Government, to the kind of society they are endeavouring to build up, one in which profit is preferred to people'. However, when he then insisted that 'we are not against "Coronation Street" or any of that kind of programme. We are not, in principle, against the advertisements used on the present Independent Television Service', he was greeted with cries of 'shame' from conference delegates.[141]

These divisions had already come out in Parliament. Patrick Gordon Walker called the Pilkington Report 'a document of great social and political importance' and then defended ITV for having produced some genuinely good popular entertainment. He concluded that 'ITV is here now. For good or ill, it is part of our national life.'[142] Woodrow Wyatt called for curbs on ITV profits but argued against the restructuring of commercial television 'because, by and large, it has given the people much of what they want'.[143] W. R. Williams, summing up the debate for the opposition, paid tribute to the work of the committee but concluded that cross-party consensus was more necessary than any particular vision of broadcasting:

> we have now left behind the old battle on the question of commercial television *v.* the BBC or some other form of corporation, that this House may decide that, in the national interest and in order to get the maximum benefit for our people out of this powerful medium, we should be able to bridge some – I do not say all – of the differences between us so that we can concentrate on ends which seem to be common to both sides of the House.[144]

Behind the scenes, such a gentlemanly approach was not always in evidence. Crossman, an influential member of the shadow Cabinet, held the private view that Pilkington's desire to restructure ITV 'can be only of academic interest; and the Labour Party would be very silly to commit itself to endorsing it'.[145] The key critic of the Pilkington Report was the party leader Hugh Gaitskell who refused to be associated with press allegations that Pilkington – and by implication Labour – was suggesting the scrapping of popular programmes. Richard Hoggart recalls that:

> Hugh Gaitskell said immediately after the Report appeared that we were unduly anti-Commercial TV. It was after all the favoured channel of 'the people'. I responded on TV that this was a mistaken and patronising view. A day or two later Crossman asked me to lunch. At least, *he* wanted to argue about the Report. He produced an ineffable snob phrase about the 'common man'. As he came in to our lunch at his house in Smith Square or nearby he was fresh from a Shadow Cabinet. He said: 'Gaitskell asked me to kick your arse.'[146]

Hoggart also recalls that he was 'not surprised but sorry' that the Labour leadership was reluctant to endorse the report. 'Funny how most of them – Gaitskell, Crossman, Crosland – were ex-public-school and Oxbridge types. Nervous patronage pretending to be honest Joe'ery.'[147]

When the Conservatives rejected Pilkington's proposals to restructure ITV and instead introduced a levy on advertising revenue, the Labour Party showed no inclination to depart from a bipartisan approach. During the passage of the 1963 Television Act, some Labour speakers appeared to be *more* concerned about the financial health of the programme companies than their Tory counterparts. Although fully behind the Conservative PMG Reginald Bevins' desire to stop excessive profits, Ness Edwards, the former Labour PMG, expressed concern that the proposed levy on advertising revenue would force the ITV companies to cut back on programme spending. 'We want good commercial television but, if we are to have it, the means of providing it must be there. I do not object to successful commercial television,' he argued, 'but I do object to bankrupt commercial television.'[148]

Ness Edwards' focus on the financial viability of the commercial television system was mirrored, in particular, by the behaviour of the ACTT. The Labour-affiliated television union agreed with Pilkington's analysis of the problems of commercial television but was less keen on the committee's recommendation to restructure the network. It was concerned that the report's proposals would undermine investment in commercial television and therefore threaten the jobs of its members.[149] ACTT general secretary, George Elvin, tried unsuccessfully at both Labour and TUC conferences to amend the motions on Pilkington so that they pressed, not for the implementation of the report's recommendations, but simply for the recognition of the ACTT inside the BBC.[150] This was then followed by a campaign by all the television unions to oppose the 1963 bill on the basis that the proposed levy on advertising would hurt ITV revenue and risk workers' jobs. The unions may well have been right to stress that a tax on ITV profits would be more effective and less likely to lead to budget cuts than a levy on advertising. However, the sectional nature of their campaign made it less appealing to those Labour MPs who, in the end, lined up behind the Conservative PMG to introduce the levy against the wishes of a few backbench Tories and television trade unionists.[151]

Labour also supported the government's decision, following the Pilkington Committee's recommendation, to authorize the BBC to run the third channel. Labour's public position, as outlined in its 1959 election manifesto, was still in favour of a new independent public corporation, a 'third way' in broadcasting. In February 1962, *The Times* reported that Labour leaders had 'come down emphatically in favour of any third television service being provided by the BBC or a new public authority'.[152] By the time of the parliamentary debate on the Pilkington Report, W. R. Williams in his summing up for Labour asserted that 'I am 100 per cent in favour of the BBC getting a third channel. I do not equivocate about this.'[153]

While there were sound economic and political reasons for the BBC to run a 'complementary' channel, Labour never provided an explanation of why it dropped its plan for a new corporation. Perhaps it was because the proposal had acquired a radical tinge as some of the evidence to the Pilkington Committee made clear. The New Left, in its submission to the committee, embraced the idea of a new organization which would cater for 'other voices, other faces, other interests, other interpretations of "entertainment", other approaches to "seriousness", other aspects of our community life'.[154] It proposed a publicly owned and democratically structured network that would take advantage of new sources of talent in the universities, local councils, drama groups and community bodies which were then 'too small or too unorthodox to catch the official eye of the BBC, too uncommercial to purchase time on ITV'.[155] This was an argument which a Labour government would have to return to in the discussions surrounding proposals for the fourth channel which took place in the 1970s. In the early 1960s, however, the idea was ahead of its time and quietly dropped.

Labour's approach towards television throughout its years in opposition in the 1950s foundered on the contradiction between its different constituencies. In attempting to reconcile anti-commercial sentiments with a defence of the mixed economy, Labour was bound to be an inconsistent champion of democratic reform. The party contained both ITV bosses and passionate critics of commercial television, supporters of private property and defenders of nationalization, those who were frightened of television and those who saw it as the pathway to a whole new world. Party supporters expressed a range of competing visions of the media and some imaginative plans for reform that prefigured later developments like Channel 4. In the end, the leadership settled on a defensive position that satisfied neither revisionists nor New Left activists.

This was a strategy designed to maximize party unity, popular appeal and electoral possibilities. Confidential committees on television policy were established before each election and dropped almost immediately afterwards, contributing to an ad hoc style of policymaking on this issue. Throughout the period, the adoption of principled positions co-existed with a tactical flexibility based on electoral requirements. By 1963, with a weakening Conservative administration, Opposition members were in a confident and co-operative mood during the passage of the television bill. 'Under the pragmatic leadership of Harold Wilson they were not going to fritter away their appeal to floating voters by a display of doctrinaire attitudes towards a popular television service.'[156] A decade of revisionism and, in particular, 13 years of opposition had convinced Labour MPs that, perhaps, commercial television was not such a bad thing after all.

NOTES

1. M. Pinto-Duschinsky, 'Bread and Circuses? The Conservatives in Office, 1951–1964', in V. Bogdanor and R. Skidelsky (eds), *The Age of Affluence, 1951–1964* (London: Macmillan, 1970), pp. 55–77, at p. 72.
2. A. Crosland, 'The Transition from Capitalism', in R. H. S. Crossman (ed.), *New Fabian Essays* (London: Turnstile Press, 1952), pp. 33–68, at pp. 38–42.
3. G. Foote, *The Labour Party's Political Thought: A History*, 3rd edn (New York: St Martin's Press, 1997), p. 205.
4. M. Jenkins, *Bevanism: Labour's High Tide* (Nottingham: Spokesman, 1979), p. 265.
5. B. Pimlott, 'The Labour Left', in C. Cook and I. Taylor (eds), *The Labour Party* (London: Longman, 1980), pp. 163–88, at p. 174.
6. V. Bogdanor, 'The Labour Party in Opposition, 1951–1964', in Bogdanor and Skidelsky, *The Age of Affluence*, pp. 78–116, at p. 113.
7. S. Haseler, *The Gaitskellites* (London: Macmillan, 1969), p. 56.
8. A. Briggs, *Sound and Vision* (vol. IV of *The History of Broadcasting in the United Kingdom*) (Oxford: Oxford University Press, 1979), p. 428.
9. H. H. Wilson, *Pressure Group: The Campaign for Commercial Television* (London: Secker & Warburg, 1961).
10. J. Whale, *The Politics of the Media* (London: Fontana, 1977).
11. Quoted in J. Curran and J. Seaton, *Power Without Responsibility*, 5th edn (London: Routledge, 1997), p. 163.
12. Briggs, *Sound and Vision*, p. 933.
13. Wilson, *Pressure Group*, p. 208.
14. T. Benn, Report to NEC on Political Broadcasting, GS/BCST/215 (General Secretary's file on broadcasting), 1953, p. 8.
15. J. Campbell, *Nye Bevan and the Mirage of British Socialism* (London: Weidenfeld & Nicolson, 1987), p. 358.
16. Ibid.
17. See T. O'Malley, 'Labour and the 1947–9 Royal Commission on the Press', in M. Bromley and T. O'Malley (eds), *A Journalism Reader* (London: Routledge, 1997), pp. 126–58, at pp. 140–41. O'Malley points out that Labour had a long record of critical interventions concerning the partisanship and monopolistic tendencies of the British press which preceded its decision to set up the 1949 Royal Commission on the Press.
18. E. Shaw, *Discipline and Discord in the Labour Party* (Manchester: Manchester University Press, 1988), p. 47.
19. According to Benn, the 'sub-committee had no official existence whatsoever, and derived its status entirely from the fact that its recommendations went to Herbert Morrison … In view of the peculiar way in which it had been established, it operated almost in secret' (Benn, Report to NEC on Political Broadcasting, p. 2).
20. Ibid., p. 14.
21. Labour Party, Evidence submitted to the Committee on Broadcasting, GS/BCST (General secretary's file on broadcasting), 1950, p. 1.
22. G. Darling, Notes for the draft evidence to be submitted to the Beveridge Committee, GS/BCST, 1950, p. 6.
23. Labour Party, Evidence submitted to the Committee on Broadcasting, p. 5.
24. B. Bain, 'Verdict on the BBC', *Tribune*, 26 January 1951, p. 9.
25. HoC Debates, 19 July 1951, col. 210
26. Ibid., col. 1530.
27. Ibid., col. 210.
28. National Television Council, *Britain Unites against Commercial TV* (London: NTC, 1953).
29. C. Mayhew, *Dear Viewer* (London: Lincolns Praeger, 1953).
30. HoC Debates, 25 March 1954, col. 1484.
31. HoC Debates, 22 June 1954, col. 336. This reflected the anti-Americanism, prevalent on the left but particularly inside the Communist Party, that fuelled the campaign against American horror comics at the same time. See M. Barker, *A Haunt of Fears: The Strange Case of the British Horror Comics Campaign* (London: Pluto Press, 1984), pp. 21–7.
32. HoC Debates, 11 June 1952, col. 250.

33. Labour Party, *Not Fit For Children*, Labour Party leaflet against commercial television (London: Labour Party, 1953).
34. Labour Party, 'Labour Says NO to Sponsored TV', *Let's Have the Truth*, 3 (London: Labour Party, 1953).
35. Ibid.
36. HoC Debates, 11 June 1952, col. 260.
37. TUC, *Report of Proceedings of the 85th Annual Trades Union Congress* (London: TUC, 1953), p. 175.
38. Wilson, *Pressure Group*, p. 42.
39. HoC Debates, 11 June 1952, col. 234.
40. Ibid., col. 242.
41. HoC Debates, 14 December 1953, col. 76.
42. Quoted in Briggs, *Sound and Vision*, p. 897.
43. Ibid., p. 930.
44. See ibid., pp. 898 and 924 for poll evidence that substantial numbers of Labour supporters would welcome commercial programmes.
45. *New Statesman and Nation*, 'TV and the Political Parties', 27 November 1954, 48, 1238, p. 680.
46. *New Statesman and Nation*, 'Television Prospect', 5 April 1952, 43, 1100, p. 396.
47. *Tribune*, 'Break up the BBC – But No Mr Muggs', 20 November 1953.
48. Ibid.
49. *Socialist Commentary*, 'Trouble over Television', December 1953, 17, p. 287.
50. Association of Cinematograph and Allied Technicians (ACT), *Report and Agenda for the 21st Annual Meeting* (London: ACT, 1954), p. 15.
51. Association of Broadcasting Staff (ABS), *ABS Bulletin*, 57, June–July 1954, p. 206.
52. ABS, *ABS Bulletin*, 63, April–May 1955.
53. TUC, *Report of Proceedings of the 86th Annual Trades Union Congress* (London: TUC, 1954), pp. 457–8.
54. Quoted in C. Moorhead, *Sidney Bernstein: A Biography* (London: Jonathan Cape, 1984), p. 215.
55. E. Fletcher, *Random Reminiscences of Lord Fletcher of Islington* (London: Bishopsgate Press, 1986), p. 178.
56. Wilson, *Pressure Group*, p. 154.
57. Fletcher, *Random Reminiscences*, p. 177.
58. Quoted in B. Sendall, *Origin and Foundation, 1946–1962*: vol. I of *Independent Television in Britain* (London: Macmillan, 1982), p. 72.
59. Ibid.
60. Ibid., p. 191 – emphasis added.
61. Bernstein with Granada which had the Northern weekday franchise, Fletcher with ABC which held the Midlands and Northern weekend franchises and King with ATV which held the London weekend and Midlands weekday franchises.
62. R. Crossman, *The Backbench Diaries of Richard Crossman* (London: Hamish Hamilton and Jonathan Cape, 1981), p. 109.
63. Quoted in P. Williams, *Hugh Gaitskell: A Biography* (London: Jonathan Cape, 1979), p. 390.
64. H. Gaitskell, 'Understanding the Electorate', *Socialist Commentary*, 19, July 1955, p. 205.
65. HoC Debates, 11 June 1952, col. 322.
66. HoC Debates, 22 June 1954, col. 1473.
67. Labour Party, Minutes of the first meeting of the Joint Committee on the Future of TV, 25 January 1955, GS/BCST.
68. Ibid.
69. Quoted in F. Craig, *British General Election Manifestos 1900–1974* (London: Macmillan, 1975), p. 206.
70. Wilson, *Pressure Group*, p. 179.
71. See ibid., pp. 201–5.
72. Sendall, *Independent Television in Britain*, vol. I, p. 34.
73. See Wilson, *Pressure Group*, p. 179.
74. Ibid., p. 206.
75. See I. Mikardo, *Back-Bencher* (London: Weidenfeld & Nicolson, 1988), p. 122.
76. T. Fyvel, 'The Age of Participation', *Socialist Commentary*, 19, March 1955, p. 70.
77. A. Crosland, *The Future of Socialism* (London: Jonathan Cape, 1980), p. 16.

78. Ibid., p. 18.
79. Ibid., p. 31.
80. Ibid., p. 35.
81. Ibid., p. 42.
82. Ibid., p. 208 – emphasis added.
83. Ibid., p. 211.
84. Ibid., p. 215.
85. Ibid., p. 216.
86. Ibid., p. 353.
87. Ibid., p. 355.
88. T. Cliff and D. Gluckstein, *The Labour Party: A Marxist History* (London: Bookmarks, 1988), p. 262.
89. R. Miliband, *Parliamentary Socialism: A Study in the Politics of Labour* (London: George Allen & Unwin, 1961), p. 344.
90. M. Abrams and R. Rose, *Must Labour Lose?* (Harmondsworth: Penguin, 1960), p. 119.
91. Ibid., p. 31.
92. Ibid., p. 42.
93. J. Cronin, *Labour and Society in Britain, 1918–1979* (London: Batsford Academic, 1984), p. 11.
94. E. P. Thompson, 'The New Left', *The New Reasoner*, Summer 1959, p. 10.
95. Ibid., p. 11.
96. R. Hoggart, *The Uses of Literacy* (Harmondsworth: Penguin, 1960), p. 191.
97. R. Williams, *The Long Revolution* (London: Chatto & Windus, 1961).
98. D. Dworkin, *Cultural Marxism in Postwar Britain* (London: Duke University Press, 1997), p. 98.
99. Cliff and Gluckstein, *The Labour Party*, p. 279.
100. See A. Briggs, *Competition, 1955–1974* (vol. V of *The History of Broadcasting in the United Kingdom*) (Oxford: Oxford University Press, 1995), pp. 114–16 for details on the abolition of the Fourteen-Day Rule, the law that prevented reporting on matters due to be debated in Parliament in the following fortnight.
101. See ABS, 'Future of TV – The Debate is On', *ABS Bulletin*, 86, Christmas 1957, p. 261.
102. T. Benn, *Years of Hope: Diaries, Letters and Papers* (London: Hutchinson, 1994), p. 253.
103. Labour Party, Minutes of the first meeting of the Sub-Committee on Television and Radio, 23 July 1958, GS/BCST.
104. Labour Party, Confidential report on the Third Programme for the Sub-Committee on Television and Radio, Re. 468/November 1958, GS/BCST, p. 5.
105. Ibid.
106. Ibid., pp. 5–6.
107. Ibid., p. 6.
108. Ibid., p. 8.
109. Ibid., p. 9 – emphasis in original.
110. Quoted in Sendall, *Independent Television in Britain*, vol. I, p. 150.
111. Labour Party, Confidential report for the Sub-Committee on Television and Radio, Re. 511/February 1959, GS/BCST, p. 3.
112. Labour Party, Confidential report, Re. 468, p.10.
113. Association of Cinematograph, Television and Allied Technicians (ACTT), *Report and Agenda for the 26th Annual General Meeting* (London: ACTT, 1959), p. 57.
114. C. Mayhew, *Commercial Television: What is to be Done?* (London: Fabian Society, 1959).
115. A. Greenwood, 'The Challenge of Leisure for Living', Labour Press Service, October 1959.
116. *Tribune*, 'Freedom of the Air', 13 July 1962.
117. A. Crosland, 'Pilkington and the Labour Party', *Socialist Commentary*, 26, August 1962.
118. Hoggart, *The Uses of Literacy*, p. 36.
119. G. Elvin, 'A Questionnaire to Candidates', *Film and Television Technician*, November 1959, p. 180.
120. Labour Party, Confidential paper on 'The Financing of a Third Television Programme', prepared for the Sub-Committee on Television and Radio, Re. 499/February 1959, GS/BCST, p. 3.
121. Ibid.
122. Ibid.
123. Labour Party, Confidential report, Re. 511, p. 3.

124. See Craig, *British General Election Manifestos*, p. 226.
125. Quoted in Sendall, *Independent Television in Britain*, vol. I, p. 298.
126. B. Harris, 'Why Should You Pay to Make These Men Rich?', *Sunday Express*, 15 March 1959.
127. *New Left Review*, 'Missing Signposts', 12, November/December 1961, p. 9.
128. Ibid., p. 10.
129. Labour Party, Minutes of the National Executive Committee, 16 May 1961, para. 168.
130. Labour Party, *Signposts for the Sixties: A Statement of Labour Party Home Policy Submitted by the NEC to the 60th Annual Conference* (London: Labour Party, 1961).
131. *New Left Review*, 'Missing Signposts', p. 10.
132. Four Labour MPs (Ness Edwards, Christopher Mayhew, Woodrow Wyatt and Denis Howell) made brief individual submissions to the committee, although only Mayhew endorsed the idea of a new public service corporation for the third channel. See H. Pilkington (chair), *Report of the Committee on Broadcasting, volume II, appendix E*, Cmnd. 1819–I (London: HMSO, 1962), p. 1138).
133. In Curran and Seaton, *Power Without Responsibility*, p. 175.
134. H. Pilkington, *Report of the Committee on Broadcasting*, Cmnd. 1753 (London: HMSO, 1962), para. 101.
135. For a summary of the recommendations of and reactions to the Pilkington Report, see Briggs, *Competition*, pp. 294–303.
136. Quoted in ibid., p. 302.
137. J. Craigie, 'Pilkington: A Second Chance for Television', *Tribune*, 6 July 1962.
138. Ibid.
139. TUC, *Report of Proceedings of the 94th Annual Trades Union Congress* (London: TUC, 1962), p. 438.
140. Labour Party, *Report of the 61st Annual Conference* (London: Labour Party, 1962), p. 147.
141. Ibid. Labour continued to be divided over its attitude towards advertising: see Chapter 3 for discussions of the NEC's study group on advertising.
142. HoC Debates, 31 July 1962, cols 435–7.
143. Ibid., col. 504.
144. Ibid., cols 526–7.
145. Quoted in D. Robinson, *Contrast on Pilkington* (London: BFI, 1962).
146. Hoggart, letter to the author, 23 March 1998.
147. Ibid.
148. HoC Debates, 25 February 1963, col. 953
149. See ACTT, 'ACTT's Policy on the Pilkington Report', *Film and Television Technician*, November 1962.
150. See TUC, *Report of Proceedings of the 94th Annual Trades Union Congress*, pp. 441–3 and Labour Party, *Report of the 61st Annual Conference*, pp. 148–9.
151. See B. Sendall, *Expansion and Change, 1958–68* (vol. II of *Independent Television in Britain*) (London: Macmillan, 1983), pp. 190–201.
152. *The Times*, 'New Broadcasting Fund Suggested', 26 February 1962.
153. HoC Debates, 31 July 1962, col. 531.
154. *New Left Review*, 'TV and the Community', 7, January/February 1961, p. 47.
155. Ibid., p. 48.
156. Sendall, *Independent Television in Britain*, Vol. 2, p. 177.

3

Harold Wilson and 'Modernization', 1964–70

THE WILSON GOVERNMENTS IN CONTEXT

The Labour government inherited substantial economic problems from the Conservatives when it came into office in 1964. Although British capitalism had expanded massively in the post-war boom, the rate of expansion had started to slow by the early 1960s putting Britain in a weaker position in relation to its international rivals. According to Clive Ponting, '[l]ow investment, wages rising faster than productivity growth and the handicap of a large number of declining industries (and an overvalued pound) lay at the root of Britain's economic problems'.[1] In other words, structural economic difficulties were to blame for poor economic growth, a declining rate of profit and an increasing rate of inflation.

Labour leader Harold Wilson's solution was to embrace economic planning; Labour's 1964 election manifesto promised a national plan that would defeat the Tories' 'stop-go economic policy'.[2] For Andrew Shonfield, whose 1965 book *Modern Capitalism* celebrated the productive benefits of indicative planning, it was 'central to Labour Party thinking that a government of the Left should assume full responsibility for the task of national planning'.[3] Wilson promised to set up new ministries of economic affairs and technology and to revitalize the National Economic Development Corporation, set up by the Conservatives in 1962.

According to Ben Pimlott, 'Wilson called for a sensible, gradualist social revolution. The instrument of that revolution was to be the centralized planning of science and technology.'[4] The soon-to-be prime minister expressed this vision most famously in his speech, 'Labour's Plan for Science', at the 1963 party conference. He argued that the choice was not *whether* but *how* to relate to technological advance:

> It is the choice between the blind imposition of technological advance, with all that means in terms of unemployment, and the conscious, planned, purposive use of scientific progress to provide undreamed of living standards and the possibility of leisure ultimately on an unbelievable scale.[5]

Wilson then went on to include developments in communications as part of this technological programme, calling for a 'University of the Air' and arguing that it is 'very nice that we should be putting so much research into colour television'.[6]

The speech has been read both as rhetoric and as evidence of Wilson's commitment to innovation and planning. Christopher Booker treats it as a brilliant piece of public relations, designed to smooth over the ideological differences inside the Labour Party which had proved so disruptive to the party throughout the 1950s and early 1960s.[7] Pimlott, on the other hand, argues that the speech genuinely struck a chord with the audience (and beyond) and represented an 'extremist' position in advocating 'government intervention in almost every aspect of the nation's economic life'.[8] Tony Benn, the first postmaster general in Wilson's government, states that Wilson was deliberately misunderstood: 'What he said was that in the white heat of the technological revolution, we will all be burned up with unemployment unless we plan it. He wasn't saying "I'll put on a white coat and get a welding machine and modernise the economy".'[9]

Both approaches contain an element of truth. Of course Wilson was eager to associate the Labour Party with the dividends of technological growth and increased leisure time; he was also profoundly serious about replacing a laissez-faire approach to technology with a more purposeful one. The left-wing journalist Paul Foot argues that what was missing from the speech, however, was an indication of how the technological revolution could be realized without treading on the toes of big business. To implement Wilson's proposals meant 'a new range of taxes and levies upon industry, considerable state representation on boards of directors and, in many cases, wholesale nationalization. Not once in his speech did Wilson indicate the extent to which his Government would interfere with industry.'[10] According to Foot, the speech was therefore not a simple public relations exercise (although it worked magnificently as one) but an example of Labour's reformist belief that 'there is nothing wrong with the machine as such. What is wrong is the driver ... [Wilson's] aim was not to scrap the machine for another one, but to steer it round the obstacles in its path.'[11]

Was this approach a break from Gaitskellite and Croslandite revisionism? Dick Crossman, a key Cabinet member in the Wilson governments, argued that it was: 'Wilson had provided the revision of Socialism and its application to modern times which Gaitskell and Crosland had tried and completely failed to do.'[12] Wilson's redefinition of socialism, that Labour's radical social objectives needed to be underpinned by planned and sustained economic growth, won acclaim from all sides of the party in the run-up to the 1964 election. The vision of a revitalized capitalism encouraged the right, while talk of trade union partnership helped to win support for an incomes policy at the 1963 Labour conference.

Others argued the opposite. In response to Labour left claims at the time that 'revisionism was not on the agenda', Paul Foot responded:

> In fact, of course, revisionism had in no sense, and not for a single moment, left the agenda. Gaitskell's policy on the Bomb had triumphed and the party's policy on economic affairs was still based on the ultra-revisionist *Industry and Society*. In more ways than one the policy of the Party, as opposed to the electoral rhetoric of its leaders, had swung, if anything, Rightwards since 1959.[13]

What had changed, it may be argued, was that Labour's revisionist objectives – those stressed by Crosland in *The Future of Socialism* concerning social legislation – were now to be intimately linked to the successful resolution of Britain's economic problems. Without a clear sign of industrial growth and an end to stop-go cycles, there could be no talk of serious social reform nor of a sustained attack on inequality and privilege. The government, therefore, attached itself to a policy of 'pragmatism': virtually anything could be justified if it could be proved to be in the national economic interest. Wages, prices, public services and electoral promises were all subordinated to the priority of restoring growth to the British economy. Pragmatism itself became the dominant theoretical position associated with the Wilson government.

Winning office and then retaining it was another central concern for Wilson as his government's economic plans hit the rocks immediately after the 1964 election. Whereas for most of the 1950s Britain's trade with the rest of the world had led to a trade surplus, a Conservative-engineered pre-election boom led to a balance-of-payments deficit of £800m in 1964.[14] The Labour government was under pressure within days of taking office to make cuts in public expenditure and to lower sterling to a rate that would make exports more competitive. Although Wilson triumphed in his first battle with the bankers (and went ahead with a budget which abolished prescription charges and raised pensions and welfare benefits), he persevered with a policy of protecting the pound at all costs. Shortly after winning the 1966 election with an increased majority, the Labour government introduced a massive deflationary package and a statutory incomes policy to support the pound. With the economy still very fragile, Wilson held out until November 1967 when devaluation of the pound was quickly followed by a savage cuts package of over £700m which included the reintroduction of prescription charges and the postponement of the raising of the school-leaving age. Further deflationary packages were imposed for the next two years together with the ultimately unsuccessful attack on union rights, *In Place of Strife*, all of which caused enormous upheavals and disappointment inside the party. 'For many in the Party, the Labour Government of 1966 to 1970 had been a failure. It had revoked its mandate commitments, ignored Conference decisions and carried through policies which ran counter to some of the basic principles of the Party.'[15]

There was more praise, however, for Labour's record in social affairs where liberalization of laws concerning abortion, homosexuality, divorce and censorship were passed in spite of the economic problems. Even a critic like Clive Ponting notes that 'the government's record [in social reform] is all the more commendable since it was achieved in the face of an awful economic legacy'.[16] To what extent did the Wilson governments demonstrate this commitment in their attempts to modernize and reform British television?

THE ROAD AHEAD: TELEVISION ISSUES IN 1964

By 1964, the outgoing Conservative administration had presided over a number of decisions affecting television. In response to the Pilkington Committee's recommendations, PMG Reginald Bevins had launched BBC2, imposed a levy on advertising revenue on the ITV companies and extended the charters of both BBC and ITA by 12 years. The Tories felt confident enough to include a separate paragraph on broadcasting in their manifesto for the 1964 election which boasted that 'we introduced ITV, authorised BBC-2, and have licensed experiments in pay-as-you-view TV by wire. We wish to extend the range of choice still further',[17] particularly through proposals for a second commercial television channel and local sound broadcasting.

The Labour Party's election manifesto, however, made no mention at all of broadcasting's role in the 'New Britain' that was to be built in the ongoing technological revolution, lacking even a reference to the 'University of the Air' that Wilson had highlighted in his 'science' speech in 1963. This was not due to ignorance of the policy challenges in the sphere of broadcasting that faced Labour. Tony Benn, the newly appointed PMG, notes in his diary that he was immediately 'confronted with important decisions over television broadcasting',[18] notably the BBC licence fee, the question of a fourth channel, pay television and the introduction of colour. Neither was it because of a lack of interest by senior party members who had already had top-level discussions with broadcasters in the run-up to the election. For example, MPs Roy Mason and George Darling (both of whom were soon to be ministers of state in the Board of Trade) met with the BBC secretary Charles Curran in July 1964 to discuss a wide range of broadcasting-related issues. The meeting revealed the Labour front bench's unhappiness with the request for an increase in the licence fee and its reluctance to endorse a fourth channel for education.[19] It seems more likely that Labour's public reticence to discuss television simply reflected the divisions which had surfaced in party discussions at the time of the Pilkington Committee and which remained unresolved, over criticisms of ITV and a defence of non-commercial television.

Wilson, as we shall see, was particularly sensitive to the increasing influence of television and sought to use Benn's professional knowledge for electoral advantage and industrial benefits. 'A mark of Wilson's seriousness about television', argues Pimlott, 'was the introduction of Anthony Wedgwood Benn, a former television producer, into the inner circle.'[20] His brief at the Post Office included not only broadcasting but also telecommunications, satellites and information technology. Decisions about television, he decided, had to be seen in the wider context of Britain's relative economic weakness and the imperative to modernize. In early 1965, he admitted that 'Defence, colour television, Concorde, rocket development – these are all issues raising economic considerations that reveal this country's basic inability to stay in the big league. We just can't afford it.'[21]

Benn's stubborn refusal to ignore harsh economic facts led him to an early and gloomy appraisal of the finances of the BBC. The departing Conservative administration had left behind not only a substantial balance-of-payments deficit but had also saddled the BBC with a rising debt in its preparations for BBC2. PMG Bevins told the

Cabinet in 1962 that 'most of his colleagues on the Ministerial Committee [on Broadcasting] shared his view that any increase in licence fee before 1965 was "politically unrealistic"' because of electoral pressure, and so left the licence fee at £4.[22] In the context of competition from pirate radio and government reluctance to increase the licence fee, Benn wrote in January 1965:

> I can see ourselves moving steadily towards the starvation of the BBC through a failure to raise the licence fee and ultimately capitulation in favour of commercial sound broadcasting. That is unless we permit the expansion of broadcasting on the basis of public service with advertising revenue to finance it.[23]

There was certainly no love lost between Benn and the BBC[24] and one of Benn's main concerns as PMG was to create a space in which a more independent system of public broadcasting could emerge, even if this meant a challenge to existing structures. Briggs writes that Benn was the only PMG who, 'while believing strongly in public service broadcasting, did not identify public service broadcasting with the BBC',[25] a definition he carried with him well after his years at the Post Office.

Benn was not the only Labour member to have reservations about the BBC, then in the throes of the 'Greene revolution', the new director general's attempt to modernize the Corporation and to compete more effectively with ITV.[26] In opposition Labour had benefited from the BBC's new-found dynamism as the latter sought to shrug off its stuffy image by commissioning a range of innovative and daring programmes. One of the most controversial examples of this was the notorious *That Was the Week that Was (TW3)* which was 'anti-pomposity, anti-sanctimony, anti-snob and – blatantly – anti-Conservative'.[27] The problem was that it was only a fine line between being anti-Conservative and being anti-government, *any* government. Now that the Labour Party was in office, there was little reason to expect that it would receive an easy ride nor that its authority would be naturally respected by the BBC. Labour's ambiguous attitude to the BBC was to be a key factor in television policy during the 1960s.

The other key area, ignored by Benn in his 'to-do' list, concerned the future of ITV. Although the Labour Party had now officially accepted the place of commercial television alongside the BBC, it would still be expected to do something to curb the tremendous profits which were being made despite the introduction of the advertising levy in 1963. Surely in Wilson's 'New Britain' where, according to the manifesto, 'we must ensure that a sufficient part of the new wealth created goes to meet urgent and now neglected human needs',[28] there would be some plans to tackle the profits of commercial television and its neglect of minority audiences? The television critic Milton Shulman expressed this most forcefully:

> The country had witnessed a major financial scandal in which, through a Government monopoly, a few men had received returns on their investments out of all proportions to either the capital they had risked or the contributions they were making to the nation. A Socialist Government would presumably have been shocked and sickened by this spectacle.[29]

Yet the government was silent on the issue. This might have been due to the fact that Wilson's favourite programme was ITV's *Coronation Street*[30] or that senior Labour politicians had by now recognized the influence of ITV. David Haworth, in an article for *Socialist Commentary* in 1965, attempted to provide an explanation for the lack of progress in government reform of television:

> I think part of the answer is that the Labour Party has never recovered from the memory of its opposition to the establishment of commercial television. As soon as the second channel became a fact, Labour found that its most enthusiastic audience was to be found among its own supporters. After that the Party found singular difficulty in allowing its considerations on broadcasting to mature in any very coherent form.[31]

The renewal of the franchises in 1967 and the debates over the size of the advertising levy at the end of the decade forced Labour to once again address the question of commercial television. Before then, in the increasingly difficult economic climate, the government had to make some firm decisions about other major areas of television policy.

HAROLD WILSON AND TELEVISION

'There is little doubt that the character and philosophy of British broadcasting as it enters the 70s has been moulded by the will and activities of Harold Wilson', wrote the TV critic Milton Shulman in 1973.[32] Wilson, it is claimed, played a decisive role in the development of Labour's television policy in the 1960s. He was an excellent television performer who appreciated the importance of the new mass medium and was keen to improve the professionalism of

Labour's broadcasts. Additionally, Wilson 'planned to use the airwaves as a major instrument of government. He would make regular broadcasts to explain his policies direct to the people.'[33] This would allow Wilson to communicate with voters without the troublesome mediation of the Fleet Street press who Wilson perceived rightly as generally anti-Labour.

The strategy, however, counted on the compliance of the broadcasting establishment at precisely the time when the BBC, in particular, was expanding its political coverage and was keen to demonstrate its independence. The skirmishes between Wilson and the BBC started almost immediately after the election when, in January 1965, Wilson was refused a ministerial broadcast without opposition right-of-reply,[34] and continued unabated. The prime minister complained regularly both about the number of left-wingers and government critics allowed by the BBC to speak on government policy and about systematic bias in BBC current affairs programmes.[35] The result was that 'Wilson was to see British television as an instrument of conspiracy against the Labour Party, and especially against himself.'[36]

The problem was that, while Labour had gained from the *TW3*'s satirical portrait of the Tories in 1963, Wilson and Labour supporters had no wish to become the object of parody now that the party was in government. Wilson's antagonism towards the BBC was initially accepted by his fellow ministers and supported even by Labour's grass roots. One resolution from the Isle of Wight Constituency Labour Party in January 1966 noted that 'whilst appreciating the need for satire in TV programmes, we have noticed an increase in political satire on the BBC TV programmes prejudicial to the Socialist point of view'.[37] Wilson may have had a point about BBC bias but his sensitivity appeared to be particularly focused on preventing open criticism of government policies as economic problems started to open up fissures among Labour supporters. By the end of the decade, Wilson's hostility to the BBC had started to disturb even his close colleagues. Crossman noted in 1969 that Wilson 'is obsessed with the BBC, and this and his obsession with leaks are his most outstanding weaknesses as a leader'.[38]

Wilson had an entirely different attitude towards ITV and spoke of the 'absolutely scrupulous impartiality' of the ITA when chaired by the former Conservative PMG, Charles Hill.[39] One of Wilson's biographers writes that 'Wilson preferred ITV from the first. It had sympathetic company bosses, such as Sidney Bernstein at Granada … [and] was widely perceived as the popular and therefore more working-class station'.[40] ITV's populism complemented Wilson's pragmatism and the prime minister was happy to do deals with commercial television at the expense of the BBC. In one celebrated incident on the morning after his 1966 election victory, Wilson refused to do a live interview with the BBC from a specially rigged train on the basis that he had not been given any warning, but was happy to accommodate ITN. This somewhat contradicts the notes of a conversation the previous day between Wilson and a senior BBC journalist, Stanley Hyland, where Wilson is quoted as saying that 'I still haven't made up my mind about the train.'[41]

Clearly, Wilson's attitude towards television structures was influenced by the state of his personal relations with broadcasters and journalists. To what extent does this mean that policy was being made not on the basis of public debate but of private passions? Michael Cockerell's view is that Wilson attempted to punish the BBC for its critical stance towards Labour, particularly in his unwillingness to sanction a licence fee increase. When BBC director-general (DG) Greene made this public in 1966, 'Wilson was enraged. He gave his backing to a Wedgwood Benn plan to reform the BBC by introducing some commercials and hiving off parts of radio.'[42] Benn then 'went to see Harold who has confused the whole thing in his mind with his current dislike of the bias in BBC programmes'.[43] However, as we shall see, this was not the plan that the government accepted, partly because Wilson himself had a more contradictory approach to the BBC than one of pure, unbridled antagonism.

Despite his comfortable relationship with commercial television bosses and his concerns about BBC bias, Wilson was fundamentally reluctant to undermine the public structure of the BBC. In a meeting between Greene and Derek Mitchell, Wilson's private secretary, immediately after the 1964 election, Mitchell reassured the DG about Labour's plans. 'I said I thought that they [the BBC] should not worry unduly. A Labour Government was bound, other things being equal, to be sympathetic to the BBC as a nationalised corporation.'[44] In the middle of heated negotiations about the licence fee, Crossman noted that Wilson 'has a conventional respect for the BBC as a public corporation and won't allow advertising … His main aim is to stay in office.'[45] Wilson's commitment to pragmatism and corporatism partially softened his desire to discipline the BBC although, of course, other things were not equal and Wilson increasingly lost patience with the Corporation during the 1960s. As Philip Ziegler, Wilson's sympathetic biographer, puts it: 'The remarkable thing is not that Wilson eventually fell out with the BBC but that it took so long for him to do so.'[46]

One of Wilson's most controversial acts was his decision in 1967, after consultation with PMG Edward Short but not the Cabinet, to appoint Charles Hill of the ITA to be the chair of the BBC. Given Hill's intimate association with both commercial television and the Conservatives, 'it was obvious, not least to Wilson himself, that the choice he was making would not appeal to many people inside the Labour Party',[47] a reaction which made little impact on the prime minister. Increasingly irritated by what he perceived as the BBC's partisanship, Wilson, according to Cockerell, selected Hill for three reasons: 'to control the exuberance and restrict the freedom of programme makers', to 'humiliate the BBC's senior executives' and finally to 'force Hugh Greene to resign'.[48] Short disagrees with any suggestion that it was a political decision:

> The press took the view that we were getting our own back at the BBC but it wasn't that at all. I think the BBC needed somebody like him – they were stodgy, they stood on their dignity about things … There wasn't a political relationship … Hill was an intelligent, cultured man. He wasn't just anybody, a great publicist, the Radio Doctor. He was never very political.[49]

This is a slightly disingenuous description of a man who was a Conservative minister for broadcasting when commercial television was first introduced in 1955 and who, according to Wilson himself, 'has already cleaned up ITV and [will] do the same to BBC now I'm appointing him chairman'.[50]

The key point is that Wilson took a keen interest in television and assumed a leadership role when it came to government policy in the field. In January 1965 he set up a ministerial committee on broadcasting to oversee television development,[51] and then took over the chair in October 1966 in order to head off opposition to his plans.[52] He met regularly with leading figures from the television world, kept a very close watch on television output and attempted to impose his will on television policy, even when he was not sure exactly where he stood. One historian has written that '[i]f Wilson believed in anything, he certainly believed in the influence of the media. And he was determined to exploit this to his own advantage.'[53] Accusations still abound that Wilson's interest in television, like a true modern-day premier, reflected an obsession with presentation more than policy and that his pragmatism suffused any firm principles. However, as I shall now attempt to illustrate, Wilson's approach to television policy, while rarely consistent, was nevertheless connected to one firm objective: to modernize and invigorate British economic and political institutions through the guidance of a Labour government. When BBC television programmes criticized this project, the entire Corporation risked the wrath of the premier; when leading figures from ITV identified themselves with Wilson, all of commercial television looked set to gain. Labour's approach to television in the 1960s was, therefore, caught between a partial desire for institutional reform and Wilson's pragmatic solutions to a declining economic situation.

PREPARING FOR THE FUTURE: PAYING FOR THE BBC

Three months into a Labour government, letters were fired off between the Post Office and Number 10. Was it true, Derek Mitchell in Wilson's office wanted to know, that Benn would 'be asking the BBC to reconsider its whole structure and policy' in response to its request for more money?[54] Benn's department replied that Benn had been 'linking this in his mind with other major broadcasting decisions that have to be reached, believing that the Government will want to look at the whole picture'.[55] Wilson reacted by setting up a ministerial committee on broadcasting, chaired by Herbert Bowden, lord president of the council, with the home secretary, the chief whip, the attorney-general, the financial secretary to the Treasury and ministers including Benn, Crossman, Jennie Lee and George Darling. The committee had a wide-ranging but crucial brief: to consider the allocation of a fourth channel, the future of the licence fee, the launch of a 'University of the Air', the possibility of local radio broadcasting and the question of television standards. In short, it was convened to plan the future of British broadcasting.

There was an immediate need for a decision about the BBC licence fee because the Corporation had been forced into debt to cope with the start-up of BBC2. Benn made it clear that any increase was contingent on the general economic situation. Benn told Greene and Lord Normanbrook, the BBC's chair, at a meeting in March 1965 that 'difficulties were being raised by the Department for Economic Affairs because of the reaction on incomes policy'. In the event that money could not be found, the PMG suggested that the BBC attempt to reduce revenue lost through licence fee evasion.[56] Wilson was even more uncompromising and placed the status of BBC2, less than a year old, in jeopardy. In response to Post Office figures that BBC2 was responsible for a large proportion of the BBC's deficit, Wilson replied that 'I do not see why we need to increase licence fees to pay for a programme that no one wants to see – and many can't see even if they wanted to.'[57] During the discussions that followed the Pilkington Report in 1962, Labour had officially supported the award of a second channel to the BBC; now, in a harsher economic climate, Wilson was less willing to back what he saw as an elitist venture.[58] Less than two weeks later, however, Wilson was persuaded to agree to a licence fee increase from £4 to £5 as an urgent measure to stem the BBC's deficit. Rather than risk unpopularity in the run-up to an election, Wilson preferred to hide the rise among the general tax increases on personal consumption in the April 1965 budget. His caution was perhaps unnecessary given that the BBC in this period produced some of its most popular and challenging programmes like *Till Death Us Do Part*, *Steptoe and Son*, *Up the Junction*, *Cathy Come Home* and the *Wars of the Roses* series.

Negotiations on BBC finances over the next 18 months highlight many of the divisions inside the Labour Party regarding its relationship to commercial forces, electoralism and pragmatism. Following more pressure on the pound that summer, the Cabinet introduced a further deflationary package in July causing Crossman to remark that '[t]his was the most violent, primitive, stupid form of "stop-go" ever thought of'.[59] Discussions on television policy seemed to be following the same cycle with short-term decisions taking precedence over long-term strategic thinking. By the autumn of 1965, the pound was in a more stable position, a situation which encouraged ministers to find a solution to the issue of BBC finances. At a meeting of the ministerial committee in November 1965, three ways of meeting the BBC's financial needs were proposed: a further increase in the licence fee, a grant from government or an injection of advertising. In the current economic circumstances, the first two were ruled out of order and so the committee opted for the latter. Benn argued that this advertising option was a 'tremendous success and if it goes through Cabinet, as I think it will, it will be the beginning of the reshaping of British broadcasting under public service conditions with some mixed revenue'.[60] The committee then gave the green light for Benn to work on a white paper incorporating the proposal.

Benn was convinced that allowing the BBC to carry a limited amount of advertising on its Light Programme (in radio) would both kill off the challenge of the illegal pirate radio stations and allow for reform of British broadcasting with local programmes and a national popular music station. Faced with the dilemma of the need to expand broadcasting at a time of public expenditure cuts, Benn felt there was no option other than attracting private finance. Short of a more radical solution and still politically attached to Wilson's programme, Benn's alternative was an entirely 'pragmatic' one: to turn to private investment and advertising despite his personal hostility towards the cash-rich ITV sector and his party's traditional antagonism towards market forces.

He immediately faced a challenge on three fronts: the conservatism of the civil service, resistance to advertising from within the party and, above all, an impending election. There was, however, no lack of debate between Labour MPs in the various broadcasting committees. In the Cabinet on 15 February 1966, those in favour of advertising included Crossman, Barbara Castle, Bowden and, according to Benn, Harold Wilson himself[61] with a majority hostile to the plan. However, given that 'no other additional source of finance was available; and in the light of the responsible attitude which the independent television companies had displayed', the Cabinet agreed that there were grounds for believing that limited advertising might be politically acceptable.[62] This was a particularly surprising admission that, not only had the ITV companies been behaving 'responsibly' but that the BBC's finances should be related to the behaviour of its commercial counterparts.

The following day, at a meeting of the backbench communications group of Labour MPs, the occasional forum for discussing broadcasting issues of the Parliamentary Labour Party (PLP), there was another split with two MPs arguing that 'the BBC should take advertising so that the public sector would not be starved of resources'.[63] The conclusion to the meeting is most interesting: 'there was a majority in favour of some advertising solution if it could be done properly but it was agreed that we shouldn't publish a White Paper at all'.[64] Although Benn had actually prepared a draft, the main task for the government was to avoid a damaging row in the run-up to a general election (planned for March 1966), even if this meant suppressing existing policy proposals. The, by now, urgent need to make some firm decisions on broadcasting was sacrificed for short-term electoral success. Crossman, despite supporting Benn's proposals in Cabinet, wrote two days afterwards that 'clearly, this is something we shall have to put under the mat until after the election'.[65] On 2 March, Wilson met Benn to brief him on the next day's broadcasting debate in the Commons and told him that he should 'certainly not suggest that the Cabinet were in any way moving towards acceptance of advertising revenue on the Light Programme'.[66]

In any case, a tentative solution to the crisis of the licence fee had been reached. Wilson called in the DG to Downing Street and:

made it clear that it was not at all in his mind to eliminate the possibility of increases in the licence fee for all time. On the other hand, the Government was not willing to accept anything in the nature of an automatic obligation to increase the licence fee to meet the rising costs of broadcasting. He said that this was particularly difficult at a time when the Government was trying to hold down public expenditure.[67]

Wilson suggested that the BBC make some efficiency savings by moving some operations out of London and by reducing licence fee evasion. Greene, somewhat surprisingly, accepted that the BBC would have to manage without an increase until 1968 as long as the government did not extend broadcasting hours.[68] Benn's reaction to the news was that this 'provided the Cabinet with an excuse for killing my proposals' and that another 'of my projects has been lost as a result of the Election'.[69] The situation appeared to be resolved.

THE WHITE PAPER AND ADVERTISING

Benn's white paper did not appear before the 1966 election and, despite the title of Labour's manifesto, *Time for Decision*, little had been decided about the general future of broadcasting. Apart from a reference to the planned expansion of higher education through a 'University of the Air', the manifesto ignored the entire question of broadcasting unlike the Conservatives who, following a well-worn theme, promised to 'provide more choice and competition in broadcasting'.[70] Having substantially increased its majority at the polls, the government immediately ran into difficulties. The seamen's strike in May 1966, opposed by the government in an effort to protect its incomes policy, compounded pressure on the pound. In July, Wilson chose to opt for a £500m deflationary package which included a six-month wage and price freeze as well as significant rises in indirect taxes. Both the parliamentary party and Labour supporters outside Parliament, who had been reluctant to criticize the government when it had only a slender majority, were now more vocal in their opposition to Wilson's policies. Backbench rebellions became more frequent, there were regular demonstrations against rising unemployment by trade unionists and the left-wing NEC was increasingly impatient with the government's handling of the economic situation. According to Lewis Minkin, 'it was prepared now, for the first time in Party history, to be publicly identified with critics and criticism of Labour Government policy'.[71]

Following Frank Cousins' resignation from the Cabinet over its handling of the seamen's strike, Benn was moved to the Ministry of Technology and his place was filled by Edward Short. This did not prevent Benn from attempting to reform broadcasting through the introduction of mixed revenue into the system and he continued to fight for the creation of a new public radio corporation, playing popular music, mainly financed by advertising.[72] This was enough to rouse the anger of those, particularly on the left, who until now had been fairly silent about the government's lack of decisions about broadcasting. First, in May 1966 a committee was set up by the Home Policy Committee of the NEC specifically to look at the increasing power of advertising in the mass communications industries. While the first draft report did not appear for another year, it was clear that any immediate increase in advertising would face a strong challenge from the Labour left. Second, *Tribune* carried a lively debate about the 'Future of Broadcasting' which, although concentrating on radio, highlighted the attitudes of those in the Labour Party towards advertising in general. Hugh Jenkins, chair of the backbench communications group, supported Benn's proposals and argued that if advertising was good enough for Tribune it should be good enough for a new public corporation. In reply to Raymond Williams' plea not to hand over 'yet another major means of communication into private and irresponsible control' through its dependence on advertising,[73] Jenkins simply applied Harold Wilson's theory of corporatism. 'Of course, advertising in the acquisitive society is often as pernicious as many other things in the market economy. That is a very good reason that the state should get itself in a position to control a section of it.'[74]

Debate continued in the Cabinet and ministerial committee throughout the autumn of 1966 with, at one point, Benn's proposals seeming likely to be accepted.[75] However, by December, after a fierce lobbying campaign by the left, advertising was rejected as an option and the white paper, finally published in December, handed over the new popular music station to the BBC. *Tribune* argued this represented 'a considerable success for the anti-commercial forces in our society'[76] while, according to Crossman, Harold Wilson 'had scored a complete triumph over his modernizing adversaries'[77] in fending off advertising on the BBC. Wilson's role was clearly vital. Always the pragmatist, he had adopted an open mind towards advertising in the early part of the year in order to put pressure on the BBC and force it to do without a licence fee increase. If he was asking workers to tighten their belts to help the country through a crisis, why should the BBC be exempt from this? The white paper warned that 'at a time when none may be content to rest upon present standards of efficiency and financial performance, good though they may be, the Government have thought it right to expect of the BBC that they should set themselves even more exacting financial objectives'.[78]

Once Wilson had forced the BBC to introduce efficiency savings, he was more able to reveal his 'true' corporatist colours. Crossman described Wilson at the time as 'a very conventional traditionalist'.[79] Advertising, he wrote later, 'has always been opposed by Harold ... on the grounds that it's immoral to permit a virtuous organisation such as the BBC to be in any way related to commercial profit'.[80] Wilson's modernizing instincts combined the need to cut back on public expenditure with the defence of a fine and upstanding British institution, even one which had antagonized him as much as the BBC.

THE OPEN UNIVERSITY AND THE FOURTH CHANNEL

Just as the post-war Attlee government is remembered for its founding of the National Health Service, the single greatest achievement of the Wilson governments in the 1960s is often reckoned to be the creation of the Open University (OU). Pimlott describes it as 'a brilliantly original and highly ambitious institution which took the ideals of social equality and equality of opportunity more seriously than any other part of the British education system'.[81] While the OU was undoubtedly a massive step forward in the expansion of higher education, it is less clear whether it was a major example of broadcasting reform. Indeed the creation of a 'University of the Air' dominated by television was severely compromised by its birth at a time of financial cutbacks and rationalization. By the time it started, the Open University was structured far more by educational principles than by a desire to transform the institutions of television.

According to Stephen Lambert, had the Conservatives won the 1964 election, they would have extended commercial television by allocating the fourth channel to the ITA.[82] The Labour Party, on the other hand, was hostile to this idea and was more interested in using an additional channel for educational purposes; indeed for most of the Cabinet, the idea of a fourth channel was intimately tied to a 'University of the Air'. This reflected the debates in the party in the late 1950s and early 1960s which had seen the consensus in favour of a new public corporation run independently of both BBC and ITA. Briggs notes that Labour's interest in educational broadcasting dates from 1962 with the setting up of Lord Taylor's study group on higher education which recommended a 'University of the Air'.[83]

Wilson embraced this idea enthusiastically as an example of the planned use of new technology for scientific gain. The 'University of the Air' was to be a meritocratic institution, symptomatic of the 'New Britain'. In February 1965, he asked the education secretary to prepare a paper on the OU for the ministerial committee on broadcasting. In handwritten notes on the report, Wilson came up with three proposals: first, that the ITA be given control of the 'University of the Air'; second that the BBC and ITA run it together with the assistance of two universities; and third 'for the BBC to run it exclusively, advertising extensively on late-night programmes and use the profits to subsidise licence revenue'.[84]

Benn described Wilson's first option as an 'appalling solution'[85] but nevertheless met informally with Lew Grade, the chair of ATV, to discuss a public–private partnership for a fourth channel. 'It would be better than giving it to the BBC, though not as good as setting up another public corporation which would be a public service and inspiration, but would be allowed to take advertising.'[86] Neither Benn nor Grade felt able to develop this proposal further but it is nevertheless another example of the model that Channel 4 was eventually based on nearly 20 years later. Backbench MP Hugh Jenkins was thinking on the same lines: he wanted to see a new public corporation, answerable to the Ministry of Education but partially financed by advertising, which would transmit 'University of the Air' programmes as well as pay-per-view programmes. 'I see no other means of getting the Fourth TV Channel going', he wrote in the ACTT's journal.[87]

In the event, initiative for the project came not from the postmaster general but from the arts minister, Jennie Lee. In March 1965 Wilson transferred Lee into the Department of Education and Science to hurry the plans along. Lee was a dynamic and enthusiastic ambassador for the project but immediately anticipated financial difficulties. 'I am convinced', she wrote to the prime minister in August, a month after the government's most recent deflationary package, 'that if you want the Open University, you can have it but only you can break through the problems raised by costs and channels.'[88] Lee lobbied hard in the ministerial committee for a fourth channel and seemed to be making some headway. Wilson wanted material for his speech at the tenth anniversary dinner of the ITA in September and agreed with Bowden that 'it should be possible for some indication to be given of the Government's firm intention to establish a fourth channel largely devoted to educational broadcasts'.[89]

Over the next few months, civil servants and ministers became increasingly nervous about the expenditure involved in setting up a fourth channel. At the same time that Wilson was pressing Lee to get a white paper out in time for the election, the ministerial committee decided that her preferred suggestion was no longer financially viable. 'The industry will simply not support a fourth television channel which the University of the Air could use during peak hours' wrote the chief secretary to the Treasury, adding that it would cost about £40m to set up the channel. The solution was to use spare evening hours on BBC2.[90] Lee wrote to Wilson the same day raging against this plan: 'I consider that to revert to a half-baked scheme, using an hour or two on BBC 2 would completely undermine the whole purpose and spirit of a University of the Air.'[91] Four days later, on 7 February 1966, Lee wrote to Bowden and made it clear that using residual hours from other channels would not be enough. 'The fourth network is indispensable', she insisted and went on to challenge the chief secretary's 'inflated' figures, suggesting that the cost would be nearer £17m. She concluded by saying that 'I am wholly convinced that unless we are prepared to establish a genuine open university, based on the fourth network, we shall expose ourselves to the charges of gimmickry.'[92]

Cabinet met the following day to discuss the project where Lee continued to argue that a fourth channel was required. She was, however, firmly in the minority: 'Concern was expressed … at the demand which the fourth television network and the University of the Air would make upon resources.'[93] With Lee's proposals soundly defeated, Wilson concluded the discussion by promising to examine both the costs of a new network and the possibility of using spare hours on BBC2. He asked Lee to ensure that the revised white paper should 'be confined to the educational aspects of the University and should omit references to finance and the fourth network'.[94] Although Benn wrote in his diary that this 'must have been a terrible set-back for Jennie',[95] Lee herself appeared to be quite cheerful the following day. She wrote to Wilson's solicitor Arnold Goodman, who was helping with the financial discussions surrounding the OU, that she now considered the use of BBC2 between 6pm and 9pm to be 'the ideal solution'[96] and was ready to amend the white paper. The next draft, three days later, dropped any references to finance, and the possibility of a fourth channel for the OU was never discussed again.

At one level, this is an excellent piece of *realpolitik* because Lee had now managed to convince the Cabinet of the need for the OU and won a place for it in the election manifesto. This is very much the standard reading of the situation. Briggs argues that Lee 'was sufficiently assured that the new university would be brought into existence that she was prepared to compromise on the introduction of a separate fourth channel'.[97] Patricia Hollis, a Labour life peer who has written a biography of Lee, presents it as a victory for skilful negotiation: 'Had Jennie persisted in demanding the fourth channel, she would have sunk the entire project. Cabinet hostility to its cost was too great. Not even Wilson could have delivered it. She capitulated.'[98]

Perhaps Hollis is right and that even a project so precious to Wilson as the OU would have been sacrificed to help balance the books. Certainly, it is true that Lee's persistence meant that civil service and establishment opposition to the project was eventually swept away. The more important point, however, is that the cost of between £17m and £40m for the OU was insignificant compared to the cost of other public projects, for example the £300m cost of maintaining Polaris at the time.[99] Given that modernization was an expensive business, some areas of policy had to be higher up the pecking order than others. A consequence of the February decision, therefore, was the scaling down of the importance of television for the university. 'The major change from Wilson's original vision', wrote the OU's first director of studies in arts, 'was the realization that it was not possible for the University to rely solely or even primarily on broadcasting … Broadcasting would have a significant role in association with other means of instruction.'[100] While the Open University is a notable example of educational reform, its status as a key development in the history of broadcasting is less certain.

With the proposed decision to move the OU to BBC2, Benn simply avoided any reference to the possibility of a fourth channel in the broadcasting debate in March 1966. The increasingly difficult economic situation throughout the summer and autumn of that year ensured that the Cabinet would not change its decision and preoccupied the minds of those who might otherwise have criticized the government for inaction. When the white paper eventually declared in December 1966 that 'the Government do not consider that another television service can be afforded a high place in the order of national priorities'[101] and delayed any decision for at least three years, there was little fuss.

The publication of the white paper meant that, after over two years in office, Labour had at last published a statement on the future of television. According to Labour's rather breathless conference report on broadcasting, 1966 had been a 'year of modernisation, development and expansion on all fronts, as befits a science-based industry in the throes of a technological revolution'.[102] True, colour television was definitely on its way, but decisions on modernizing BBC finances, developing a fourth channel and expanding broadcasting hours had all been put on hold. The problem was that Wilson's technological revolution had coincided with a prolonged period of economic turbulence that meant that the Labour government's priority was survival rather than innovation. Despite the appearance of the document, there was, therefore, little evidence of a strategic and co-ordinated plan for television reform.

LABOUR, THE ITV FRANCHISES AND THE LEVY

Apart from its refusal to hand over a second channel to the ITA, commercial television had little reason so far to worry about life under a Labour government. Wilson attended the tenth anniversary dinner of the ITA in September 1965 and publicly praised the achievements of commercial television. Relations between Brompton Road (ITA headquarters) and Downing Street were uniformly friendly with even Tony Benn privately admitting that he was fond of the ITA chairman, Charles Hill.[103] More importantly, while an ITV franchise was no longer a 'licence to print money', it was certainly an invitation to spend money. In the first ten years of operations, ITV bosses had embarked on an £80m programme of diversification snapping up 'sports stadiums, television-rental shops, property companies, optical firms, publishing houses, sweet shops, hotels, agencies and a host of other businesses'.[104] Television, in the minds of many ITV entrepreneurs, was a business that required accountability to both audiences *and* shareholders.

The introduction of the levy on advertising revenue by the Conservatives in 1963 had proved to be only a slight inconvenience. 'The programme companies had learned to live with the additional burden of discriminatory taxation', writes the official historian of commercial television, 'and – despite their earlier cries of doom and gloom – they had continued to prosper.'[105] Annual profits of the ITV companies between 1964 and 1968 averaged £18.3m, a profit rate of 50 per cent on capital as against the average of 13 per cent in industry generally.[106] Harold Wilson was more than happy to see this example of dynamic accumulation, particularly because his Exchequer was reaping the rewards, some £40m going back into government funds in 1966 alone.[107]

In a climate in which the prime minister was calling for pay restraint and belt-tightening, it was the trade unions which provided some of the most vocal criticism of ITV's greed. At the 1965 TUC conference, Alan Sapper from the Television and Screenwriters' Guild attacked the use of ITV profits for diversification together with the deteriorating quality of programmes. At the following year's conference, Sapper called on the government to 'ensure that the major proportion of television company's [sic] profits are used for the benefits of British television'.[108] The ACTT seconded the resolution and criticized the ITV companies for making vast profits and then withholding them from television production.[109] The issue was not debated, however, by Labour conferences.

In December 1966, Hill invited applications for the 15 commercial television franchises, now due for renewal. Any worries in the British economy caused by July's deflationary package failed to deter entrepreneurs enthusiastic about the possibility of earning easy returns of investment. 'The frenzied scramble that followed', according to Shulman, 'was a genteel British version of such other financial stampedes as the gold rush in Alaska, the uranium panic in Canada, and the nickel dash in Australia.'[110] While the majority of the applicants were leading figures from the world of business and banking, individuals and institutions close to Labour including Arnold Goodman, Sidney Bernstein and the *New Statesman* were in the queue.[111]

The government made no attempt to interfere with the decisions of the ITA because Wilson had full confidence in Hill's ability. Some on the left were not so optimistic. *Tribune* complained that 'so long as profit is the main concern of the promoters we are unlikely to get a better commercial television service. The ITA could help by insisting that a fixed percentage of the profits be ploughed back into the industry.'[112] When the franchises were announced two weeks later, *Tribune*, unlike the majority of Fleet Street who were generally 'pleased by Lord Hill's new look for commercial TV',[113] criticized the arbitrary and unaccountable process of dishing out television monopolies, particularly to politicians.[114] The *New Statesman*, not surprisingly given its participation in the process, was less outraged but still deplored 'the general spectacle of a scramble for bids'.[115] Even Cabinet minister Richard Crossman declared that this was 'an extraordinary part of our so-called free enterprise – the feudal deal in TV franchises which has been given to ITA … I wish our Labour Government had done something about it, but we didn't.'[116]

Indeed, the PMG vigorously defended the deal in Parliament shortly afterwards. To those who called for transparency in the allocation of franchises, Edward Short replied that secrecy was needed to fend off the prying eyes of the media who would inevitably take sides. 'The consequence of open adjudication, therefore, would seem to be the exclusion of the Press from the programme companies.'[117] Given the growing dangers of media concentration and the high levels of press investment in ITV at the time, this might have been a sensible proposal. Short, however, welcomed the fact that the press now had financial interests in more television franchises than before because this provided for an additional source of income which would only add to the security and diversity of the British press.[118] He was supported by the backbench Labour MP Christopher Rowland who attempted to divert attention away from criticisms of the commercial motives of ITV: 'I strongly take the view that the question of profits is not the most important point to watch. Throughout broadcasting, the most important thing is the programmes and their quality and standard.'[119] He then went on to defend the right of MPs to be chairmen of ITV companies and congratulated the ITA on its 'shake-up' of commercial television.

Labour had, in practice, accommodated to the commercial television companies while the left was busy either attempting to buy its way into ITV or calling on the ITA, rather than the government, to insist that profits be reinvested back into programmes. Yet, just weeks after the new franchises were awarded, the NEC's advertising sub-committee produced its first draft report which proved to be extremely critical of ITV. Recognizing the crucial influence that advertising revenue exerted on television, the committee stuck by the findings of the 1962 Pilkington Committee that the needs of advertising clashed with the public's right to choose from a diverse range of quality programmes. The report finished by stating:

> We do not believe that the passage of time has done anything to soften the force of this hard criticism [of commercial television in the Pilkington Report]. Nor does the ITV auction of licences to print money which we have recently witnessed encourage us to believe that the implication of the Pilkington Report was ever squarely faced. We still think that a greater degree of public control and public accountability is necessary in commercial television.[120]

While the government had missed the opportunity to reform commercial television by taking advertising sales away from the ITV companies, restricting cross-media ownership or introducing some transparency into the franchise process, the NEC's anti-commercial beliefs now came to the fore. This was just one of the differences that emerged between the NEC and the government in the period after 1966.[121]

Devaluation of the pound in November 1967 and the subsequent cuts in public expenditure threw the Wilson government into disarray. Divisions in the Cabinet echoed massive dissension in Labour's grass roots. Time and again, the government turned on its own supporters to pay the price of economic crisis, implementing incomes policies and spending cuts. The theme of betrayal was taken up not just in the pages of *Tribune* but also in a series of leader articles in *The Times* in June 1968 by an anonymous civil servant. On one occasion, 'C' used the example of commercial television to illustrate Labour's failure to sustain the hopes of its supporters and its retreat from substantial reform. It is worth quoting at length:

> As an example [of Wilson's pragmatism] the Government's attitude (or rather lack of attitude) to commercial television which the Labour Party had persistently attacked in opposition, is not inapposite. Nothing epitomized more ostentatiously the candy-floss society, nothing else, to pile Pelion on Ossa, had been such a Thrasonic demonstration of crude capitalism. Yet no change was made in the way the franchises were allotted and the consequent fortunes distributed according to the whim of the ITA. No one denies that the profits made out of commercial television were a national scandal which should have undermined the position of the Macmillan Government more seriously than the Profumo affair. What is beyond comprehension is that the same procedure should have been allowed to repeat itself under a Labour Government without a murmur.[122]

By 1969, the tide was starting to turn against the commercial companies: advertising revenue was declining because of economic uncertainty while one of the new franchise companies, London Weekend Television, was on the brink of collapse after financial mismanagement. Most disastrously for the ITV employers, the government, desperate for revenue to prop up the economy, increased the advertising levy by £3m in the April budget. The chancellor, Roy Jenkins, could no longer justify ITV's huge profits and argued that '[i]n my view the community should have a bigger share in the value of these publicly created concessions'.[123]

This announcement was met with cries of horror from the ITV companies who warned of impending bankruptcy with a fall in profits from £15m in the mid-1960s to some £3–5m in 1969. Veteran opponents of ITV like Christopher Mayhew and Milton Shulman urged the public not to feel any pity while even *The Economist* warned not 'to exaggerate that crisis. ITV is not on the verge of utter financial collapse.'[124] The Labour-supporting *New Statesman*, however, adopted a more pragmatic approach: 'It is hard to weep for a bonanza industry which could once weigh itself in diamonds. But the balancing-up process is swinging too heavily the other way: if you rock the boat hard and often enough, it will capsize.'[125] Although commercial television had not been rocked hard or often by Labour, ITV bosses organized a high-profile lobby to rescue their ailing craft. Former Labour minister, Lord Aylestone, complained that the levy was too high, while figures like Peter Cadbury of Westward threatened that he 'would not apply for a licence again in 1974 if current problems continued. The levy is nothing but confiscation.'[126]

Private Eye replied in an article called 'Con the Nation Street' that not enough confiscation had taken place. It pointed out that Westward's profits had consistently risen as had its dividends to shareholders and that the enormous profits of ITV over the years had never been invested back into quality programmes. It concluded:

> In the last three years the Chancellor has taken some £1,800m from the taxpayers. In this situation, it was hardly surprising that he should seek to take an extra £3m from the rising revenue of some of the most profitable monopolies in the country. The result was a great chorus of rich men's protest, massive cuts in all forms of productive television, a lowering of already rock-bottom television standards, creation of widespread unemployment in the film industry, threats of total closure of TV stations, and perhaps more relevantly, a discreet reminder that this is the year in which a General Election will be fought, like none other, on the 'television image' of the protagonists.[127]

Private Eye's warning was prescient. Several months later, John Stonehouse, the new minister of posts and telecommunications, refunded not only the £3m cut of the previous year but handed back an additional £3m to the ITV companies.[128] In reply to an outraged Mayhew, Stonehouse said that '[w]e are not giving a handout. We are taking less from the programme contractors than we announced we would take a year ago. That is not a handout. It is simply adjusting the amount we take from them.'[129] The decision to come to the rescue of the ITV companies had not been discussed in Cabinet or in the strategic economic policy group, where financial planning was supposed to be concentrated: 'The deal was fixed between the Chancellor and Stonehouse.'[130] Even George Elvin, president of the ACTT whose members were directly affected by the temporarily troubled state of ITV's finances and who had therefore been reluctant to endorse a higher levy, criticized the government for not tying the levy cut to a requirement to invest more in production.[131]

After all of Wilson's exhortations to workers to share in the nation's drive to economize and make sacrifices, it was perhaps to be expected that such an act of charity to television's top entrepreneurs should coincide with an impending election. Stuart Hood, the former controller of BBC Television and prominent left-wing commentator on broadcasting issues, argues that the concession to commercial television could be 'explained in part by the fact that Labour voters watch ITV and in part by the close links between the Wilson circle and show business interests'.[132] The gradual upturn in the fortunes of the ITV companies in the following years further proved that there was no need for generosity on the part of the chancellor. It is, nevertheless, a revealing lesson that it 'took a Labour government to feel pity for the contractors'[133] and to ensure their continuing profitability.

A MOOD FOR CHANGE

Not all the issues dealt with in the 1966 white paper had been resolved by the late 1960s. In particular, the problem of BBC finances remained high on the broadcasting agenda. Having promised the BBC a further licence increase in 1968, the government seemed anxious to postpone a decision. At the beginning of the year, Greene wrote to his chair, Charles Hill that the PMG's attitude to the £1 rise 'which was formerly positive seems, for unknown reasons, to have become negative'. Reflecting on this dilemma, he continued that '[o]ne wonders whether he has changed his mind or whether he has run into great difficulties on Cabinet level'.[134] It was more likely that Wilson, gripped by the economic traumas of the time, was simply not prepared to sanction an increase. Philip Ziegler, quoting Wilson's private papers, notes that it was almost like a medical condition. On 19 March 1968, Wilson declared that he was 'allergic to any increase in BBC revenue' and that the Corporation should make itself more efficient.[135]

With the BBC's situation increasingly desperate, Cabinet discussed the matter again in May. As Crossman sighed to his diary, 'Up to the P.M.'s room to discuss the BBC licence fee, which we've already been discussing for two years [actually nearer four years] … The P.M. chose to indulge in one of his tirades [against the BBC]' and went on to compare the good old days of ITV under Hill to the bias of today's BBC.[136] And yet, despite his vocal opposition to raising the licence fee, Wilson was eventually persuaded to agree to the increase which was finally introduced in January 1969, one year late. The same situation reoccurred the following year when Wilson only agreed to a further rise only as long as it was postponed until after the next election.

Labour was much more supportive of public service broadcasting when it came to the matter of pay television. The previous Conservative government had licensed some pay-per-view experiments that Labour had allowed to continue. Despite fierce lobbying by Lords Mountbatten and Brabourne and some prevarication by PMGs Short and Stonehouse, the NEC's Home Affairs Committee decided in October 1968 to reject any extension to Pay TV Ltd's licence. It argued that pay television was likely to hegemonize live sporting events and that 'if Pay-TV made a success of their venture it would be necessary to license other commercial companies to provide a pay service, and that commercial consider-ations not subject to the restraints imposed on the BBC and ITV might thus predominate over considerations of public service'.[137] This decisive course of action was in stark contrast to Wilson's intervention in the matter. Having heard the HPC's rejection of pay television, Lord Moutbatten, stepfather of Lord Brabourne, the chairman of Pay TV Ltd, phoned Downing Street in a fury:

> Lord Moutbatten said that he had discussed this question with the Prime Minister at Lord Thompson's lunch on Thursday, October 17 [eight days before]. The Prime Minister had given him to understand on that occasion that he had no need to worry. From this he had gathered that the question had been settled favourably. He was wondering who was in fact in charge of the Government.[138]

This was, of course, a question that was starting to gain some currency. Who was in charge of broadcasting policy? Was there a strategic plan or was government policy in the field of television designed to cope with crisis management? To what extent was policy led by Wilson's whims or party principles? With both the BBC and ITV under increased financial pressure, with debates on advertising still running under the surface, with no decision about the future of a fourth channel and with a growing lack of trust in the broadcasting authorities, there was an urgent need for a co-ordinated strategy for the broadcasting industry.

The possibility of a systematic overhaul of broadcasting was originally raised by PMG Edward Short in his statement on the ITV franchise allocations in June 1967. Noting that the charters of both the ITA and the BBC were due to be renewed in 1976, he argued that 'nine years from now, an opportunity will arise for a fundamental review of the whole system'. In the short term, he hoped that 'in the spring of 1969, a long, cool look will begin at the whole system of broadcasting in this country'.[139] Before then, however, there were plenty of opportunities to criticize the current arrangements. Commenting on the disappointing opening week of the new ITV regime, the *New Statesman* called for urgent government action to think of ways of making television a 'genuinely independent public service'. 'Whatever may have been done for the arts', went the cover story, 'the record on broadcasting suggests that the difficulties of interfering to increase independence have been too much for Downing Street's thinking.'[140]

The temperature was raised by speeches by key Labour figures, Tony Benn and Richard Crossman, in October 1968 that called for broadcasting reform. Benn addressed 30 people in his local constituency on the theme of 'Broadcasting in a Participatory Democracy'. While his words were taken to be a public attack on the BBC in particular, Benn was in fact demanding a wider restructuring of the airwaves:

> Broadcasting is too important to be left to the broadcasters, and somehow we must find some new way of using radio and television to allow us to talk to each other. We've got to fight all over again the same battles that we fought centuries ago to get rid of the licence to print and the same battles to establish representative broadcasting in place of the benevolent paternalism by the constitutional monarchs who reside in the palatial Broadcasting House.[141]

Jenkins claims that the speech was part of a build-up for a resolution demanding media reform at the 1968 Labour conference, although no such motion was ever put. Crossman's speech, on the other hand, was far more moderate simply demanding 'a new atmosphere between the BBC, the Independent Television companies and ourselves'.[142] While Crossman's speech was praised by Hugh Greene and Hugh Cudlipp of the *Daily Mirror*, Benn's was attacked by Wilson who, according to

Benn, 'wrote me a memo saying "gurus should be confined to Wolverhampton" trying to muddle me up with [Enoch] Powell. I wrote him a reply signed "the guru of Millbank Tower"'.[143]

Benn's calls for deep-rooted broadcasting reform tapped into a mood of wider political radicalization. The student revolt and general strike in France in May 1968 together with growing protests against the Vietnam War had led to a critical concern with the political role of television.[144] In the UK, this connected to the revival of New Left ideas and the centrality of culture as a political battleground. *New Left Review* editor Perry Anderson had outlined the specific demands of the New Left in relation to television in 1964: full implementation of the Pilkington proposals, 'the fullest freedom for producers to create and the fullest free availability of works for the community to experience'.[145] Now, in the more militant atmosphere of the late 1960s where a space had developed for challenging the status quo, arguments for fundamental reform of broadcasting were beginning to circulate more widely.

The left-wing academic Stuart Hall questioned the entire framework of British broadcasting in an article for the *New Statesman* in July 1969. He advised readers to reject the 'narrow framework' of the usual debates about broadcasting which accepted predetermined notions of what was possible and what was not. Challenging the myth of choice in British television, he argued that it was a mistake to 'see the alternatives as confined to either bureaucratic, administratively top-heavy, executive-oriented, paternalist broadcasting organised in a monolithic unit; or robber-baron, advertising-conscious, programme-starved, profit-oriented contracting companies'. The key was to 'transcend this set of alternatives'.[146]

Labour's response was clear, if not exactly bold. While rejecting specific commitments to reform ITV or to find additional finance for the BBC, it promised in its 1970 election manifesto 'to establish a high-powered Committee of Enquiry to report on The Future of Broadcasting'.[147] Why did the Labour government suggest, at that particular time, a full investigation into the structures of British broadcasting? Partly, following the events of 1968, it was a response to the left-wing critique of the lack of accountability in broadcasting and of key institutions in general. Yet it was also due to some fierce lobbying by programme makers who were increasingly alienated by the complacency of the broadcasting duopoly. In late 1969, they launched a pressure group called the 76 Group, named after the year in which both the ITA licence and the BBC Charter were due to run out. According to Stephen Lambert, their aim was to urge the Government to appoint a Royal Commission to review the structure, finance and organisation of broadcasting. They believed that there was a general crisis in the industry and that two recent controversial events – the publication of the BBC's plans for *Broadcasting in the Seventies* and the LWT debacle – were symptomatic of this crisis.[148]

Broadcasting in the Seventies outlined the BBC's controversial plans to rationalize its radio output by replacing the Home, Light and Third Services with Radios 1, 2, 3 and 4 in an effort to free up resources for local radio and undermine demands for commercial local radio. The 76 Group argued that the changes were explicitly concerned with efficiency savings and attacked the new 'managerialism' in the BBC which meant that 'everyone who has worked for BBC-TV over the last five years will have first-hand evidence of an atmosphere in which programme standards have increasingly suffered in the race for ratings'.[149] In March 1970, the 76 Group placed an advertisement in the *Guardian* with the headline, 'Crisis in Television and Radio – A Royal Commission Now!' The text criticized both 'the subservience of programmes to profits' in ITV and the BBC's response to financial problems as one that favoured 'business rather than programme values'. The call for a Royal Commission 'to review the structure, finance and organisation of broadcasting'[150] was signed by a long list of broadcasting luminaries, including Jim Allen, Humphrey Burton, Stuart Hood, Dennis Potter, Milton Shulman and Phillip Whitehead, as well as two Labour MPs, Douglas Houghton and James Dickens, and one Liberal MP, Richard Wainwright.

Pressure for an inquiry was starting to worry senior broadcasting figures. 'What had begun as a revolt against changes in radio generally', wrote the BBC chair, 'was developing into a fundamental attack on the whole system, BBC and ITV alike.'[151] Grace Wyndham Goldie, head of television talks at the BBC, was even more alarmed. Such an inquiry 'could put the whole of British broadcasting into a melting pot and recommend to Parliament something quite different from anything resembling the kind of British broadcasting which so far had existed'.[152] Except that it did not. In reality, a Royal Commission must have seemed to the government like an excellent short-term strategy to head off any immediate decisions about broadcasting.

The reformers got their way when, in May 1970, PMG Stonehouse announced to Parliament the creation of an inquiry under the chair of Lord Annan who had sat on the advisory committee of the Open University some years earlier. Crossman, once again, was puzzled when he heard the news in Cabinet: 'I asked why colleagues weren't consulted and Harold said some colleagues were. Here is another instance of a major decision being privately taken by Harold and a few others.[153]

The irony is that Wilson himself had initially opposed the idea, even though he is now generally credited with pushing it through. The new BBC director general, Charles Curran, recalled that Wilson 'did not favour the setting up of a further Committee of Inquiry and had not been pleased when the Minister [Stonehouse] had mentioned this prospect in the course of the debate'. Wilson favoured resolution of urgent matters by the existing broadcasting authorities and 'thought that to set up a Committee of Inquiry was simply to inject an amateur body in an area where professional knowledge was essential'.[154] This was classic Wilson: what was needed was a body of scientists and experts who would take a purposeful look at the situation and not be put off by any ideological differences. What persuaded Wilson to change his mind is unclear. Perhaps Stonehouse convinced him that any changes 'could be made more acceptable to the public if they were made as a result of recommendations by an independent committee rather than as the result of an internal Government review'.[155] Perhaps Wilson thought that the threat of a full review would be a useful lever to have during the course of the 1970 election. In any case, Wilson lost the election and Heath, anxious to avoid any negative publicity for commercial sound broadcasting, immediately cancelled the inquiry.

In what ways had almost six years of Labour government transformed British television? On the one hand, it had introduced the Open University; on the other hand, it had bailed out the ITV companies and constantly delayed licence fee increases for the BBC. Wilson had come to power on the back of popular enthusiasm for technological innovation and the modernization of Britain's political and social institutions. Both Wilson and Benn had wanted television to be associated with these objectives and to play its part in an industrial and cultural revolution. In 1964, satirical shows were mocking the Tories for being obsolete while, within two years of Labour being in office, programmes like *Up the Junction* and *Cathy Come Home* demonstrated how television could play an important progressive role in public life.

By the end of the decade, some critics were claiming that innovation had turned into stagnation, boldness into caution, idealism into pragmatism. Milton Shulman noted evidence of a 'creeping conformity, a growing reluctance to cause trouble, a greater emphasis on light entertainment and sport'.[156] Christopher Booker, the former writer on *TW3*, later described the prevailing mood as 'one at least of confusion and disillusionment, if not of considerable gloom':[157]

> The atmosphere of apparently limitless novelty in which television in the late Fifties and early Sixties established itself as such as dominant force in the social and political life of the nation, had dwindled by the end of the decade into a kind of general resigned acceptance of the predominant triviality.[158]

While such a picture exaggerates both the creativity of an earlier 'golden age' and the bleakness of the picture in 1970, it is certainly true that government policy under Wilson did little to actively promote an atmosphere of confidence and experimentation. That British television did not go backwards was due more to the efforts of producers, directors and scriptwriters attempting to relate to the profound political and social changes of the 1960s than to creative government steering of broadcasting. Tony Benn argues that the period was one in which *all* reforms had to be fought for in very difficult circumstances. People who wanted reform 'were struggling against a hostile press, a prime minister who began by being very radical and then very conservative, against a Treasury who hated your guts, against the right wing of the Labour Party who thought the whole thing was totally wrong – the early modernizers – so it wasn't exactly easy'.[159] However, in some areas, there *was* real evidence of social reform with the liberalization of laws concerning abortion, homosexuality, divorce and censorship. Why did this not extend to BBC television?

Partly, this was due to the fact that television *policy*, as opposed to output, was still not seen as central by many in the Labour Party. Housing, unemployment, health and education were all seen as important areas in which government *ought* to legislate. Television, on the other hand, was an area of private enjoyment in which Labour, still scarred from its initial opposition to the now successful ITV system, was reluctant to intervene.

Another explanation for Labour's failure to transform broadcasting in the 1960s lies with the contradictory role of Harold Wilson himself. On the one hand, Wilson sought to punish the BBC for its frequent criticisms of his government by blocking licence fee increases and supporting Benn's plan to introduce advertising on the BBC. At the same time, he was reluctant to allow advertising on the BBC in order to protect its status as a public corporation and to highlight the value of corporatism and was always persuaded, after some argument, to agree to licence fee increases. Wilson was extremely sensitive to the growing political importance of television and therefore infuriated by individual instances of BBC behaviour, but he was simultaneously protective of the Corporation's cultural heritage. In practice, despite his animosity towards a range of programmes and journalists, Wilson demonstrated a very inconsistent commitment to reform the BBC and to modernize the institutions of broadcasting.

More important than Wilson's personal shortcomings was the economic context in which decisions about television were being made. In the 1960s, broadcasting was affected by the declining state of Britain's finances and the government's response of a programme of public spending cuts. Labour's main contribution to the modernization of the BBC in the 1960s, consisted of a relentless financial squeeze that made it very difficult for the Corporation either to expand or to prepare a long-term strategy. Wilson's government recognized that real reform of British television would eat up precious resources. According to former PMG Edward Short, 'there was no real intention of changing it [television]. I don't think we could have done it without a great upheaval and finding some way of paying for alternative channels.'[160] Faced with contradictory pressures from different constituencies in the party, the result of Wilson's approach was both an economy and a television policy that mirrored the 'stop-go' cycles of the early 1960s. Bound by an economic and political consensus that put profitability and efficiency at the heart of all decision-making, the legacy of the 1960s Labour governments' approach to British television appears to be one of hesitation rather than modernization and of pragmatism rather than transformation.

NOTES

1.   C. Ponting, *Breach of Promise: Labour in Power, 1964–1970* (London: Hamish Hamilton, 1989), p. 393.
2.   Labour Party, *Manifesto for the 1964 General Election* (London: Labour Party, 1964), p. 6.
3.   A. Shonfield, *Modern Capitalism: The Changing Balance of Public and Private Power* (New York: Oxford University Press, 1969), p. 154.
4.   B. Pimlott, *Harold Wilson* (London: Harper Collins, 1993), p. 272.
5.   H. Wilson, 'Labour's Plan for Science', speech to the annual conference of the Labour Party, Scarborough, 1 October 1963, p. 3.
6.   Ibid., p. 6.
7.   C. Booker, *The Neophiliacs: The Revolution in English Life in the Fifties and Sixties*, 2nd edn (London: Pimlico, 1992), p. 213.
8.   Pimlott, *Harold Wilson*, p. 305.
9.   T. Benn, interview with the author, 19 February 1997.
10. P. Foot, *The Politics of Harold Wilson* (Harmondsworth: Penguin, 1968), p. 153.
11. Ibid.
12. R. Crossman, *The Backbench Diaries of Richard Crossman* (London: Hamish Hamilton and Jonathan Cape, 1981), p. 1026.

13.   P. Foot, 'Harold Wilson and the Labour Left', *International Socialism*, 33, Summer 1968, p. 19.
14.   H. Wilson, *The Labour Government 1964–70* (Harmondsworth: Pelican, 1974), p. 27.
15.   L. Minkin, *The Labour Party Conference* (Manchester: Manchester University Press, 1980), p. 330.
16.   Ponting, *Breach of Promise*, p. 392.
17.   F. Craig, *British General Election Manifestos 1900–1974* (London: Macmillan, 1975), p. 41.
18.   T. Benn, *Out of the Wilderness: Diaries 1963–67* (London: Arrow, 1988), p. 165.
19.   Memo from Curran to Grisewood, 30 July 1964, BBC Written Archives, R78/2/1.
20.   Pimlott, *Harold Wilson*, p. 270.
21.   Benn, *Out of the Wilderness*, p. 204.
22.   See ibid., p. 306.
23.   Ibid., p. 212.
24.   Benn described the BBC as 'wildly right wing' and Lord Normanbrook, its chair, as 'a real old Establishment figure and not at all knowledgeable on broadcasting' (ibid., p. 183).
25.   A. Briggs, *Competition, 1955–1974* (vol. V of *The History of Broadcasting in the United Kingdom* (Oxford: Oxford University Press, 1995), p. 517.
26.   For a full discussion of Hugh Greene's impact as BBC director general, see ibid., pp. 309–454.
27.   Pimlott, *Harold Wilson*, p. 269.
28.   Labour Party, *Let's Go with Labour for the New Britain*, Manifesto for the 1964 general election (London: Labour Party, 1964), p. 8.
29.   M. Shulman, *The Least Worst Television in the World* (London: Barrie & Jenkins, 1973), p. 23.
30.   See Pimlott, *Harold Wilson*, p. 267.
31.   D. Haworth, 'Labour and Television', *Socialist Commentary*, 29, May 1965, p. 32.
32.   Shulman, *Least Worst Television*, p. 26.
33.   M. Cockerell, *Live from Number 10: The Inside Story of Prime Ministers and Television* (London: Faber & Faber, 1989), p. 113.
34.   Ibid., p. 115.
35.   See for example Briggs, *Competition*, pp. 546–58, Cockerell, *Live from Number Ten*, pp. 113–51 and Shulman, *Least Worst Television*, pp. 25–54 for more detailed accounts of the stormy relationship between Wilson and the BBC.
36.   Pimlott, *Harold Wilson*, p. 269.
37.   Labour Party NEC, Resolutions to the Publicity Sub-Committee of the NEC, 23 February 1966.
38.   R. Crossman, *The Diaries of a Cabinet Minister*, vol. III (London: Hamish Hamilton and Jonathan Cape, 1977), pp. 387–8.
39.   Quoted in Cockerell, *Live from Number Ten*, p. 125.
40.   A. Morgan, *Harold Wilson* (London: Pluto, 1992), p. 332.
41.   D. Edwards, Note on Prime Minister's Allegations Against BBC, 7 April 1966, BBC written archives, R78/1, 825/1.
42.   Cockerell, *Live from Number 10*, p. 134.
43.   Benn, *Out of the Wilderness*, p. 387.
44.   Notes of a meeting between Greene and Mitchell, 12 November 1964, Public Record Office (henceforth PRO) PREM 13/141.
45.   R. Crossman, *The Diaries of a Cabinet Minister*, vol. II (London: Hamish Hamilton and Jonathan Cape, 1976), p. 160.
46.   P. Ziegler, *Wilson: The Authorised Life* (London: Weidenfeld & Nicolson, 1993), p. 203.
47.   Briggs, *Competition*, p. 599.
48.   Cockerell, *Live from Number 10*, p. 135.
49.   E. Short, interview with the author, 21 April 1998.
50.   Quoted in Crossman, *The Diaries of a Cabinet Minister*, vol. II, pp. 442–3.
51.   See letter from Mitchell to McIndoe in the Cabinet Office, 8 January 1965, PRO PREM 13/142.
52.   Briggs, *Competition*, p. 563n.
53.   D. Childs, *Britain since 1945: A Political History*, 4th edn (London: Routledge, 1997), p. 111.
54.   Letter from Mitchell to G. Tilling of the GPO, 4 January 1965, PRO PREM 13/142.
55.   Letter from Tilling to Mitchell, 7 January 1965, PRO PREM 13/142.
56.   Letter from Lord Normanbrook to Greene, 15 March 1965, BBC written archives, R78/2/1.
57.   Handwritten comments by Wilson on a letter from H. Reid to Tilling, 1 April 1965, PRO PREM 13/735.

58. He was not alone in thinking this. Benn acknowledged at the time that 'there may be a case for taking BBC2 away from the BBC' (Benn, *Out of the Wilderness*, p. 239) while, according to Tam Dalywell MP, to 'save money, and the embarrassment of a Labour Government having to put up the licence, Dick [Crossman] wants to do away with BBC2' (quoted in ibid., pp. 310–11).
59. R. Crossman, *The Diaries of a Cabinet Minister*, vol. I (London: Hamish Hamilton and Jonathan Cape, 1975), pp. 268–9.
60. Benn, *Out of the Wilderness*, p. 353.
61. Ibid., p. 388.
62. Cabinet minutes, Discussion of the broadcasting white paper, 15 February 1966, PRO CAB 128/41.
63. Benn, *Out of the Wilderness*, p. 389.
64. Ibid., p. 390.
65. Crossman, *The Diaries of a Cabinet Minister*, vol. I, p. 459.
66. Notes of a meeting between Wilson and Benn, 2 March 1966, PRO PREM 13/735.
67. Notes of a meeting between Greene and Wilson, 16 February 1966, BBC Written Archives, R78/3/1.
68. PMG Benn had proposed in February 1966 to extend broadcasting hours on all channels (Letter from Benn to Lord Fulton, 1 February 1966, BBC written archives, R78/3/1). Perhaps ironically, it was the Conservatives who, in January 1972, finally abolished all restrictions on broadcasting hours.
69. Benn, *Out of the Wilderness*, p. 394.
70. Craig, *British General Election Manifestos 1900–1974*, p. 76.
71. Minkin, *Labour Party Conference*, p. 300.
72. The creation of a new radio corporation hinged on what to do with the pirate radio stations. While hostile to the entrepreneurial attitudes and unlawfulness of the pirates, most Labour MPs also recognized their increasing popularity and were therefore unwilling to ban them just before a general election. By the time that legislation banning the pirates was introduced in July 1966, Labour MPs were pressing for a 'sweetener', some sort of new, legal popular music channel to replace them (see Briggs, *Competition*, p. 562).
73. R. Williams, 'What Happens after the "Pirates" Walk the Plank?', *Tribune*, 7 October 1966.
74. H. Jenkins, 'My plan for a national music programme', *Tribune*, 14 October 1966.
75. See Crossman, *Diaries of a Cabinet Minister*, vol. II, p. 71.
76. *Tribune*, 'Broadcasting: A Sigh of Relief', 30 December 1966.
77. Crossman, *Diaries of a Cabinet Minister*, vol. II, p. 154.
78. White paper, *Broadcasting*, Cmnd. 3169 (London: HMSO, 1966), para. 11.
79. Crossman, *Diaries of a Cabinet Minister*, vol. II, p. 71.
80. Crossman, *Diaries of a Cabinet Minister*, vol. III, p. 84. Wilson, as ever, maintained a tactical approach to the subject. Having passed over advertising at that time, Wilson specifically insisted that the 'White Paper should also avoid any indication that advertising had been rejected in principle as a source of finance' (Cabinet minutes, Discussion of the broadcasting white paper, 8 November 1966, PRO CAB 128/41).
81. Pimlott, *Harold Wilson*, p. 515.
82. S. Lambert, *Channel Four: Television with a Difference?* (London: BFI, 1982), p. 17.
83. Briggs, *Competition*, p. 491n.
84. Handwritten comments on a paper prepared by the education secretary for the Ministerial Committee on Broadcasting [B(65)5], 9 February 1965, PRO PREM 13/735.
85. Benn, *Out of the Wilderness*, p. 236.
86. Ibid., p. 239.
87. H. Jenkins, 'Financing the Fourth TV Channel', *Film and Television Technician*, May 1966.
88. Letter from Lee to Wilson, 13 August 1965, PRO PREM 13/740.
89. Letter from Mitchell to Trevelyan in the lord president of the council's office, 9 September 1965, PRO PREM 13/740.
90. Letter from Diamond to Bowden, 3 February 1966, PRO PREM 13/740.
91. Letter from Lee to Wilson, 3 February 1966, PRO PREM 13/740.
92. Letter from Lee to Bowden, 7 February 1966, PRO PREM 13/740.
93. Cabinet minutes, Discussion of the Open University, 8 February 1966, PRO CAB 128/41.
94. Ibid.
95. Benn, *Out of the Wilderness*, p. 385.

96. Letter from Lee to Goodman, 8 February 1966, PRO PREM 13/740.
97. Briggs, *Competition*, p. 498.
98. P. Hollis, *Jennie Lee: A Life* (Oxford: Oxford University Press, 1997), p. 317.
99. Ponting, *Breach of Promise*, p. 88.
100. J. Ferguson, *The Open University from Within* (London: University of London Press, 1975), p. 15.
101. White paper, *Broadcasting*, para. 17.
102. Labour Party, *Report of the 65th Annual Conference* (London: Labour Party, 1966), pp. 102–3.
103. Benn, *Out of the Wilderness*, p. 321.
104. Shulman, *Least Worst Television*, p. 23.
105. B. Sendall, *Expansion and Change, 1958–68*, vol. II of *Independent Television in Britain* (London: Macmillan, 1983), p. 335.
106. See ibid., pp. 319 and 370.
107. M. Donne, 'The Lines are Drawn for the TV Contract Battle', *Financial Times*, 1 March 1967.
108. A. Sapper, speech to TUC conference, *Report of the 98th Annual Trades Union Congress* (London: TUC, 1966), p. 485.
109. The motion was remitted after the General Council asked for more time to consider precisely where the money should go. No further action was taken because of the franchise renewals the following year.
110. Shulman, *Least Worst Television*, p. 56.
111. Alan Sapper had previously called on the TUC to support a trades union channel because 'it is really imperative that this one-eyed serpent is constructively tamed'. See A. Sapper, speech to TUC conference, *Report of the 97th Annual Trades Union Congress* (London: TUC, 1965), p. 517. This call had been firmly rejected by the General Council.
112. *Tribune*, 'Scramble for TV stations', 2 June 1967.
113. Shulman, *Least Worst Television*, p. 62.
114. *Tribune*, 'Television: Clear Out the Tycoons', 16 June 1967.
115. *New Statesman*, 'The Other Side of Lord Hill', 16 June 1967.
116. Crossman, *Diaries of a Cabinet Minister*, vol. II, p. 377.
117. HoC Debates, 28 June 1967, col. 449.
118. Ibid., col. 453.
119. Ibid., col. 434.
120. Labour Party NEC, First Draft Report of the Advertising Committee of the NEC, Re. 169, June 1967, p. 23.
121. See Minkin, *Labour Party Conference*, pp. 298–300.
122. 'C', 'Why is Labour so Reluctant to Govern?', *The Times*, 10 June 1968.
123. HoC Debates, 15 April 1969, col. 1014.
124. *The Economist*, 'Pay Now, View Later', 27 September 1969.
125. P. Hunt, 'ITV Faces the Crunch: Pros and Cons of the Big Five's Network Monopoly', *New Statesman*, 2 May 1969, p. 725.
126. Quoted in A. Moreton, 'Stonehouse to Hear Protest by ITA on Advertising Levy', *Financial Times*, 3 January 1970.
127. *Private Eye*, 'Con the Nation Street', 16 January 1970.
128. Headlines the following day (17 March 1970) ran 'ITV Firms Given Levy Lifesaver' (*Sun*), '£6m Boost for the Needy TV Men' (*Evening News*) and 'TV Shares Soar as Whitehall Steps Down on Levy' (*Daily Express*).
129. HoC Debates, 23 March 1970, col. 1144.
130. Crossman, *Diaries of a Cabinet Minister*, vol. III, p. 863.
131. *TV Today*, 'Should Have Imposed Conditions on Levy Concession', 23 April 1970.
132. S. Hood, *On Television* (London: Pluto, 1987), p. 76.
133. Ibid.
134. Memo from Greene to Hill about the licence fee, 26 January 1968, BBC Written Archives, R78/3/1.
135. Quoted in Ziegler, *Wilson: The Authorised Life*, p. 269.
136. Crossman, *Diaries of a Cabinet Minister*, vol. III, p. 84.
137. Memo from J. Nunn to M. Halls on Pay Television Ltd, 23 October 1968, PRO PREM 13/1951.
138. Note of a conversation between Halls and Lord Mountbatten, 25 October 1968, PRO PREM 13/1951.

139. HoC Debates, 28 June 1967, col. 456.
140. *New Statesman*, 'Trouble in the Air', 9 August 1968.
141. Quoted in R. Jenkins, *Tony Benn: A Political Biography* (London: Writers & Readers, 1980), p. 144.
142. Crossman, *Diaries of a Cabinet Minister*, vol. III, p. 229.
143. T. Benn, interview with the author, 19 February 1997.
144. See, for example, V. Fisera, *Writing on the Wall: France, May 1968, A Documentary Anthology* (London: Allison & Busby, 1978), pp. 305–7.
145. P. Anderson, 'Critique of Wilsonism', *New Left Review*, 27, September/October 1964, p. 27.
146. S. Hall, 'The Real BBC Crisis', *New Statesman*, 18 July 1969, p. 69.
147. Craig, *British General Election Manifestos 1900–1974*, p. 363.
148. Lambert, *Channel Four*, p. 39.
149. Quoted in ibid., p. 41.
150. 76 Group, 'Crisis in Television and Radio – A Royal Commission Now!' advertisement in the *Guardian*, 17 March 1970.
151. Lord Hill, *Behind the Screen: The Broadcasting Memoirs of Lord Hill of Luton* (London: Sidgwick & Jackson, 1974), p. 138.
152. G. W. Goldie, *Facing the Nation: Television and Politics 1936–1976* (London: Bodley Head, 1977), p. 304.
153. Crossman, *Diaries of a Cabinet Minister*, vol. III, p. 921.
154. Notes of a conversation between Curran and Wilson on 7 December 1970, written on 22 December 1970, BBC Written Archives, R78/1, 825/1.
155. Quoted in Lord Hill's notes of a meeting at the Ministry of Posts and Telecommunications, 21 January 1970, BBC written archives, R78/6/1.
156. Shulman, *Least Worst Television*, p. 103.
157. Booker, *The Neophiliacs*, p. 303.
158. Ibid., p. 308.
159. T. Benn, interview with the author, 19 February 1997.
160. E. Short, interview with the author, 21 April 1998.

4

The Rise of the Left, 1970–79

DEMANDS FOR REFORM

Calls for fundamental reform of British television found some resonance inside the Labour Party at the start of the 1970s – the speeches by then Cabinet members Benn and Crossman in 1968, attacking the lack of accountability and creeping trivialization of television respectively, were still relatively fresh. However, the mood for reform was far more urgently expressed outside parliamentary bodies, particularly by those groups motivated by the radical possibilities of the struggles of 1968. While conservative groups like Mary Whitehouse's National Viewers and Listeners Association (NVLA) urged reform to 'clean up' television, the main critics of the existing structures of broadcasting came from the left. More accountability in decision-making, more diverse representations of minority groups, a less antagonistic portrayal of trade unionists and socialists were all 'New Left' demands that emerged at the start of the decade. The fact that some of the most popular programmes at the time included *Dad's Army*, *Colditz* and *The Onedin Line* – what Briggs calls 'the appeal to history'[1] – simply fuelled the desire for more contemporary and relevant output.

One of the most militant groups that combined the desire for a new social order with a programme of media reform was the Free Communications Group. The FCG devoted itself to opening up public debate on key questions concerning the media – for example, ownership, workers' control and editorial coverage – from the perspective of workers in the media industries themselves. According to the FCG, 'newspaper, television and radio should be under the control of all the people who produce them'.[2] Co-ordinated by a steering committee composed of journalists and broadcasters,[3] the group organized a series of public meetings (one of which was addressed by Tony Benn) which received extensive publicity and within a year had recruited 700 members and earned a considerable degree of influence in broadcasting debates.

The FCG challenged the lack of transparency in broadcasting decision-making by publishing the controversial (and hitherto secret) 1967 franchise submissions of London Weekend Television and Harlech, together with proposals by journalists across Europe for increased control over the editorial process. It helped to organize a 'teach-in' of rank-and-file BBC workers in 1970 and published the ensuing discussions about democratic control over programme content and organizational structures under the headline of 'They Farted in the Cathedral – or How 35 BBC Employees Asked for Democracy in the Corporation'.[4] Briggs confirms that the FCG 'had a footing inside the BBC' and that its activities helped to stimulate debates even among the governors about increased participation and accountability.[5] By its fifth issue, the *Open Secret* was claiming that the group can 'lay a fair claim to have initiated the debate that is now agitating almost all quarters of the communications industry'.[6]

These debates, vigorously pursued by ordinary broadcasting workers, had permeated through to the official trade union movement by the early part of the decade. The Association of Broadcasting Staff, which represented staff at the BBC, successfully proposed a motion at the 1971 TUC conference calling for a committee to study television coverage of the trade union movement.[7] The ACTT launched its own commission examining alternative structures for television and carried a resolution at its 1971 conference calling for the nationalization of the film industry without compensation and under workers' control.

Demands for radical media reform, therefore, were starting to be articulated in the early part of the 1970s, particularly by media workers and activists engaged in extra-parliamentary movements. Their concerns were not simply confined to legislative questions about the status of the BBC Charter or the ITA but dealt with fundamental questions of accountability, ownership, content and control of broadcasting. In a period in which the post-war consensus was cracking under the tensions caused by industrial militancy, economic decline and political struggle, broadcasting's role as a unifying cultural force was less assured. How would Labour answer the challenge of attempting to transform British television to meet the needs of a less consensual and increasingly highly politically charged social order?

THE RISE OF THE LEFT INSIDE THE LABOUR PARTY, 1970-74

The incoming Conservative government of Edward Heath was greeted with a wave of militancy. The industrial relations bill of December 1970 banned the closed shop and unofficial strikes, introduced secret ballots, a register of unions and a 60-day 'cooling-off' period before strike action could be taken. Massive demonstrations and protest strikes were organized against the proposals and brought more and more workers into political action. In June 1971, workers at the Upper Clyde Shipbuilders (UCS) were sacked and responded later that summer by occupying the yards, winning solidarity from workers across the country. In July 1972, the TUC called a one-day general strike in response to the imprisonment of five London dockers for breaking the industrial relations law. The dockers were freed. In both 1972 and 1974, miners went on strike for higher pay, in the latter instance contributing to the downfall of the Heath government.

Twenty-four million working days were lost through strikes in 1972, the highest since 1926, the year of the General Strike.[8] This huge increase in working-class militancy spread from matters of pay and conditions to more political questions of workers' control as some workers, according to Royden Harrison, 'began to exhibit an ominous concern with the conditions of *distribution* as well as production'.[9]

Union militancy was supplemented by the rise of the women's movement and gay liberation together with the increasing influence of grass-roots movements and the revolutionary left. Initiatives for change, therefore, were more likely to come from outside the Labour Party itself so that, while large numbers of Labour members were involved in the various activities, they were not organized as party members but as trade unionists, socialists or feminists. Even those activists who were attempting to influence official party policies acknowledged the 'intellectual lethargy' of the leadership of the Labour movement. In their 1972 book on the 'new unionism', Ken Coates and Tony Topham argued that

> it is fair to say that the bulk of creative socialist thinking and writing goes on either outside the Labour Party or in its under-ground. Writers like E. P. Thompson, Raymond Williams, Perry Anderson and Ralph Miliband [leading New Left figures] are scarcely less outsiders in the present climate than such maverick Fabians as John Hughes or Peter Townsend. No one in the higher councils of the Party takes any notice of what the latter say.[10]

Even if the Labour Party leadership was not in the forefront of developing this militancy, the party was not immune from its effects and it swung massively to the left in the opening years of the decade. Successive Labour conferences passed resolutions extending public ownership and adopting unilateral disarmament, and condemned the party leadership's decision not to implement the more radical conference decisions. This shift was reflected in the unions where 'the most powerful men in the movement were now both left-wingers':[11] Jack Jones and Hugh Scanlon, leaders of the Transport and General Workers' Union (TGWU) and Amalgamated Engineering Union (AEU) respectively. By 1973, even the right-wing shadow chancellor Denis Healey promised, in the heat of conference, that the party's aim was 'to bring about a fundamental and irreversible shift in the balance of power and wealth in favour of working people and their families'.[12]

The most high-profile left-wing Labour MP was Tony Benn, party chairman in 1971, who associated himself with the UCS occupation and the jailed dockers and spoke of the urgent need for increased participation in political and industrial decision-making. According to Phillip Whitehead's history of the 1970s, the Labour Party was energized by Benn as its chair: 'A hundred sub-committees bloomed in the exercise *Participation 72*[13] and the chairman was everywhere, encouraging here, prompting there.'[14] Benn's involvement in grass-roots political activities and his support for industrial democracy was to be crucial in later initiating Labour's media reform programme.

This was the context in which the National Executive Committee drew up the document that was to become, for Pelling and Reid,[15] the most left-wing policy statement in the party's history, *Labour's Programme 1973*.[16] The document proposed a strategy based on an expanded public sector, an interventionist National Enterprise Board co-ordinating economic activity, compulsory planning agreements involving government, employers and workers and foreign exchange controls to protect sterling. Embracing the language of industrial democracy and participation, the document promised action in a whole series of policy areas – from prices, pensions and income distribution, to industrial relations, full employment and communications. Labour's aim, in the words of the programme, was 'no less than a new social order'.[17]

The adoption of this programme, later known as the Alternative Economic Strategy (AES), was motivated both by the militancy of the period but also by the debates which had followed Labour's defeat in 1970. While the traditional Labour revisionists like Crosland and Roy Jenkins called for a renewed commitment to social justice and egalitarianism to compensate for Wilson's indecision and failure, another group of Labour theorists called for a much more decisive form of economic planning. Writers and activists like Ken Coates, Michael Barratt Brown and Stuart Holland organized around the Institute for Workers' Control, were influenced by the New Left emphasis on participation and democratization and argued for strong state intervention into the private, not just the public, sector.[18] However, whereas the original New Left was 'highly suspicious of Labour as a parliamentary party hostile to extra-parliamentary activity, the new Labour left saw no reason why parliamentary *and* extra-parliamentary activity could not go together hand in hand'.[19] Labour was to be the vehicle for radical economic change. It was in this atmosphere, of an increasing attachment to concepts of industrial democracy, participation and planning, that a commitment to television reform at last began to be seriously debated inside the Labour Party.

TELEVISION ISSUES IN THE EARLY 1970S

Labour and the BBC

The stormy relationship between the Labour Party and the BBC that had developed in the 1960s continued into the following decade. Wilson's highly personal vendetta against what he saw as systematic anti-Labour bias by the Corporation remained at an intense level. His controversial appointment of Lord Hill as chairman in 1967 appeared to have made little difference to the BBC's coverage and he held the Corporation partially responsible for Labour's defeat in the 1970 election.[20] Immediately afterwards, one senior BBC figure reported that 'Wilson is extremely bitter about the BBC, so bitter that he wishes in the future that Labour Party Political Broadcasts should be done by Granada Television.'[21]

The situation was inflamed the following year by the broadcast of a programme in the *24 Hours* documentary strand about Labour's fall from power. *Yesterday's Men* dealt with the consequences of losing power and took its title from Labour's portrayal of its Conservative opponents in the run-up to the 1970 election. According to Anthony Smith, it provoked 'the biggest and most furious row that a television programme in the English language has ever provoked'.[22] While the programme was intended to be a fresh examination of the mixed fortunes of the political class, it appeared to Wilson and the Labour

Party to be a simple hatchet job. Tony Benn described the programme as a 'complete send-up' and claimed that the producers had 'knifed Harold as hard as they could'.[23] Outraged by the provocative questioning about his personal finances, the satirical incidental music and the trivial tone of the whole programme, Wilson asked his solicitor Arnold Goodman to seek an injunction against the BBC. While this was not successful, the huge uproar that followed the programme forced the governors to issue a partial apology and led to a more cautious approach to current affairs output. 'For a long time afterwards,' wrote Ben Pimlott, 'television pulled its punches when dealing with politicians. "Better be safe than imaginative" became the bitter motto.'[24]

Partly because of the consequences of *Yesterday's Men* and partly because Labour was now in opposition and therefore only a secondary media target, Wilson's high-profile campaign against the BBC declined in the following years. Nineteen months after the BBC apologized to Wilson, he met Sir Michael Swann, the new BBC chair, for lunch. 'Mr. Wilson started by saying he had had no serious causes for complaint in the last eighteen months, and that he felt the BBC had been making strenuous efforts to be fair.' As distinct from his earlier accusation of systematic bias, Wilson argued that 'alleged unfairnesses' were due not to 'malice or political partisanship' but to 'political inexperience'.[25] Just as trade unionists and the left inside the Labour Party were starting to agitate around demands for balanced broadcasting coverage, Wilson and the Labour leadership were now making conciliatory noises to the BBC.

Labour and ITV

The Free Communications Group's publication of LWT's franchise submission highlighted the lack of transparency in the awarding of licences as well as the failure of some ITV broadcasters to stick to their promises. Meanwhile, the question of excess ITV profits had not disappeared. The short-lived downturn in advertising revenue of 1970–71 had turned around by 1972 so that, once again, the ITV system was awash with money. Profits increased by 40 per cent for Thames TV, 46 per cent for Scottish TV and 50 per cent for Granada and Westward, while Border doubled and Anglia tripled their rates of return.[26] This was no doubt helped by the Conservative government's cut in the exchequer levy in February 1971. While Labour had done precisely the same thing the previous year, this time its MPs were extremely critical. 'Disgraceful' shouted Labour MPs in Parliament when the cut was announced, while the shadow telecommunications minister, Ivor Richard, called the move 'extraordinarily regressive'.[27]

One of the last acts of the Labour government in 1970 had been to set up a Prices and Incomes Board to examine the costs and revenue of commercial television. When it reported at the end of the year it made a number of recommendations about how to restore profitability but also drew attention, according to the ACTT's Caroline Heller, to 'the problem of what level of profit is socially acceptable in the interest of stability'.[28] This was pursued by an even more extensive investigation in 1971–72 into commercial television undertaken by the Select Committee on Nationalized Industries, chaired by left-wing Labour MP Russell Kerr. While one historian described the committee's report as 'Pilkingtonian in flavour', excessively aggressive towards ITV and therefore counter-productive,[29] the committee made it clear what had changed since the 1960s:

> There has been a shift of emphasis from considering the broadcasting media solely in terms of the programmes they produce to one in which the BBC and the [Independent Broadcasting] Authority are seen as powerful institutions in their own right, whose style of decision-making and action profoundly affects the community. It is this view which has led to the demand for public accountability and for increased public participation and access.[30]

The committee was extremely critical of the current system and proposed a number of changes, including stronger regulation, more experimentation and education in programming, more opportunities for the smaller ITV companies and the reduction of pressure for high ratings. No wonder that, according to Anthony Smith, 'the document pleased the more radical wing of the broadcasting world'.[31]

The report clearly echoed the concerns of the broadcasting unions, the Free Communications Group and the growing left inside the Labour Party about the need for industrial democracy, a qualification of the overriding drive for profits and an interest in alternative structures. Indeed, Kerr himself in a letter to *The Times*, made it clear that the system itself was up for grabs. 'Do you need, for example, an IBA at all? Do we wish to continue with a system whereby roughly half of the nation's TV is controlled by a handful of companies making very substantial profits indeed? Are these "ground rules" for the operation of this most powerful of all media divinely ordained and immutable?'[32] Thus, while the relationship between the Labour leadership and individual ITV employers continued to be a close one, the commercial television system as a whole was increasingly subject to critical investigation by the Labour movement.

Labour and the fourth channel

The allocation of a fourth channel was a central issue to all those interested in television policy in the early 1970s. Since the previous Labour government had postponed a decision because of its economic difficulties, the Conservatives now threatened to hand it over to ITV. When the ITA published proposals for an ITV2 in December 1971, opponents of commercial television swung into action to prevent a precious national resource being handed over to private entrepreneurs. Research produced by Caroline Heller for the ACTT union showed that there was a weak economic rationale for an advertising-led ITV2 in the light of the Tory introduction of local commercial radio.[33] The Free Communications Group expressed its concern that advertising revenue would be diverted from upmarket newspapers and 'if it is the quality press which will suffer most, do we really want a fourth channel?'[34] Similarly, the *New Statesman* declared its total opposition to a commercial fourth channel because of the 'parlous state of the British press, which cannot sustain the loss of further millions of advertising revenue'.[35]

Opposition to an ITV2 cemented around the cross-party TV4 campaign that was backed by the FCG, Mary Whitehouse's NVLA, various unions and sympathetic Labour MPs like John Golding, Phillip Whitehead and Hugh Jenkins. The latter group tabled an early day motion which argued that 'the fourth television channel should not be allocated to the present independent television contractors' and won the support of about 100 MPs.[36] According to Labour MP Ivor Richard, the Opposition was 'firmly and definitely opposed to the allocation of the fourth channel to ITV at this stage'.[37]

What vision of the fourth channel was the opposition in favour of? One important contribution to the debate was Anthony Smith's vision of an electronic publishing house in the form of a 'National Television Foundation' (NTF). Endorsed by the ABS union, Smith's plan was to provide a 'right to broadcast' to a range of social groups so that the NTF 'would then play a kind of impresario role, merely by allocating resources to some, but fitting producers, writers, technicians, to others who arrived only with an idea, a grievance, a cause'.[38] Despite a lack of detail about how to fund such an operation, the model fitted with contemporary concerns to open up broadcasting to new voices on a more decentralized basis than existing broadcasting institutions and was to prove extremely influential in later discussions about the fourth channel. Others argued for an education-based channel or for a network of local community stations, while one piece of academic research found that 63 per cent of the public simply did not think that there should be a fourth channel.[39]

Perhaps not surprisingly, then, the other suggestion from the Labour movement at the time was to do nothing. Phillip Whitehead MP, while welcoming the spirit of the NTF model, criticized the financial problems associated with the plan and argued that 'the best thing we can do about that fourth button on the set is not to press it. Not for anyone.'[40] The ACTT, deeply concerned about the impact of a fourth channel on employment prospects in the industry, also decided that postponement was the best option. It would be 'improper to commit the Union to any particular scheme without opportunity for detailed analysis and comparison of the benefits offered to workers in the industry'.[41] In the early 1970s, therefore, the Labour Party was far more united about what it did *not* want than what it did want from a fourth channel.

Labour and a public inquiry

The issue that galvanized all of those around the Labour Party who were interested in broadcasting policy was the demand for a public inquiry into broadcasting. Almost every decision that had any connection to television was linked to the need for a full and open debate on the future of broadcasting. Since the Conservatives had scrapped Labour's plan for such a committee back in 1970, the clamour for an inquiry from Labour quarters was now even more deafening. The problem was that, having introduced local commercial radio (as promised in its manifesto), the new Conservative government was not keen to enter into a protracted debate on the role of broadcasting in a climate in which the left was setting the intellectual agenda.

Labour seized every opportunity to raise the issue. The early day motion rejecting an ITV2 in December 1971 tied the future of the fourth channel to a public inquiry as, for Philip Whitehead, all the possible alternatives for a new channel 'ought to be sifted through the fine mesh of a public inquiry'.[42] The Labour chairman of the Select Committee on Nationalized Industries, Russell Kerr, argued that his concerns about the IBA were tied to the 'urgent need for a wide-ranging enquiry'.[43] The Free Communications Group, the TV-4 campaign and the ACTT all pressed for an inquiry while the 1971 TUC conference called for a 'process of public enquiry into the ownership and control of the mass media'.[44] When in March 1973 the Conservatives announced the extension of both the BBC Charter and Independent Television Act from 1976 to 1981, 'the Labour Party immediately declared that if it returned to power it would not be bound by it'[45] *without* an inquiry. MPs kept up the pressure on the Conservatives so that, by October 1973, Phillip Whitehead was promising:

> I shall do everything I can to persuade the Labour Party not merely to oppose the coming legislation to extend the Charter and the Act in 1981, but to pledge that one of the first acts in government should be to announce that wide-ranging inquiry ... We must not have a repetition of the abandonment of Pilkington once Labour came to office in 1964.[46]

Why was there such a consensus about the need for an inquiry? Anthony Smith argues that 'there was need then and there is now. If you're trying to find independent institutions within the public sector to run everything but particularly a cultural enterprise, the periodic inquiry is an essential form of public accountability'.[47] Nicholas Garnham, an influential supporter of an inquiry at the time, wrote later of the 'liberal belief in an inquiry for its own sake as a way of letting the people into the debate on the future of British broadcasting'.[48] Calls for an inquiry in the early 1970s fitted Benn and the left's demands for increased accountability in the television industry while it provided opponents of Benn inside the Labour Party with the opportunity to take the heat out of the situation. The need for a comprehensive review of broadcasting was one that all sections of the party could agree on.

THE LABOUR PARTY STUDY GROUP ON THE MEDIA AND *THE PEOPLE AND THE MEDIA (TPATM)*

It was, however, the left inside the party who provided the backbone of Labour's first systematic broadcasting policy. In April 1972, the Home Policy Committee of the NEC under the supervision of Tony Benn invited about 40 members of the Labour movement to a meeting on 'communications' to discuss many of the issues raised above and to establish a study group on the media. Noting that it was not yet clear whether the government would launch an inquiry, the introductory document suggests that it was nevertheless time the party began to 'clarify its view on future policy' and sketch out some of the key areas for debate for publication in a green paper. These included relations between the media and politicians, questions of bias, finance and ownership, the role of advertising[49] and the issues of access to, 'worker participation' in and 'alternative structures' for the media. Heavily influenced by left-wing critiques of commercialism and media concentration, the document argues that what is needed is a 'thorough examination of the alternatives *across the board*, and the development of a comprehensive policy as to future structure'.[50]

Labour MPs invited included James Callaghan, Ian Mikardo and Tom Driberg from the NEC together with a dozen other MPs, among them Crossman, Mayhew, Whitehead, Stonehouse and Kaufman, as well as representatives from media unions. The largest single group was listed as 'others': intellectuals, academics and industry people who had contributed to the recent media debates. This group included Neal Ascherson and Gus MacDonald from the FCG Steering Committee, Hilda Himmelweit from the London School of Economics and James Curran from the Polytechnic of Central London, and New Left figures like Raymond Williams and Stuart Hall.[51] Although neither Williams nor Hall attended any of the meetings, the fact that they were invited onto an official Labour Party committee at all demonstrates the influence of the left in party discussions of media reform.

The study group drew explicitly on ideological critiques of the media influenced by Marxism so much so that the original document contained a lengthy quote from Hall on the need to transcend the existing set of broadcasting alternatives. While Hall did not make his physical presence felt on the study group, another theorist with a similar ideological critique of broadcasting consensus came to play a decisive role in drawing up Labour policy. Nicholas Garnham was the head of communications at the Polytechnic of Central London and had been active in ACTT debates about democratizing the media. In *Structures of Television*, first published in 1973, he launched a savage critique of the existing broadcasting arrangements. The duopoly for Garnham was a

> system in which two powerful institutions responsible not to the public but to the real, though hidden, pressures of the power elite, big business and the cultural establishment, manipulate the public in the interest of that power elite and socialise the individual broadcaster so that he collaborates in this process almost unconsciously.[52]

Garnham attacked the myth of the independence of broadcasters and contrasted it with the real interventionist role of the state in determining the level of the licence fee or the levy or coverage of political matters. Instead of hiding the political control structures of the media, Garnham argued to make them transparent through an ongoing democratization of media organizations. Television should be restructured into regional, independent non-profitmaking corporations where day-to-day control is in the 'hands of a works committee elected by all the workers' and where longer-term decisions are made by boards elected by both workers and local people.[53]

Another significant influence on the study group was Caroline Heller who had drafted the ACTT's Television Commission report. This too proposed the social ownership of mass communications and highlighted the urgent need for open access to financial information, increased democracy in decision-making, security of employment in the industry, the centralized collection of advertising revenue, the abolition of spot advertising and the decentralization of production units in broadcasting. It concluded that the ACTT looks forward to a 'system which will not only facilitate and encourage programme makers in their efforts to inform and interpret society but also a system which thinks of broadcasting as a means by which society can hold a dialogue with itself'.[54]

While the radical voices of Garnham and Heller were clearly heard on the study group, there were also conflicting points of view. Christopher Mayhew perhaps best represented the other extreme, telling Benn that the study group's proposals were 'disgusting, woolly, Marxist stuff'[55] and eventually resigning from the Labour Party to join the Liberals. In between were individuals like Anthony Smith and Philip Whitehead who wanted to see serious reform but were very sceptical of what they saw as Benn's unrealistic and undesirable plans to nationalize the media. The debate between the 'radicals' and 'reformists' was a vigorous one. For example, during the period of the study group, Garnham wrote to the *Guardian* championing the need for total structural reform of broadcasting and condemning Smith's idea of a National Television Foundation proposal as 'tinkering at the edges' and therefore 'diversionary'. 'It is like building a small village in which to eke out a living at the mercy of the feudal barons, rather than laying siege to their fortresses.'[56] Smith replied the following day, accusing Garnham of 'revolutionary inertia' and of underestimating the importance that a different model of television, which might be introduced after a full-scale broadcasting inquiry, might make to the overall broadcasting system.[57] However, while there were different political positions played out in the study group, the group as a whole was perceived as firmly belonging to the left. According to Garnham, the issue of media reform was then 'seen as a platform by the left of the party and that it was no accident that Benn was chairing it'.[58]

The first meeting took place on 17 May 1972 in the House of Commons, lasted nearly three hours and was attended by 23 people. It was resolved to reject a general formulation of media policy in favour of '*separate and detailed studies* of the different aspects' of the media. The next question was whether to concentrate on the press or broadcasting:

> Some felt that broadcasting should have first priority for study in view of the opportunity for changing the structure that 1976 presented; on the other hand, it was argued that the majority of trade unionists saw the Press as the major problem – partly because of the extent of anti-Union bias shown over the Industrial Relations issue.[59]

Whilst this issue was not resolved there and then, the view of both Phillip Whitehead[60] and James Curran is that it was clearly 'the press that was the leading edge in terms of the evolution of [Labour Party] media policy. It was concern about the press that led to *The People and the Media* rather than about broadcasting.'[61] The group agreed to discuss press and broadcasting at separate meetings and to produce a statement on media issues for publication in the forthcoming party policy document, *Labour's Programme 1973*.

This document contained one page on 'Communications', drawn up after consultation with the study group, which acknowledged the danger of 'market distortions' on freedom of expression in the media. It referred to the activities of the study group but added that 'more work will be necessary before we are in a position to propose any definite solutions to the problems in this complex field'.[62] However, *Labour's Programme* did confirm some firm principles on which party policy on the media would be based – industrial democracy, public ownership and accountability – and, in the spirit of the times, insisted on the need for a 'full-ranging inquiry into the future of broadcasting'.[63] As vague as these comments were, it was already clear that the study group was firmly aligned with Tony Benn's way of thinking rather than the more conservative approach, embraced by Wilson and the majority of the shadow Cabinet, of generally leaving broadcasting institutions alone.

A meeting between Wilson, Labour's broadcasting spokesperson John Grant and the BBC chairman, Sir Michael Swann, reveals some of the differences of opinion. The Labour leader insisted that the party 'really didn't have any firm ideas and were trying to evolve a policy … they were implacably opposed to the fourth channel going to IBA and would rescind this when they got into power. They were also firmly opposed to advertising on the BBC, except possibly paid-for Government advertising.'[64] When Swann raised the topical issue of public accountability,

> Wilson was vague but Grant came out firmly for a broadcasting council. I went over our arguments, i.e. that a council without power would only be yet another critical voice, while a council with power would undermine the Governors. Grant said this was 'swimming against the tide', but after a good deal of argument, Mr Wilson was, I felt fairly sure, firmly on my side. Indeed, discussion about the authority of the Governors, the DG and senior staff seemed to cheer him up no end.[65]

Of course, Swann may have misinterpreted Wilson's thoughts on the issue, but it would hardly be surprising had Wilson supported the authority of the BBC governors and the broadcasting establishment against left-wing proposals for full accountability, as the lesser of two evils.

In May 1973, the study group resolved to draft a green paper in the next few months. Four weeks later this decision was reversed. The NEC's Home Policy Committee considered a draft report from the group and agreed to publish it as a discussion paper and not a green paper because the party had already published too many of them on various other subjects. The profile of the study group suffered another reverse when Labour's election manifesto in February 1974 excluded all mention of broadcasting, omitting even the party's support for a public inquiry. Despite the discussions on television policy taking place inside and outside the Labour Party, only the Conservative manifesto referred to television and pledged to 'bring forward proposals for the allocation of a fourth TV channel when economic circumstances permit'.[66]

The final draft was presented to the study group on 3 April 1974, over a month after Labour had narrowly won the general election. The broadcasting section was written by Nicholas Garnham and Caroline Heller and amended by committee in the light 'of the fact that the report now had a rather different relationship to a possible enquiry into broadcasting',[67] an event confirmed by the home secretary's announcement that such an inquiry would now take place. With pressure to complete and publish the report, the group met again at the end of the month and agreed to accept Heller's redraft on broadcasting. The document, eventually called *The People and the Media (TPATM)*, was published in July 1974, no longer a green paper but a 'discussion paper' designed both to 'stimulate thought outside the stricter confines of the Labour Movement' and to 'assist [members of the inquiry] in their deliberations'.[68]

Two points are worth stressing about the document as a whole. First, it is evident that press reform and not broadcasting is the driving force behind *TPATM* with nearly 18 pages devoted to the former and only five to the latter. *Tribune*, the house magazine of the Labour left, greeted the report with the headline 'Don't Just Save the Press – Change It' and completely ignored all the recommendations about television in its hurry to assess the impact on the press.[69]

Second, the ideas of the 'radicals' permeate *TPATM* far more than those of the 'moderates', to the extent that Anthony Smith is not even a signatory to the document. There is no mention at all of the spirited debates outside the party about the fate of the fourth channel, a sure sign that the views of Garnham and the ACTT Television Commission of a reluctance to endorse expansion at any cost had triumphed, for the moment, over Smith's plan for a National Television Foundation. On issues concerning the licence fee, regulation and programme sources, it was radical ideas that predominated.

The document opens with an expression of concern about the current state of the media. Economic concentration, the domination of the profit motive, the absence of accountability in decision-making, the lack of diversity of content, and the influence of government secrecy are all constraints on a genuinely free media. It highlights the need for decentralization and industrial democracy:

> As for the dangers of governmental control, there seems little doubt to us that alternative structures of broadcasting, based on smaller units and more open decision-making … would provide a far more effective safeguard for freedom of communications than is provided by these supposedly well-intentioned, anonymous and unaccountable guardians. Our aim must be to devise a framework for the media that avoids the twin dangers of government and commercial control.[70]

TPATM suggested radical reforms. It called for a Public Broadcasting Commission (PBC), replacing both BBC and IBA boards, which would be the overall administrative and funding agency for television and radio together with a new Communications Council to review the operations of all media. *TPATM* proposed to phase out the licence fee on the basis that broadcasting services 'should not be subjected to severe instability of advertising revenues, but neither should they be shielded from economic realities and the need to order national priorities'. The solution, partially in the spirit of the Pilkington Report, was to centralize both the collection of advertising revenue and Exchequer grant.[71] Perhaps most controversially of all, the BBC and ITV networks would be scrapped in favour of two new television corporations that would each run one national and one regional channel. 'Programme-making itself would be carried out by a wide variety of dispersed *programme units* reflecting the creative talent of all parts of the UK.'[72] These developments would be supplemented by the creation of a national publicly owned cable network, freedom of information legislation and the abolition of both the Official Secrets Act and local commercial radio.[73]

The report met with a hostile response, particularly from the broadcasting establishment. Lord Hill thundered in the *Listener* against the 'acts of vandalism' proposed by *TPATM* and 'the authors' doctrinal urge to weaken the broadcasting organisations in the interests of what they call "real internal democracy"'.[74] 'Was it significant', Grace Wyndham Goldie astutely asked, 'that in the Labour Party's broadcasting plans there was so little mention of Parliament or the need to maintain Parliament's ultimate responsibility for broadcasting?'[75] Lord Annan continued this line of thinking when he later wrote of calls for internal democracy that 'to claim that the authorities should be largely comprised of members elected by, and answerable to, outside bodies because these bodies alone can discern the public interest, is really an attack upon the power of the minister and Parliament'.[76] Of course this was precisely the political point behind the document: to express a more militant, producerist conception of democracy which involved new sorts of extra-parliamentary structures and a wider range of voices taking part in the democratic process.

Commentators in the broadsheet press were not quite as dismissive as those in the upper echelons of broadcasting. An editorial in *The Times* sympathized with the desire to tackle the future of media but argued that the proposals, if implemented, would lead to increased state intervention and further instability in the industries. It added that 'it is dangerous to seek improvement by pulling down existing institutions with a tradition behind them'.[77] The *Guardian* took the debates rather more seriously and only criticized *TPATM* for excluding film, publishing and the theatre from the report and for not having enough input from the press and broadcasting fields.[78]

Broadcast, the industry magazine, attacked the proposals as unrealistic and unable to deal with concrete questions of financing television, although the main problem lay elsewhere, with the intellectual fallacies of the argument: 'It is so strongly based on doctrinaire views about "internal democracy" and concepts of accountability that nobody has bothered to question those beliefs objectively.'[79]

Even those involved in the study group expressed reservations. Eric Moonman, a Labour MP on the group, argued later that they had 'ducked intellectual issues in favour of platitudes'[80] while Phillip Whitehead signed *TPATM*

> with some misgivings about one part of it which was the idea of an overarching broadcasting authority that could control everything. I didn't write a minority report because I felt strongly that the ideas in the document were sufficiently good and radical that it could carry one single proposal that I thought then was unworkable.[81]

Anthony Smith is more critical and argues that *TPATM*

> was a vengeful plan. It wasn't a plan produced from a position of total detachment on the part of people thinking what would be best for this medium. It was produced by a group of people who felt that the system was against them and wanted a structure that would make it fair for them ... Also they were concerned primarily with the political role of television and not with its entertainment and cultural role. As a former professional in the medium, I realised that news and current affairs is a by-product of television and that the real role of television is to enthral, to entertain and to compensate for hours of drudgery at work.[82]

How valid are these criticisms? First, the report rejects 'a position of total detachment' in favour of a partisan critique of the way in which the media legitimize certain agendas while rejecting others. The media, according to *TPATM*, 'are confining themselves to the narrow middle ground of what their controllers consider acceptable and uncontroversial'.[83] A greater variety of programme sources, it argues, would lead to the nurturing of creativity and a proliferation of views within the system. So, while there may well have been a perception on the part of the left that the 'system was against them', *TPATM* sought to add to the diversity of voices available, through the creation of a decentralized production network and an emphasis on increasing access, and not to wipe out those offending ones. Second, the report marginalizes popular entertainment not simply because of perceptions of its low political status, but because challenging, minority-interest programmes (like investigative current affairs) are more likely to suffer in pure ratings-led television. *TPATM*, therefore, did not seek to limit what sort of programmes and genres should be produced, but it did seek to protect those areas of programming threatened by the logic of market-led broadcasting and to expand the range of opinions within the system.

Third, while the majority of the broadcasting establishment savaged *TPATM* for centralizing and politicizing broadcasting, the stated intention of the document was merely to extend the accountability of the mechanisms of decision-making beyond traditional political appointees. Instead of BBC governors or IBA board members appointed by the relevant secretary of state, the PBC would have a membership 'made up of elected representatives from the broadcasting organisations and local government, plus members of parliament, in equal proportions, with the addition of nominees from important national organisations'.[84] Far from placing broadcasting under the control of the Labour Party NEC, *TPATM* dared to challenge the accepted convention of supreme parliamentary control, reflecting the dominant political current at the time of grass roots-led democratization and participation. Fourth, the idea that the proposals had been drawn up in a hurry and without any professional input ignores the fact that no political party up to that time had held ten lengthy meetings, produced a number of discussion documents and consulted with a wide range of politicians, technology experts, broadcasters and academics on the issue of broadcasting. While *TPATM* was not 'objective' or indeed popular, it nevertheless contained a coherent set of proposals informed by a genuine consultative process and was intended to stimulate further discussion about television policy.

A more valid criticism of the document is its lack of detail about sources of revenue to replace the licence fee and the precise structure of the new television corporations. However, since it was endlessly repeated afterwards that *TPATM* was a discussion document and not a blueprint, this is an understandable omission. Perhaps the most serious accusation is that the document was a naive attempt at democratic reform and that the proposals would never have been implemented by a Labour government. Whitehead recalls that the 'word going out from anybody on the industrial/financial side, apart from Tony [Benn], was that this was unrealistic and you should not take it too seriously'.[85] Smith is adamant that these were 'not implementable proposals in the real world of politics. In power they would have been confronted by all the commercial interests, all the other industrial interests which lie behind broadcasting.'[86]

At one level, Smith is correct to point out that, if Labour failed to confront these interests, *TPATM* would indeed be a utopian dream and, as Labour was extremely unlikely, in practice, to antagonize such a powerful range of forces, the document was more hot air than practical politics. But it is also the case that *any* proposal for radical reform is likely to be attacked by establishment politicians and press as being unrealistic, poorly conceived and dangerous. This is particularly the case when such reform involves the abolition of media institutions like the BBC and ITV and which threatens the position of other media bodies in both press and broadcasting. A sympathetic hearing from these 'opinion-formers' is unlikely. The point is that these proposals were conceived as part of a generalized political challenge to market structures and traditional social democratic government and reflected a growing mood inside the country to press for alternative social and political structures. With hindsight, it is easy to write off *TPATM* as misguided and hopeless; at the time, as Stephen Lambert argues, 'structural reform was in the air'.[87]

TPATM faced its first test with the Cabinet during the discussions of the party's manifesto for the October 1974 election which Wilson called in response to the establishment of a minority government earlier that year. Given that Labour finally had something approaching a media policy and that the government had announced the formation of a public inquiry into broadcasting, surely the inclusion of a paragraph or two on broadcasting would be appropriate. Indeed, a joint meeting of the Cabinet and the NEC in June discussed a draft manifesto that contained several paragraphs on 'communications and the media'. Drawing attention to the forthcoming inquiry and the study group report on the media, the manifesto promised that Labour would scrap the licence fee and 'ensure that a new and more open structure is built for the media'.[88]

However, after a summer in which 'Wilson and his advisers were embarked upon a careful exercise: mellowing the manifesto',[89] the entire section about communications had disappeared by the time the manifesto eventually appeared three months later. Perhaps, television policy was simply not important enough to justify inclusion in the manifesto or perhaps the proposals were found to be too left-wing for the party leadership. In the year in which the Labour Party had spent longer than ever discussing television policy and in which the party's first systematic statement on the mass media had been produced, neither manifesto in 1974 included a single mention of what the party planned to do with television. Now that the party was back in government, would *TPATM* form the basis of legislative action or would its more radical findings disappear under the strain of political office?

THE IMPACT OF THE 1974–79 GOVERNMENT

Speaking to the Labour conference in opposition in 1973, Denis Healey had promised a savage attack on the wealth and privilege of the rich. The following year, speaking to the Confederation of British Industry, Healey as chancellor declared that Labour wanted 'a private sector which is vigorous, alert, imaginative – and profitable'.[90] Having entered office just as a world economic recession was developing, Healey and the Labour government needed all the friends they could get. By October 1974, inflation was up to 17 per cent with wage increases running up to 22 per cent.[91] As both unemployment and the balance of payments deficit increased, the demands for deflation grew stronger from the employers while the left found it increasingly difficult to win support for its programme of import controls and state-directed investment. 'To the right of the Labour Party,' as one critic put it, 'the "alternative strategy" was neither an alternative nor a strategy.'[92] Far from leading an offensive against capital, Tony Benn found himself increasingly isolated in a government that claimed it was forced to take desperate measures to protect the economy. Benn's defeat in the referendum on Common Market membership in March 1975 only added to his marginalization in Cabinet.

Instead of the anticipated expansion of the public sector, the left found itself confronted with repeated cuts in public spending throughout 1975 and 1976. By autumn 1976, with sterling in steep decline, the chancellor negotiated a rescue package with the International Monetary Fund (IMF) in return for £2.5 billion worth of cuts over two years. When the new prime minister, James Callaghan, told the 1976 Labour conference that the old Keynesian method of increasing public spending as a solution to economic crisis was no longer an option, the period of Labour revisionism – of equality founded on economic growth – was firmly at an end. Union leaders who had previously called for social planning in industry now called for a 'social contract' between workers and the government, which involved holding down wages to help the country through its difficulties. Nationalization was now less about taking control of the 'commanding heights' than about bailing out unprofitable firms.

According to one government adviser, the National Enterprise Board, the cornerstone of the left's economic strategy, 'became a convenient casualty ward for firms the Government wished to rescue from bankruptcy'.[93]

While more recent writers like Martin Holmes[94] argue that the government had little choice but to deflate and pass on the cuts, there was huge bitterness at the time from inside and outside the Labour Party. One supporter of the left complained that the IMF measures did little to halt economic decline but marked the end of any hint of progressive government: 'From the defeat of the Labour government by the IMF in December 1976 to its electoral defeat in May 1979 there is little else but a sordid and wearying tale of a government without any coherent strategy or policy, except to struggle for its own survival.'[95] Backbench revolts became increasingly familiar – between 1974 and 1979 there were 309 divisions with Labour MPs voting against their government compared to 109 between 1966 and 1970.[96] Annual conferences regularly voted against the executive while, perhaps most seriously, union members started to resist the pay norms until, in 1979, following the 'winter of discontent', Callaghan's government was defeated by Margaret Thatcher's Conservatives.

In contrast to the grand plans for modernization and innovation of the Labour government of the 1960s, the 1974–79 government made fewer promises. Both governments were confronted by serious economic difficulties and both were forced to capitulate to public spending cuts and an abandonment of reform programmes. But, as Phillip Whitehead notes about the later period, there was a 'growth of pessimism about future prospects [which] left its mark on the government. Times of contraction do not produce an enthusiasm for radical experiment.'[97] According to Roy Jenkins, while his main aim as home secretary in the 1960s had been 'the opening of windows of freedom and innovation', in his second term between 1974 and 1976, 'I saw my primary task as the maintenance of the proper authority of the state'.[98] The commitment to progressive legislation which had seen the introduction of a Health and Safety at Work Act, the Employment Protection Act and the repeal of the Tory anti-union laws by 1975, petered out under the strain of maintaining office and keeping the economy afloat. The dream of the Croslandite revisionists for progressive social reform underpinned by economic growth turned into the opposite. By 1976, there had been a 'sea-change' in British politics: '[p]ermissiveness, collectivism and social reform, it was thought, had produced a crisis of authority. Governments were at best weak, at worst corrupt. Subversives lurked everywhere. The terrorist was at the gates.'[99] It was at this time that the public inquiry into the future of broadcasting, desired for so long by Labour supporters, was launched.

LABOUR AND THE ANNAN COMMITTEE

One of the first acts of the incoming Labour government in March 1974 was to abolish the Ministry of Posts and Telecommunications and to place broadcasting policy under the remit of Roy Jenkins in the Home Office and technical matters in the Department of Trade and Industry. Neither Wilson nor Jenkins make any reference to this shift in their memoirs although Garnham is convinced that the purpose of the move was 'to make sure that Benn was not the minister in charge of broadcasting',[100] despite his credentials for the job. One month later, Jenkins announced the establishment of a committee to examine the future of broadcasting to be chaired by Lord Annan. Given the narrow majority of the government and the pressure of far more urgent matters, for example the state of the economy and Britain's membership of the European Economic Community (EEC), it is curious that it acted so quickly to revive the committee.

This may be explained in part in terms of practical necessity. With the BBC Charter and IBA legislation due to expire in 1976, some firm decisions were needed about broadcasting and the development of new technologies. The government therefore extended the lives of both broadcasting bodies until 1979 when the committee would have reported on its deliberations. Anthony Smith argues that a decision on the fourth channel was getting to be a priority by 1974 and that the government 'could see that industrially it was quite important. Setting up a new channel meant that there was a lot of industrial potential in manufacturing and they wanted to help British manufacturing'.[101]

Given that deliberations about the industrial benefits of broadcasting were largely absent from the ensuing discussions, a more persuasive argument is that reviving the committee was an easy way of exacting revenge on the Conservatives who had scrapped the Annan Committee upon winning the 1970 election. Annan himself agrees that it was 'a tit-for-tat. You know "you've slapped us down and now we're bloody well going to do it". I don't know that Wilson was all that involved but Roy [Jenkins] certainly was and was extremely helpful and supportive.'[102] Phillip Whitehead concurs that one of the ways of wiping the Tory slate clean was to bring Annan back. But I think the main influence behind the scenes in 1974 was quite a complicated interplay of forces. There was a strong push among academics for, at the very least, a re-examination of what we wanted from an ITV2 … and you can't underestimate Roy Jenkins. He had been a radical Home Secretary but now he didn't want to be Home Secretary again and didn't want to go through that tour of picking up on particular issues but here he had a ready-made issue.[103]

As Whitehead suggests, academics were starting to take up broadcasting issues. In 1973, academics committed to media reform and an official inquiry came together in the Standing Conference on Broadcasting (SCoB) and conducted a series of lively interventions into the debate. Billed as the 'alternative Annan', SCoB was an influential pressure group and consisted both of academics involved in the Labour Party study group, like Garnham, Smith and Curran, as well as other leading figures in the field – Stuart Hall, Jay Blumler, Tom Burns, James Halloran, Hilda Himmelweit, Stuart Hood, Denis McQuail, Colin Seymour-Ure and Raymond Williams.

The mid-1970s, therefore, was marked by a high level of intellectual and political pressure in the Labour movement highlighting the need for media reform. It was in this climate that the Labour government set up both the Annan Committee and a Royal Commission on the Press to examine questions of press control and monopoly. However, as much as these inquiries were concessions to the left, they could also be seen as fitting the needs of the right. James Curran argues that the 'concern of the Labour leadership has always been to have a good press and having a radical press policy was counter-productive in their eyes. Indeed what the Labour leadership did was to kick the issue into touch, quite consciously by setting up a Royal Commission.'[104] The same case could be made for broadcasting. 'Wilson's strategy', according to Garnham, 'was first to move broadcasting into the Home Office and get it away from Benn and then secondly set up Annan which meant that the whole thing was under wraps for three or four years. They didn't have to make any decisions – it became a non-political question.'[105] Wilson aimed to take media reform out of the hands of impatient broadcasting workers and activists and into the more trusted hands of Lord Annan and his committee.

'Politics' was still an issue when it came to the membership of the inquiry team. Breaking the unwritten rule that 'nobody who has expressed any strong views on a subject should ever be on a committee',[106] Jenkins insisted that his political ally, Phillip Whitehead, should be on the Annan Committee. Whitehead had not only expressed strong views on broadcasting but had actually been a signatory to *The People and the Media* and appeared to be a card-carrying member of the group to abolish the BBC and the IBA. Whitehead recounts how the deal was done:

> Annan's real terror was of politicians. Roy Jenkins got me on and overruled him on this. They were old mates and Jenkins said 'I know this man and he's all right and you can have a right-wing broadcaster and a right-wing politician' and he put both of those on. So I was neutralised by having Sir Marcus Worsley [MP] and Anthony Jay ... and it left me with fewer natural allies – Hilda Himmelweit was really the only other person who had been in the Labour Party strand.[107]

This was despite the inclusion of two trade unionists, one of whom, John Pollock, was the former chair of the Scottish Labour Party but who had no recorded ideas on broadcasting. The other, Tom Jackson, the general secretary of the Union of Post Office Workers and a former BBC governor, was a significant rebuff to those inside the Labour movement who wanted a more vocal opponent of the duopoly. So, despite the massive contributions the left had made to media debates, Jeremy Potter is right to argue that 'the membership of the committee reflected the moderate Labour leadership's desire for reform, not the revolutionary zeal of those behind *The People and the Media* and SCoB'.[108]

The most significant absence from the committee was Anthony Smith, then a research fellow at St Antony's College, Oxford and a member of both SCoB and the Labour Party study group. His model of a National Television Foundation was one of the few coherent proposals for a fourth channel and Smith himself was an influential figure in broadcasting debates. Indeed, until quite a late stage, Smith was on the list and certainly was not blocked by Annan who was in favour of his presence on the committee.[109] According to Smith, 'the civil servant in charge of broadcasting at that time came to see me about being on the committee and was surprised that the night before the announcement, the thing came back from Downing Street with this name scratched out'.[110] Having argued with Wilson over the latter's support for the Stalinist regime of Husak in Czechoslovakia against the democratic opposition, 'the next time Wilson saw my name on a piece of paper he crossed it out'.[111]

Labour's submission consisted entirely of suggestions taken from *TPATM*: the abolition of the licence fee and the replacement of the BBC and IBA by a Public Broadcasting Commission. Did this submission represent *official* Labour Party policy on broadcasting? While Wilson was not prepared to make any manifesto commitments along the lines of *TPATM*, he was less disturbed by the thought of these proposals being one small part of many contributions to a wide-ranging inquiry on which a Labour government would later legislate. The status of *TPATM* was clarified by a letter to *The Times* by John Grant, Labour's broadcasting spokesperson, who insisted that *TPATM*

> is a discussion document. It commits neither the party nor the individuals who sign it, although they were in broad agreement with its general approach and felt it could usefully stimulate much further thought about this important subject. *It is, of course, in no sense Government policy which is to await the findings of the Royal Commission on the Press and the Annan Broadcasting Committee* which were set up after the working party had completed most of its work.[112]

In a clear example of the gap between party and government, the Labour government's media policy was not the one proposed by the party's study group but one to be agreed following the recommendations of the public inquiry. Several months after Labour's submission was delivered to the Annan Committee, the 1975 party conference passed a resolution that firmly welcomed the publication of *TPATM* although both the motion and the debate concentrated exclusively on the state of the newspaper industry and ignored the study group's proposals for broadcasting reform. The ideas contained in *TPATM* therefore remained in limbo: acknowledged by annual conference as providing the basis of the party's media policy but seen by the leadership as a mere discussion document.

Labour's submission was complemented by that of the Standing Conference on Broadcasting, which argued that 'the BBC and IBA do not have a privileged place in society; they act as stewards of a public service. Whether they remain or whether alternative structures are set up to replace them, a reappraisal of the present system seems to us inevitable.'[113] SCoB called for centralized collection of advertising revenue, an emphasis on accountability and the creation of a 'National Broadcasting Policy Council' to advise on policy and a 'National Broadcasting Commission' to take over executive control. Such was the standing of what were fairly radical ideas that the committee gave over two whole days to considering SCoB's proposals after which, interestingly, SCoB organized a press conference at which Lord Annan was present. 'When asked why he was there, Lord Annan replied that

SCoB's submissions contained "some very interesting proposals" …
The unstated implication was that Lord Annan welcomed such
thinking from an allegedly non-aligned group.'[114]

Whilst this is not the place for a detailed analysis of the Annan
Report,[115] it is nevertheless important to stress how seriously the
committee took the more radical submissions, particularly those from
the left and the labour movement. In some ways, the whole premise of
the report, finally published in March 1977, was based on the need, not
simply for modernization or renewal, but for the democratization of
broadcasting. 'It has been put to us', the report states towards the
beginning, 'that broadcasting should be "opened up".'[116] The duopoly,
according to the committee, was proving to be a straitjacket on
creativity and audiences so that 'major changes should take place in
the structure of broadcasting if good programmes are to continue to be
made for audiences who will be more varied, fragmented and perhaps
better educated'.[117] In a direct acknowledgement of the left critique of
the narrowness of the broadcasting agenda, the report argues that
contemporary culture 'is now multi-racial and pluralist: that is to say,
people adhere to different views of the nature and purpose of life and
expect their own views to be exposed in some form or other. The
structure of broadcasting must reflect this variety.'[118]

The skill of the Annan Committee is that it embraced the need for
change without undermining the basic authority of the existing broadcasting organizations and structures. Having recognized the left's
critique, the report, in the main, rejected their proposals. An executive
broadcasting commission was ruled out as too centralist; workers'
representation on governing bodies was seen as undesirable; and the
abolition of the BBC and IBA considered unnecessary. The key demands
of the left for structural reform were confronted and turned down.

The Annan Committee did, however, propose one major change:
the launch of an 'Open Broadcasting Authority' (OBA) to run the
fourth channel. As we have seen, the official Labour Party submission
was silent on this issue while most of the labour movement was more
united on what it did not want (an ITV-2), than on what it did
(generally, an educational channel). Some, like SCoB, argued that a
fourth channel was not a priority in the current economic
circumstances and that any decision should be postponed. However,
heavily influenced by Anthony Smith, who had participated in but
who had not signed up to Labour's *TPATM*, and his vision of a
National Television Foundation, the committee agreed on a new
authority to oversee an approach to scheduling and programming that
would cater to the demand for diversity and difference in television:

> We do not see the fourth channel merely as an addition to the plurality of outlets, but as a force for plurality in a deeper sense. Not only could it be a nursery for new forms and new methods of presenting ideas, it could also open the door to a new kind of broadcast publishing.[119]

The OBA would commission programmes from a range of producers, including the ITV companies, the Open University and, most importantly for the champions of diversity, independent producers. Mixed sources of programming would be complemented by a mixed revenue base of sponsorship, block advertising, subscriptions and government grants. Furthermore, the OBA would act as a publisher, not a broadcaster, and therefore need not be responsible for ensuring balance in individual programmes but across its schedule as a whole. Such a structure would allow for the transmission of opinions not normally sanctioned by the other channels and therefore appeared to be at the heart of the committee's stated aim to 'open up' broadcasting. This was complemented by the report's support for a fourth channel in Wales broadcasting in the Welsh language.

The committee's concession to the radical demands for democratization and access was countered by its insistence that the channel should not associate itself with any one political position and that 'if it allowed its service to be taken over by political extremists, it would soon lose its remit from Parliament ... In general, we recommend the [Open Broadcasting] Authority should have the maximum freedom which *Parliament is prepared to allow.'*[120] Annan was determined that while new voices were to be heard, including those which expressed the breakdown of consensus, they must be organized according to the terms of the existing political consensus. The pressure for an expanded broadcasting sphere that arose in part from the extra-parliamentary struggles of the late 1960s and early 1970s was to be accommodated in a new channel whose parameters of acceptability would have to complement those of Parliament.

The Annan Report was, therefore, a model of compromise: urging evolutionary proposals to marginalize more revolutionary ones, embracing change while preserving existing structures and encouraging new voices while retaining the former gatekeepers. According to Annan himself, 'the report was not a crusading one like Pilkington. This one was "look, steady as she goes, one great venture – Channel Four – is enough, and there is nothing very much more that we ought to be doing at the moment".'[121] Phillip Whitehead, described by Annan as the 'hero of our report',[122] was equally cautious. Far from boasting that the committee's proposals were set to revolutionize broadcasting, he argued in Parliament that the report 'is not a prescription for instant action or an attempt to say that certain things are terribly wrong now and must changed overnight'.[123]

Despite the fact that the report firmly rejected the Labour Party's unofficial media policy, most Labour MPs welcomed the committee's findings. Eric Moonman, a signatory to *TPATM*, praised both the proposal for the fourth channel and the report's conclusion that 'competition between the BBC and ITV has not benefited the public.[124] The reaction of home secretary Merlyn Rees was even more revealing: 'What impressed me most about the report … is what the Committee did not recommend. It did not recommend any fundamental change in the constitutional arrangements for broadcasting in this country.'[125] Annan's decisive backing of the existing framework of British broadcasting was a relief for those in the government who had little appetite for implementing radical broadcasting reforms. The re-emergence of a consensus about broadcasting policy was confirmed by the warm responses to Annan of Willie Whitelaw, the shadow home secretary, and the TUC respectively.

Garnham, writing three years after the report, argued that this was precisely what Wilson had hoped for when launching the inquiry:

> Annan, like all such Committees of Inquiry, was expressly designed to lance the boil of radical discontent (and in particular to head off proposals for radical reform from within the Labour Party itself) by allowing all voices to express themselves in evidence to the Committee, there to be nullified, because by their nature unstructured and unfocussed, by the 'on the one hand and on the other' of committee compromise.[126]

Labour had pursued a similar path in terms of press policy. With *TPATM*'s press proposals backed by party conference, the creation of a Royal Commission on the Press was evidence of the seriousness of Labour's intentions but also a useful way of postponing any immediate decisions. James Curran, who actually drew up the terms of reference, recalls that when the Commission had completed its work in 1977, 'I had lunch with a senior civil servant and he said nothing will come of the report. I asked why and he said there was no political will behind it. He said that it would be in the inter-departmental committee where the findings would get lost and it turned out he was exactly right.'[127] Proposals for a change in monopoly law and ownership rules were quietly dropped.

The Annan Report was therefore both a full-blooded engagement with and a firm rejection of the critique of the broadcasting duopoly developed by socialist intellectuals and activists in the Free Communications Group, media unions, SCoB and the Labour Party study group. It recognized the need for change but only so long as its proposals, in the words of the report, 'would help to take the heat out of a number of controversies which rage today'.[128] 'It was a genuine attempt to evolve the structures of broadcasting', as Anthony Smith puts it, yet its principal achievement 'was to confirm the idea of the broadcasting authority'.[129]

In conclusion, while the Annan Report was not official Labour Party policy, *it may as well have been*. First, it focused the principles of access, accountability and diversity, all of which underlay Labour's policy debates at the time, into a neat compromise package. Second, it largely satisfied both Labour radicals with promise of an OBA and Labour moderates with appeals to the preservation of public service broadcasting and structural stability. Finally, it aimed not to antagonize its ideological foes too much: 'ITV received the report with more relief than dismay. It was not the threatened end of the world as they knew it.'[130]

FROM ANNAN COMMITTEE TO WHITE PAPER

During the parliamentary debate on Annan in May 1977, the Labour home secretary Merlyn Rees claimed that he intended to implement proposals based on the report in the lifetime of the present government. However, he also made it clear that he had reservations about two aspects of the OBA: the uncertainty of its revenue base and the relaxation of the requirement to produce 'impartial' programmes. These criticisms were mirrored by civil servants in the Home Office but also by the Treasury, which was anxious about backing a new public project at a time of great economic instability. According to Phillip Whitehead, 'the Treasury feared that there would be a financial shortfall and that we would end up bailing out another public service. Merlyn Rees was just a desperately cautious person and wasn't going to do anything within the Home Office if he could avoid it.'[131] Instead, Rees passed on the bulk of the responsibility for drawing up a white paper to his minister of state, Lord Harris. 'Together with the Home Office civil servants,' notes Lambert, 'Harris ... favoured an extension of the existing ITV network' and indeed he went on to become the chair of Westward Television[132] as well as leaving the Labour Party to join the Social Democrats. This was not an auspicious development for supporters of Annan, anxious to see the spirit of the committee embodied in future legislation.

The first rumours emanating from the Home Office suggested that a possible way forward lay in postponing the fourth channel until the economy picked up. Unwilling to antagonize the left by scrapping the OBA in favour of IBA control and unable to convince the Treasury that this was the right time to use public funds for broadcasting, the government was accused of stalling on a decision 'at least until the restoration of an upbeat economy'.[133] In January 1978, however, a leak of Harris' draft white paper confirmed that the Home Office had decided to defer a fourth channel for three years and then hand it over to the IBA, not the OBA. Both Annan and Whitehead still admit to being surprised at the Home Office's decision. Whitehead confesses to being 'amazed that senior Labour Party people were going around parroting the words of Sir Brian Young [IBA director-general] and the IBA'[134] while Annan claims that 'I don't know what the pressures on him [Rees] were or why he wanted this. It was absolutely against the whole tenor of our report.'[135] At the time, Annan supporters were even more horrified. The industry magazine *Campaign* carried the dramatic headline, 'Labour MPs Fight for OBA' and quoted Whitehead raging that 'we are all people who have thought a lot about broadcasting reform and we are angry at these stories coming out of the Home Office'.[136] *Broadcast* argued that the government had decided not to expand television services and that this had 'long been the assumption of the more pessimistic of the industry's observers, who could not see a Government faced with an election and still surrounded by economic problems devoting too much time, or money, to broadcasting'.[137]

The battle reached the highest levels as Rees failed to win over the Cabinet to the proposals and indeed produced one of Prime Minister Callaghan's few decisions on broadcasting. Heavily lobbied by Whitehead, former arts minister Hugh Jenkins, Tony Benn and others, Callaghan agreed to set up and chair a new Cabinet sub-committee on broadcasting to make recommendations on the white paper.[138] In particular, Callaghan asked Bernard Donoghue and David Lipsey from his Downing Street research staff to prepare a paper on the fourth channel that eventually favoured the OBA. By May 1978, the tide had turned and, to the relief of the reformers, the OBA had been reinstated and the concerns of the Treasury about increasing public borrowing had been defeated. This was partly due to new figures showing that the cost of a new service would be much lower than previously thought and partly due to persistent campaigning by Whitehead,

Anthony Smith and others about the need for increased diversity. Stephen Lambert argues that the decision may also have had more internal political roots:

> Whether Callaghan was persuaded of the need for a new Authority for the fourth channel because of the merits of the argument, or more because it would be a relatively easy concession to the left wing of the Party at a time when such concessions were few and far between, is difficult to determine.[139]

Six months after the Cabinet committee was launched and 16 months after the publication of the Annan Report, Labour's white paper on broadcasting appeared and it soon became clear that, with the important exception of the OBA and support for a Welsh-language channel, concessions to the left *were* 'few and far between'.

Rees presented the white paper as reflecting the spirit of the Annan Committee that broadcasting 'should continue to be provided as public services and the responsibility of public authorities. But', he continued, 'our proposals are also designed to encourage diversity in the range and variety of material available to the public and to enhance the accountability of the broadcasting authorities.'[140] Using the popular language of broadcasting reform, the white paper committed itself to both increased pluralism *and* the existing structures of BBC and ITV, the licence fee *and* the levy. However, while in some places the white paper and the Annan Report were very similar,[141] the former also contained a number of important deviations from the latter.

First, in terms of financing the OBA, the white paper extended the range of revenue sources to include spot advertising and rentals from programme-makers selling advertising in their own programmes. Given that the ITV companies were likely to be a major source of OBA programming, this would greatly increase the influence of commercial forces on the channel. Both of these proposals 'represent a critical departure from Annan's thinking and caused a few gulps even among the paper's enthusiastic supporters'.[142] Second, the white paper also challenged the OBA's editorial independence by insisting that the new authority should ensure that 'due impartiality is preserved in the treatment of controversial matters and that nothing should be broadcast which incites to crime or is offensive to public feeling'.[143] This was a major blow not just to Annan's concept of pluralism but to the radical demands for a challenge to the establishment's control over what was deemed 'controversial' or 'acceptable'. Programmes which adopted a partisan stance on, for example, Northern Ireland, trade unions, anti-racism and, of course, the policies of government were now more likely to be ruled out of order. The white paper aimed to reinforce the power of public authorities to decide what was offensive and assumed, despite the pages of Annan which talked of the increasing pluralism of social life, that there existed just one 'public feeling'. This was a top-down interpretation of diversity that led *Broadcast* to summarize the proposal as a demand for 'NO "committed journalism" on OBA'.[144]

Any ideas that the white paper would cater to the demands for increased accountability of the authorities themselves were also crushed. Far from OBA members being drawn from a variety of representative groups, it would be up to the home secretary to appoint members who would need to include people with 'experience in broadcasting and business'.[145] The Home Office would also be kept busy with the proposed creation of three 'Service Management Boards' for the BBC to supervise and co-ordinate its television, radio and external services, ostensibly to improve management control and cut down on bureaucracy. Given that half of the boards' members would be appointed by the home secretary from outside the BBC, this was seen as a highly political attack on the independence of the BBC, too much for even the *News of the World* to bear:

> The idea of peak-time Fourth Channel broadcasts of Moslem madrigals, recipes for curried caviar, and hints for gay joggers is a laugh. But the proposal in the Government's off-White Paper to intimidate the proud BBC into craven impotence is no laughing matter. It is malicious. It is sinister. It is appalling.[146]

One of the most curious changes from Annan concerned the future of cable television. While *TPATM* had called for a publicly owned cable network and Annan had suggested locating community cable services within a 'Local Broadcasting Authority', Labour's white paper adopted a very different approach. It placed existing cable services under the authority of the commercial regulator, the IBA, and stated that the 'Government is not prepared at this stage to dismiss the possible advantages of pay-TV, or to conclude that the disadvantages which it might hold could not be overcome'.[147] Whereas Annan had described pay-TV as a 'ravenous parasite', the white paper promised to look favourably on new pilot schemes and considered the 'possibility that regulated pay-TV might increase the range and quality of television in this country'.[148] This approach was not entirely unforeseen because, in 1975, Labour had allowed advertising on cable and permitted cable systems with extra capacity to carry ITV programmes from other regions.

The white paper, therefore, was a mixed blessing for the advocates of reform. While it acknowledged the tone of the Annan Report, it sought to increase state intervention into broadcasting, strengthen the grip of the existing broadcasting authorities and restrict the possibilities of access to and participation in broadcasting. For Anthony Smith:

> Where Annan gave us pluralism, the white paper substitutes triopoly with a dash of state direction. The white paper gives us an Open Broadcasting Authority, but one that is pretty heavily enmeshed with existing commercial operators; it gives us cable, pay tv and local radio but inside the IBA and the BBC, so that these will grow in the next decades into vast supra-media conglomerates. It gives up public accountability but by way of Home Office appointees.[149]

The OBA was the key remaining link back to the ideas of the television reformers and was a significant achievement but, by then, it was not just the property of the left. Although shadow home secretary Willie Whitelaw may have been sceptical of the OBA's financial structure he was nevertheless supportive of its main purpose. With a growing consensus about the need to open up broadcasting, Labour did eventually take a bold decision by backing the OBA. However, those radical policies which had been conceived in the early 1970s out of a desire to see genuinely new structures and new sorts of television had been transformed by the end of the decade into a relatively narrow and cautious plan for the rest of broadcasting. The white paper was the outcome of a long series of passionate debates for radical reform of broadcasting, twisted through years of public inquiries, cabinet committees, backroom deals and economic crisis.

It was no surprise that the white paper's proposals had not been implemented by the time the Conservatives, led by Margaret Thatcher, won the general election of May 1979. Labour had lost its parliamentary majority and was relying on Liberal votes to keep it afloat. Broadcasting was neither a central issue for the party leadership nor one that was guaranteed to be uncontroversial. The 1978 Queen's Speech was non-committal about broadcasting while the Commons debate on the white paper took place at the end of March 1979, by which time Labour had lost a vote of no confidence and was preparing to fight the election. Despite the near irrelevance of the debate, Rees nevertheless promised that 'the Government remain convinced that the fourth television channel should be run by an Open Broadcasting Authority, as proposed in the White Paper, and that the legislation we shall introduce in the new Parliament will contain provisions to that effect'.[150] Labour's election manifesto briefly confirmed this pledge but there was little urgency to press for legislation in the short term. 'While inflation and industrial relations and devolution are matters that demand more or less immediate attention,' wrote one commentator at the time, 'television and radio seem to be going along quite nicely as they are.'[151] The Labour leadership's broad satisfaction with the existing state of television meant that it would be another 18 years before the party had another opportunity to transform broadcasting.

How significant were Labour's achievements in the area of television in the 1970s? Intellectual debate about broadcasting reform was dominated by a left-wing movement energized by the revolts of the late 1960s and early 1970s and anxious to stimulate a broadcasting culture that reflected the breakdown of what it saw as a stifling parliamentary consensus. Figures around the New Left conceptualized broadcasting as a means of democratic exchange and mass publishing instead of the more hierarchical structures represented by the BBC and IBA. In many ways, the Labour Party was peripheral to this movement as campaigning bodies like the Free Communications Group looked to industrial activity and political militancy to press for change. For example, one of the most influential critiques of the existing duopoly was written by Nicholas Garnham in 1973 at the same time as his involvement in the Labour Party study group. *Structures of Television*,[152] however, mentions the Labour Party only once (critically), concentrating instead on broadcasting workers as key agents of change.

However, inasmuch as these debates *were* expressed in parliamentary contexts, it was certainly the Labour Party that articulated them best. The establishment of the party's study group on the media with the involvement of a wide range of politicians, activists and intellectuals, and its publication of *The People and the Media* confirmed the issue of media reform as one belonging to the left of the party. While the suggestion to abolish the BBC and IBA was greeted with horror by the broadcasting establishment and with silence by the Labour leadership, it provides one of the few examples of a strategy for an entirely different vision of British broadcasting. The whole tenor of the Annan Committee borrowed heavily from these debates and placed broadcasting accountability and democracy at the heart of the mainstream political agenda in the latter part of the decade.

Another notable achievement was the creation of an Open Broadcasting Authority which, although never introduced by Labour, owed its roots to debates conducted in the labour movement and which was given respectability by Labour's white paper in 1978. According to Phillip Whitehead, Labour's contribution to the debate

> changed the terms of broadcasting in the area in which it focused. I'm still intensely proud of Channel Four and S4C [Welsh language channel]. We had two things that mattered at a time when we could still do them. The first was to have an open channel that operated as a publishing channel where there were by definition many voices and where the remit was to let minorities be heard. And for S4C, we proved you could run a channel in the other national language and makes a success of that and revive the language in the process.[153]

These gains need to be offset against the far more substantial reforms proposed by the left of the party which were published and then buried by the leadership. We have argued that the process of a public inquiry and extended executive and parliamentary discussion proved to be an effective way of taking the heat out of more radical demands. But it must also be true that, while the Labour left seized upon broadcasting reform, it was never a top priority as compared to issues of industrial relations, economic policy and nationalization. In 1978, the trade union official and future Labour MP Denis MacShane sighed that '[s]ince 1970 the Labour Party and TUC have managed to spend a total of three and a half hours on the ownership, control and role of the media at their respective conferences'.[154] In any case, when the labour movement did discuss media policy, it consistently privileged press over television policy, as demonstrated by the reactions to *TPATM*.

A more important reason for the lack of commitment to a radical television policy is that the socialists on the Labour left shared the party with both moderates and right-wingers. Indeed the left itself was divided between those who favoured the abolition of the BBC and IBA and those who wanted more narrow reforms of the broadcasting authorities. Just as Labour's opposition to the introduction of commercial television in the 1950s was compromised because of these conflicting interests, the party's attitude towards television in the 1970s still had to accommodate the views of both left and right. Instead of a television policy, we may say that Labour had several different policies. Anthony Smith speaks of the 'several coherent' plans that Labour had at the time and argues that the party was 'always very divided because there were those in the party who wanted commercialism – very few – there were others who wanted control, and there were some who were simply bewildered and did not know how to get what they wanted which was a level playing field'.[155]

The consequence of having these conflicting positions was to allow the government to strike a 'balance' which neutralized the more radical demands of the left but gave it concessions (some of them important, like the OBA) to keep it on board the Labour project. In times of economic growth, governments are more prepared to consider the expansion of services like television. In times of crisis, like that of 1974 to 1979, the space for a radical restructuring of television through parliamentary means becomes increasingly limited. Having set the agenda for broadcasting reform at the start of the decade, those radicals who pinned their hopes on Labour's ability to shake up broadcasting and usher in a new age of openness and diversity were sorely disappointed. There were some successes, such as the Open Broadcasting Authority, but at the end of the decade broadcasting was largely controlled by the same authorities and the same voices whose domination had produced the original demands for reform some ten years earlier. 'What is remarkable about the Wilson and Callaghan years', reflects Phillip Whitehead, 'is that they constitute a virtual holiday from institutional reform of any kind.'[156] Television appears to be no exception.

NOTES

1. A. Briggs, *Competition, 1955–1974:* vol. V of *The History of Broadcasting in the United Kingdom* (Oxford: Oxford University Press, 1995), p. 946.
2. FCG, *Open Secret*, 1, 1969, p. 1.
3. The Steering Committee of Neal Ascherson, Alexander Cockburn, Gus Macdonald and Bruce Page supported an elected council of 24 members.
4. FCG, *Open Secret*, 5, 1970, p. 21.
5. Briggs, *Competition*, p. 795.
6. FCG, *Open Secret*, 5, p. 1.
7. TUC, *Report of the 103rd Annual Trades Union Congress* (London: TUC, 1971), p. 591.
8. H. Pelling and A. Reid, *A Short History of the Labour Party*, 11th edn (London: Macmillan, 1996), p. 145.
9. R. Harrison, 'Introduction', in R. Harrison (ed.), *The Independent Collier* (Hassocks: Harvester Press, 1978), pp. 1–16, at p. 1 – emphasis in original.
10. K. Coates and T. Topham, *The New Unionism: The Case for Workers' Control* (London: Peter Owen, 1972), p. 185.
11. Pelling and Reid, *A Short History*, p. 132.
12. D. Healey, speech to Labour Conference, *Report of the 72nd Annual Conference of the Labour Party* (London: Labour Party, 1973), p. 128.
13. 'Participation 72' was the Benn-inspired attempt to involve ordinary party members in prioritizing issues to be addressed. See M. Hatfield, *The House the Left Built: Inside Labour Policy Making 1970–1975* (London: Victor Gollancz, 1978), pp. 72–5.
14. P. Whitehead, *The Writing on the Wall: Britain in the Seventies* (London: Michael Joseph, 1985), p. 119.

15.   Pelling and Reid, *A Short History*, p. 146.
16.   Labour Party, *Labour's Programme 1973* (London: Labour Party, 1973).
17.   Quoted in Hatfield, *The House the Left Built*, p. 174.
18.   See S. Holland, *The Socialist Challenge* (London: Quartet, 1975).
19.   G. Foote, *The Labour Party's Political Thought: A History*, 3rd edn (New York: St Martin's Press, 1997), pp. 306–7 – emphasis in original.
20.   See Briggs, *Competition*, p. 880.
21.   Memo from J. Grist to DG, 14 July 1970, BBC written archives, R78/1, 826/1.
22.   A. Smith, 'The "Yesterday's Men" Affair', *New Statesman*, 16 June 1972, p. 820. Also see J. Seaton, 'Politics and Television: The Case of *Yesterday's Men*', *Contemporary British History*, 10, 4 (1996), pp. 87–107 and P. Catterall, 'Reassessing the Impact of *Yesterday's Men*', *Contemporary British History*, 10, 4 (1996), pp. 108–38.
23.   T. Benn, *Office without Power: Diaries 1968–1972* (London: Hutchinson, 1988), p. 350.
24.   B. Pimlott, *Harold Wilson* (London: Harper Collins, 1993), p. 578.
25.   M. Swann, Note by the chair on a lunch with Harold Wilson on 20 March, written 21 March 1973, BBC written archives, R78/1, 826/1.
26.   *Campaign*, 'The Changing Picture behind ITV Profits', 13 October 1972.
27.   HoC Debates, 15 February 1971, col. 1212.
28.   C. Heller, 'Half an Equation is Better than None', *Film and Television Technician*, November 1970, p. 12.
29.   J. Potter, *Politics and Control, 1968–80* (vol. III of *Independent Television in Britain* (London: Macmillan, 1989), p. 64.
30.   House of Commons, Second Report from the Select Committee on Nationalized Industries, Session 1971–72, *Independent Broadcasting Authority* (London: HMSO, 1972), para. 145.
31.   A. Smith (ed.), *British Broadcasting* (Newton Abbot: David & Charles, 1974), p. 222.
32.   R. Kerr, 'Inquiry into the Future of Broadcasting', letter to *The Times*, 26 October 1972. The Independent Broadcasting Authority (IBA) was set up in 1972, replacing the ITA and regulating both commercial television and radio broadcasting.
33.   ACTT, *A Report on the Allocation of the 4th Channel*, ACTT Television Commission (London: ACTT, 1971).
34.   FCG, *Open Secret*, 7, 1971, p. 36.
35.   *New Statesman*, 'Greedy TV Tycoons', 24 December 1971, p. 878.
36.   S. Lambert, *Channel Four: Television with a Difference?* (London: BFI, 1982), p. 45.
37.   HoC Debates, 15 December 1971, col. 557. We may assume that the Opposition was not entirely united about this. Only three years previously, Labour PMG John Stonehouse told a broadcasting symposium that he supported a fourth channel going to ITV because 'it could provide an excellent opportunity for existing and new independent companies to experiment even more with adventurous programmes'. See J. Stonehouse 'Broadcasting in the 1970s' in E. Wedell (ed.), *Structures of Broadcasting: A Symposium* (Manchester: Manchester University Press, 1970), p. 6.
38.   A. Smith, *The Shadow in the Cave* (London: Quartet, 1976), p. 296.
39.   J. Halloran, 'Research Findings on Broadcasting', in Lord Annan, *Report of the Committee on the Future of Broadcasting*, Appendix F, Cmnd. 6753-1 (London: HMSO, 1977).
40.   P. Whitehead, 'The Fourth Channel', *Listener*, 6 January 1972, p. 3.
41.   ACTT, 'Television: The Competitors for Control', *Film and Television Technician*, February 1973, p. 29.
42.   HoC Debates, 15 December 1971, col. 532.
43.   Kerr, 'Inquiry into the Future of Broadcasting'.
44.   TUC, *Report of the 103rd Annual Trades Union Congress*, p. 591.
45.   Briggs, *Competition*, p. 888.
46.   P. Whitehead, 'A Debatable Point', *Listener*, 11 October 1973, p. 488.
47.   A. Smith, interview with the author, 6 May 1999.
48.   N. Garnham, *Structures of Television* (London: BFI, 1980), p. 47.
49.   In February 1972, the party had finally published its green paper on advertising which contained seven paragraphs on television. It repeated the Pilkington Report's criticism of ITV's relentless search for maximum ratings and argued that 'commercial television can best be understood as an adjunct of the industrial system, rather than as a service of broadcasting with the responsibilities that entails'. See Labour Party, green paper, *Advertising* (London: Labour Party, 1972), p. 49.

50. Labour Party, 'Introductory Note on Communications', Minutes of the Home Policy Committee, April 1972, RD 324, p. 6 – emphasis added.
51. Labour Party, 'Meeting on Communications: Preliminary List', Minutes of the Home Policy Committee, April 1972, RD 326.
52. Garnham, *Structures of Television*, p. 16.
53. Ibid., p. 45.
54. ACTT, 'Television: The Competitors for Control', p. 28.
55. T. Benn, *Against the Tide: Diaries 1973–76* (London: Arrow, 1990), p. 98.
56. N. Garnham, 'Television: Living with the Feudal Barons', letter to *Guardian*, 11 August 1973.
57. A. Smith, 'An Open Door Policy for the Fourth TV Channel', letter to *Guardian*, 18 August 1973.
58. N. Garnham, interview with the author, 27 February 1997.
59. Labour Party, 'Note on Communications Meeting', Minutes of the Home Policy Committee, June 1972, RD 370, p. 2.
60. P. Whitehead, interview with the author, 22 April 1999.
61. J. Curran, interview with the author, 17 February 1997.
62. Labour Party, *Labour's Programme 1973*, p. 88.
63. Ibid.
64. M. Swann, Note by the chair on a lunch with Harold Wilson.
65. Ibid.
66. F. Craig, *British General Election Manifestos 1900–1974* (London: Macmillan, 1975), p. 389.
67. Labour Party, Minutes of the seventh meeting on Communications, Home Policy Committee, 3 April 1974.
68. Labour Party, Foreword and Preface to *The People and the Media*, Res. 83, June 1974.
69. R. Clements, 'Don't Just Save the Press – Change It', *Tribune*, 19 July 1974, p. 9.
70. Labour Party, *The People and the Media* (London: Labour Party, 1974), p. 7.
71. Ibid., p. 15.
72. Ibid., p. 14.
73. Proposals for the press adopted the same principles and included the establishment of an Advertising Revenue Board to collect and redistribute advertising revenue, a subsidy to launch new non-commercial publications, a publicly owned national printing corporation and a commitment to industrial democracy in press structures (ibid., pp. 16–33).
74. Lord Hill, 'A Labour View of Broadcasting – Examined by Lord Hill', *Listener*, 19 July 1974, pp. 66–7.
75. G. W. Goldie, *Facing the Nation: Television and Politics 1936–1976* (London: Bodley Head, 1977), p. 327.
76. Lord Annan, 'The Politics of Broadcasting', Encyclopaedia Britannica Lecture, Edinburgh University, 7 November 1977, p. 25.
77. *The Times*, editorial, 'Labour Looks at the Media', 11 July 1974.
78. *Guardian*, 'Labour Aims to Screen Media, End Monopoly', 11 July 1974.
79. *Broadcast*, 'Labour Policy Group Calls for Total Reorganisation of Broadcasting Structures', 15 July 1974, p. 4.
80. HoC Debates, 23 May 1977, col. 1060.
81. Whitehead, interview.
82. A. Smith, interview.
83. Labour Party, *The People and the Media*, p. 6.
84. Ibid., p. 14.
85. Whitehead, interview.
86. A. Smith, interview.
87. Lambert, *Channel Four*, p. 57.
88. Labour Party, 'Revised outline of manifesto', Minutes of a joint meeting of the NEC and the Cabinet, 25 June 1974, Res. 130/July, p. 36.
89. Whitehead, *Writing on the Wall*, p. 129.
90. Quoted in *Socialist Commentary*, 'Profit and Socialism', June 1974, p. 1.
91. P. Whitehead, 'The Labour Governments: 1974–1979', in P. Hennessy and A. Seldon (eds), *Ruling Performance: British Governments from Attlee to Thatcher* (Oxford: Basil Blackwell, 1989), pp. 241–73, at p. 246.
92. M. Holmes, *The Labour Government: 1974–79: Political Aims and Economic Reality* (London: Macmillan, 1985), p. 96.

93. B. Donoghue, *Prime Minister* (London: Cape, 1987), p. 149.
94. Holmes, *The Labour Government*.
95. G. Hodgson, *Labour at the Crossroads* (Oxford: Martin Robertson, 1981), p. 114.
96. P. Norton, *Dissension in the House of Commons, 1974–1979* (Oxford: Clarendon Press, 1980), p. 428.
97. Whitehead, 'The Labour Governments', pp. 254–5.
98. R. Jenkins, *A Life at the Centre* (London: Macmillan, 1991), p. 376.
99. Whitehead, *Writing on the Wall*, p. 202.
100. Garnham, interview.
101. A. Smith, interview.
102. Lord Annan, interview with the author, 29 April 1999.
103. Whitehead, interview.
104. Curran, interview.
105. Garnham, interview.
106. Annan, interview.
107. Whitehead, interview.
108. Potter, *Independent Television*, p. 241.
109. Annan, interview.
110. A. Smith, interview.
111. Ibid.
112. J. Grant, 'Press Freedom', letter to *The Times*, 16 April 1975 – emphasis added.
113. Quoted in *Broadcast*, 'The Medium', 2 June 1975.
114. *Broadcast*, 'The Medium', 7 July 1975.
115. See, for example, Potter, *Independent Television*, pp. 243–60 and Garnham, *Structures of Television*, pp. 47–57, for contrasting critiques of the report.
116. Lord Annan, *Report of the Committee on the Future of Broadcasting*, Cmnd. 6753 (London: HMSO, 1977), p. 16.
117. Ibid., p. 28.
118. Ibid., p. 30.
119. Ibid., p. 235.
120. Ibid., p. 236 – emphasis added.
121. Annan, interview.
122. Annan, *The Politics of a Broadcasting Inquiry*, 1981 Ulster Television Lecture, 29 May 1981, p. 17.
123. Potter, *Independent Television*, p. 255.
124. HoC Debates, 23 May 1977, cols 1062–3.
125. Ibid., col. 1019.
126. Garnham, *Structures of Television*, p. 47.
127. Curran, interview.
128. Annan, *Report*, p. 241.
129. A. Smith, interview.
130. Potter, *Independent Television*, p. 251.
131. Whitehead, interview.
132. Lambert, *Channel Four*, p. 78.
133. *Variety*, 'A 4th Net, Content, Coin Squeeze', 21 September 1977.
134. Whitehead, interview.
135. Annan, interview.
136. *Campaign*, 'Labour MPs Fight for OBA', 13 January 1978.
137. *Broadcast*, untitled report on the OBA, 16 January 1978.
138. The committee was called GEN 114 and contained senior Labour ministers such as Merlyn Rees, Tony Benn (energy), David Owen (foreign secretary), Roy Hattersley (prices), Shirley Williams (education), William Rodgers (transport) and Joel Barnett (Treasury). See P. Hennessy, 'No Background Papers on Broadcasting Available', *The Times*, 26 July 1978. Callaghan vetoed the original membership list prepared by the Home Office which *excluded* Benn, Hattersley and Rodgers, the leading proponents of broadcasting reform. See B. Page, 'The Secret Constitution', *New Statesman*, 21 July 1978.
139. Lambert, *Channel Four*, p. 79.
140. Quoted in *The Times*, 'Open Broadcasting Authority to Have Role of Publisher', 27 July 1978.

141. This is particularly true about the purpose of the OBA. For example, Annan: 'A great opportunity would be missed if the fourth channel were seen solely in terms of extending the *present* range of programmes' (Annan, *Report*, p. 235). White paper: 'A unique opportunity will be missed if the fourth channel is not used to explore the possibilities of programme which say something new in new ways' (Home Office, white paper, *Broadcasting*, Cmnd. 7294 (London: HMSO, 1978), p. 9).
142. Broadcast, 'TV4 Goes to the OBA', 31 July 1978.
143. Home Office, *Broadcasting*, p. 10.
144. *Broadcast*, 'TV4 Goes to the OBA'.
145. Home Office, *Broadcasting*, p. 11.
146. *News of the World*, 'The BBC in Peril', 30 July 1978.
147. Home Office, *Broadcasting*, p. 62.
148. Ibid.
149. A. Smith, 'Why Governments Must Meddle in the Media', *New Statesman*, 4 August 1978.
150. HoC Debates, 29 March 1979, col. 681.
151. *Television Today*, untitled report on television legislation, 5 April 1979.
152. Garnham, *Structures of Television*.
153. Whitehead, interview.
154. D. MacShane, 'Review of *Putting Reality Together*', *Film and Television Technician*, May 1978, p. 5.
155. Smith, interview.
156. Whitehead, 'The Labour Governments', p. 266.

In the Shadow of the Tories, 1979–92

Just as the disappointments of the 1964–70 Wilson governments had led to a left-wing shift in the early 1970s, experience of the collapse of the Wilson–Callaghan administration under the pressure of public spending cuts and pay restraint left a bitter taste in the mouths of many Labour supporters. Yet, whereas left activists in the earlier period had turned their attention to questions of industrial democracy and participation in growing social and political struggles, they now turned towards constitutional battles to change internal party procedures to allow for more grass-roots involvement and democracy at all levels of the party. Activists set their targets on achieving compulsory reselection of MPs, a more democratic way of selecting the party leader and forcing the leadership to include conference policies in the party manifesto.

Rising inflation and unemployment together with negative economic growth boosted the opportunities for the left. The victory of Michael Foot over Denis Healey as party leader in November 1980, the success of the constitutional reformers at the special Wembley conference in January 1981 and the near-election of Tony Benn as deputy leader in October 1981 all confirmed its rising influence. Policy-making flourished as over 50 sub-committees – composed of MPs, trade unionists, academics and supporters – were convened by the left-dominated NEC to draw up the radical proposals for *Labour's Programme 1982*, the basis for the following year's manifesto.

The shift to the left produced a sharp reaction inside the party. Four senior party members, including the former home secretary Roy Jenkins, split away from Labour to form the Social Democratic

Party (SDP) in 1981, leading two academics to ask 'can the Labour Party hold together?'[1] Others have since argued that the strength of the left was exaggerated; witness the election of a right-wing majority to the NEC in 1981 and the comfortable victory for Roy Hattersley over the left-wing candidate, Michael Meacher, as deputy leader in 1983.[2] According to this view, the Bennite left always had a fragile grip on power inside the party and, indeed, depended on the unreliable support of sympathetic left-wing trade union general secretaries.

The strength of the left was tested in the 1983 election, which Labour fought on a manifesto famously dubbed by shadow minister Gerald Kaufman as 'the longest suicide note in history'.[3] Once again, Labour historians have claimed that its radical reputation was overstated. Pelling and Reid describe the 1983 manifesto as 'an ambiguous document'[4] while Eric Shaw argues that it was far less left-wing than its 1970s counterparts with fewer commitments to public ownership and calls it a 'hybrid' compromise between Bennism and acceptance of a market economy.[5]

Labour's poor performance in the election, where it only narrowly beat the SDP–Liberal Alliance into second place, demanded that the party reconsider its strategies for change at a national level. Influenced by the idea that local government successes could 'provide an important test-bed for new socialist ideas, and ... become significant arenas in which to mount effective resistance to Conservative governments',[6] the left now redirected its attention towards the sizeable number of local authorities controlled by Labour, like London, Liverpool, Sheffield and Manchester. The concept of 'municipal socialism' suggested both a shield against Tory policies as well as a chance to launch innovative social and economic programmes appropriate to specific communities. Its key themes were decentralization of local services and increased opportunities for participation, particularly for minority populations, in the life of the local area. Training schemes, cultural programmes and support for co-operatives were among the policies favoured by the municipal left, headed by the Greater London Council (GLC) and its industrial agency the Greater London Enterprise Board (GLEB).

In response, the Conservative government imposed restrictive upper limits on the amount of money local authorities could raise through the rates. Under the pressure of this 'ratecapping' in 1984/85, the councils conceded defeat one by one and set legal rates. Although there were some limited cultural and economic achievements, significant gains were constrained by the status of local councils as, what Goodwin and Duncan call, 'small left-wing hillocks of power on a vast capitalist plain'.[7]

Municipal socialism's ideology of local democracy and community involvement proved to be an influential although short-lived development of left Labour thinking. In an effort to rid Labour nationally of its militant reputation, the recently elected 'soft left' Labour leader, Neil Kinnock, refused to sanction a confrontation between Labour local authorities and central government. Kinnock had pursued a similar strategy, firstly during the 1984–85 miners' strike when he distanced Labour as far as possible from the views of the miners' leader, Arthur Scargill, and subsequently in his attacks on 'hard left' *Militant* supporters inside the party. Kinnock had won the leadership after the party's disastrous performance in the 1983 election and was determined to drag Labour towards the centre, ditching left-wing commitments and professionalizing the party's image and campaigning strategies. Immediately after his election, he scrapped the myriad of NEC study groups and sub-committees which had been a bastion of the left and replaced them with a more centralized structure of joint policy committees, composed of representatives from the PLP, NEC and 'expert' party members. Furthermore, in 1985, a new campaigns and communications directorate was set up with Peter Mandelson as its director. By 1986, Kinnock, with Mandelson's approval, launched the shadow communications agency, whose role was to modernize Labour's PR strategy

From the moment of his election, Kinnock attempted to reduce the identification of the Labour Party with nationalization and hostility towards the market. Quizzed about the theme of his leadership some years later, he replied that his overarching objective was 'the enlargement of individual liberty ... feasible by the involvement of the collective contribution of the community'.[8] Combining the individualism of Thatcherism with the collectivism of the Labourist tradition, Kinnock sought to find a new role for the market in this relationship. Interviewed in October 1984, Kinnock claimed:

> The first thing to understand is that we are in a market, it is called the world economy. We will to a great extent make our living by selling in that market and it therefore requires the most efficient organisation of our resources, human and material, in order to satisfy need at home and in order to be effective in that market abroad.[9]

Kinnock made these comments in an interview with Eric Hobsbawm in the magazine of the British Communist Party, *Marxism Today*, the main vehicle for a contemporary, if not new, set of ideas concerning the need for ideological reorientation in the working-class movement. According to Hobsbawm, the decline of manual occupations, the rise of the service sector, the fragmentation of class consciousness and the rapid rise in living standards had eroded Labour's support to such an extent that new alliances and new priorities were urgently required if Labour was to have any significant future.[10] *Marxism Today* analysed the phenomenon which it named 'Thatcherism' as a virtually unstoppable new sort of consumer capitalism combining economic libertarianism with social populism. The left, it argued, needed to join forces with all anti-Thatcher elements, including the SDP, 'wet' Tories and the clergy to form a 'progressive' movement against the Conservative government.

The magazine updated the 'embourgeoisiement' thesis of the earlier revisionists, who had argued that Labour had to shed its class image if it was to win power, and insisted that the left needed to relate to the consumerist aspirations of those voters increasingly drawn to Thatcherism. The traditional language and icons of Labourism were less relevant to a population defined by share ownership, foreign holidays and, importantly, cultural consumption. The ideas of *Marxism Today*, particularly in its sympathetic attitude to commercialism and consumerism, certainly provided part of the theoretical backdrop for Labour's shift towards acceptance of the market. Martin Jacques, the magazine's editor, wrote later that the 'Communist Party in the eighties acted like the Labour revisionists of the fifties'[11] while A. J. Davies argues that Hobsbawm provided 'intellectual sustenance for the Labour Party' and that 'the magazine did have some influence on Neil Kinnock'.[12]

The Labour leadership took defeat in the 1987 election as an opportunity not to re-examine its rightward shift but to accelerate it. Traditional Labour icons were dropped – the red flag, the word 'comrade' and red membership cards all disappeared[13] – while, following the defeat of industrial struggles like the miners' strike and the 1986 printers' strike at Wapping, the leadership attempted to weaken Labour's links with the trade union movement. Kinnock then announced the launch of an extensive policy review to further 'modernize' the party's image and to develop a programme for the 1990s. At one level, this was simply a continuation of previous efforts, following Gaitskell and Wilson in the 1950s and 1960s, to shed the party's working-class roots and to reposition itself as a national, social democratic party. What was new about Kinnock's revisionism, however, was the extent to which Labour was ready to embrace the market, as revealed by its 1988 consultation paper *Democratic Socialist*

Aims and Values. This stated that, apart from a few areas like health care, education and social services, 'the operation of the market, where properly regulated, is a generally satisfactory means of determining provision and consumption',[14] an argument the Conservatives could scarcely have disagreed with.

Although the mass movement against the poll tax in 1990 and the subsequent resignation of Thatcher herself might have suggested a growing dissatisfaction with Tory policies, Kinnock was determined to proceed with Labour's courtship of the market. By 1992, any remaining calls for public ownership had been replaced by talk of 'public control' and the need to engage with debates around 'wealth creation' rather than traditional concerns about income redistribution. Labour confidently entered the 1992 election, therefore, as a very different party than the one that had lost power in 1979. It had moved away from its old appeals to nationalization and high taxation, brushed up its image, reduced the influence of the left and the unions, and recruited the services of some of the most talented communications specialists in the country.

Nevertheless, it lost the election. The party leadership blamed the defeat in 1992 on the impact of the anti-Labour press (see Chapter 6) and a Tory campaign which had successfully managed to portray Labour as a high-spending party. Further internal reform and ideological revision, it appeared, was necessary. Left-wing Labour supporters, on the other hand, argued that concessions to the market had undermined the ability of the party to offer a distinctive alternative to the government. The leadership, claimed two activists, 'threw away' the election and its 'strategy of appeasing the establishment, capping working-class aspirations and taming the membership left Labour vulnerable to the Tories on polling day'.[15] Had the leadership gone too far or not far enough in pulling Labour to the right? Labour's television policy throughout the 1980s was caught up in this tension between those determined to embrace 'social market' principles and those committed to defending public ownership – a battle overwhelmingly resolved in favour of the 'new revisionists'.

1979–83: THE FOURTH CHANNEL, THE STUDY GROUP AND
NEW TECHNOLOGY

The most pressing television-related issue for the incoming Tory government in 1979 was the question of the fourth channel. The

Labour government, acting on the recommendations of the 1977 Annan Report, had thrown its weight behind proposals for an Open Broadcasting Authority to oversee a channel, funded by advertising, grants and sponsorship, that aimed to provide experimentation in broadcasting and to cater to minority audiences. In opposition, William Whitelaw, the Tory shadow home secretary, had backed the remit of the channel but disagreed with the strategy of a new television corporation, arguing instead that the service should be controlled by the IBA, the commercial television regulator. As home secretary, he fleshed out his vision in a speech in September 1979 at the Royal Television Society convention in Cambridge. Far from envisaging a mainstream commercial service, Whitelaw repeated his desire for a distinctive channel with 'programmes appealing to and, we hope, stimulating tastes and interests not adequately provided for on the existing channels'.[16] ITV companies would fund the channel by selling advertising in their regions, thus removing any threat of commercial rivalry between ITV and the new channel. He made it clear that he saw a significant role for a new generation of independent producers as programme suppliers to the channel, but retreated on the principle of a separate Welsh-language service. Although Whitelaw had decisively rejected Labour's *official* position, he appeared to have stuck fairly closely to the spirit of the OBA.

Indeed, appointments to the fourth channel over the next year confirmed its identification with Labour. Edmund Dell, a former Labour Cabinet minister, was selected as chair of the Channel 4 board with Richard Attenborough, another Labour supporter, as his deputy. The appointment of yet another Labour Party member, Jeremy Isaacs, as the channel's chief executive in September 1980 further undermined the ability of the party to argue against Whitelaw's plans. The only really effective opposition was posed not by Labour but by the Welsh nationalist Plaid Cymru party whose leader promised to fast until the government backed down on its refusal to allow a Welsh-language channel. Goodwin argues that the issue 'generated perhaps the only genuinely mass campaign on a television issue during the Thatcher and Major governments, that went beyond the ranks of the broadcasting industry and the political elite'.[17]

So, on the first key issue of the decade involving television, there was more consensus than conflict between the two main parties. The left was happy that a commitment to diversity and innovation had been embedded in the remit of the new service while the government was persuaded that, according to Stephen Lambert, a fourth channel supplied largely by independent producers would diversify television production in Britain and perhaps, at the same time, break the union's grip on the industry and alleviate the existing hidebound industrial relations. It was a persuasive line of argument to certain elements in the Conservative Party, and helps explain the support that the independent producers received from free marketeers such as Keith Joseph's Conservative policy group.[18]

The left and the labour movement were, however, interested in much more than the fate of the fourth channel at the turn of the decade. By 1980, the Glasgow University Media Group (GUMG) had produced two books highlighting the systematic anti-trade union bias in BBC and ITV news.[19] The TUC's media working group, set up in 1977 under the influence of earlier GUMG research, published a discussion document on the media in September 1980. *Behind the Headlines* noted the growing monopolization of the media industries and the regular editorial distortion against trade unionists and posed a general question about balance. 'We are not just asking whether the trade union Movement is getting a fair deal from the press, but whether the media as a whole are "doing the job they are paid to do".'[20] In 1981, Tony Benn penned an extensive critique of the fundamentally anti-democratic nature of British press and broadcasting which condemned the ideological conformity of what he called the 'consensus media' and their unremitting hostility to groups and ideas which challenged the 'centre'.[21]

It was in this atmosphere that, in May 1980, the Labour Party NEC decided to convene a second study group on the media with the aim of publishing a discussion document. This was one of the many sub-committees launched at that time by the left-dominated NEC as part of the process of internal democratization and wider participation in policy formation. Given the publication of the Annan Report and the Royal Commission on the Press together with technological developments around cable and satellite, an update of the policy proposed in the first study group's document, *The People and the Media*, was now necessary. The new study group's terms of reference were:

To propose ways of achieving a more balanced presentation of news and opinion in the media by improving opportunities to publish and broadcast a diversity of views; to consider the implications of new technology and the development of new services such as local radio and the fourth channel; and to examine alternative forms of ownership, organisation and finance of the press and broadcasting services, which would guarantee freedom from both government and commercial ownership.[22]

In terms of television in particular, the group was to examine the structure of the BBC, the licence fee, the fourth channel, industrial democracy, new technology and a complaints procedure. Omitted from the NEC's list, however, was any mention of restructuring ITV or of considering the role of advertising as a source of broadcasting finance, although these were confronted in subsequent discussions.

The study group was chaired by NEC member Frank Allaun and included a number of left-wing Labour MPs, like Tony Benn, Eric Heffer, Bob Cryer and Michael Meacher, as well as academics like Nicholas Garnham and James Curran who had served on the first group and who were deeply critical of the existing duopoly:

> There was a tendency within the Labour Party at that time of people who came out of the 1960s and remembered the BBC as rationing pop music and having an enormous store of resentment against that tradition of public service broadcasting. The second thing was that they remembered the way in which broadcasting had joined with the press in the attacks on trade unions. So we were terribly hostile to the institution of public service broadcasting while being very strongly in favour of public broadcasting. That was the central dilemma at the heart of the period.[23]

They were joined on the group by others, including Austin Mitchell MP and a layer of trade union officials – for example Alan Sapper from the ACTT, Ted O'Brien from the National Society of Operative Printers and Assistants (NATSOPA) and Paddy Leach from the ABS – who were more sympathetic to or had vested interests in the present organization of television.

As in the 1970s, the main emphasis of the 1980s study group concerned press reform. Frank Allaun recalls that 'the most important matter we discussed and agreed on was the diversification of the press'[24] and proposals for an 'Open Press Authority' that would award newspaper franchises.[25] There were, however, a number of noticeable differences between the two study groups. First, while the 1970s study group had been encouraged to examine 'the alternatives across the board', the terms of reference eight years later were more narrowly focused on achieving 'balance' and examining largely predetermined options for reform. Next, whereas the first study group had met during a time of heightened class struggle and had been deeply influenced by militant and syndicalist ideas, the 1980s group coincided with a decline of workers' confidence and the rise of a left whose power lay largely *inside* the Labour Party and the trade union leadership. Third, while the first group met only ten times in two years, the confidence of the left allowed it to produce a coherent, if unpopular, document at the end of its deliberations, with an impressive range of signatories across the Labour movement. Such was the atmosphere of experimentation that MPs and others were willing to put their names to *TPATM*, if only to stimulate an open discussion about the media. The 1980s group, on the other hand, met more than 20 times over three years and never produced a public document in its own name. This was partly because an election intervened before discussions were finished but was also because irreconcilable internal disagreements about how to reform broadcasting emerged in the study group.

The group did agree on some issues, for example on the need to develop some sort of mechanism to achieve balanced coverage of the labour movement. One of the first decisions of the study group was to initiate a monitoring exercise of specific radio and television programmes and 'to report any bias, unfair reporting or choice of subject which might justify a complaint'.[26] By the ninth meeting in May 1981, the group agreed to support a legal right of reply across press and broadcasting as a means of correcting biased reporting against the labour movement. The idea that systematic bias against the left could be corrected through statutory remedies was itself a step away from the proposals in *TPATM* to tackle the *causes* of bias through a radical restructuring of the press industry itself.[27] The policy was, however, warmly welcomed by the NEC which published a statement on the right to reply in March 1982.[28] There was also general agreement in the group on the need for a communications ministry, despite some reservations about its Stalinist connotations: 'Most members felt, however, that a centralised ministry which would coordinate the separate responsibilities of the Home Office and the Department of Trade was badly needed if the public interest was to be adequately defended.'[29]

While the study group was able to coalesce around constitutional and legal reform of the media, there was a polarization around issues concerning the financing and structures of television. Radical ideas which took their cue from *The People and the Media* attracted some of the strongest opposition. Nicholas Garnham's proposal for a 'National Communications Authority' and a 'National Communications Commission' supplemented by regional commissions which would supersede existing regulatory arrangements,[30] were sharply criticized for involving 'too great a concentration of power'.[31] Demands for a reduction in advertising were described 'as being out of touch with the realities of the broadcasting industry since a significant cut in advertising would necessitate large sums from the Treasury'. Furthermore, there was 'disagreement about whether the introduction of advertising had led to a drop in standards'[32] and the left's preferred option of the centralized collection of advertising was generally rejected.

A key critic of the left was Paddy Leach of the BBC staff union, the ABS, who 'did not wish to see the break-up of the BBC/IBA set up or the abolition of the licence fee which he felt insulated broadcasting from Government interference'.[33] Similarly, Labour MPs Phillip Whitehead and Austin Mitchell opted for a strategy of decentralization within the *existing* broadcasting structure and the creation of separate regulatory bodies for national and local radio, ITV, BBC and cable. '[R]ather than establish a new central body,' argued Whitehead, 'it would be better to develop the best elements of the present system. This would avoid opposition from the trade unions and the public.'[34]

On some issues there was little discussion. The fourth channel was barely mentioned, presumably because there was little to complain about. The new technologies of cable and satellite were broached only towards the end of the group's life (as I shall discuss later) and there was only a brief attempt to debate industrial democracy in the television industries. Legalistic and constitutional remedies therefore coexisted in the study group with far more radical suggestions for democratizing the media. Trade union sectionalism and political pragmatism blunted the edge of attempts to launch a fundamental restructuring of the current broadcasting structures. This impasse certainly undermined the possibility of publishing the discussions in any coherent form and indeed its proposals, as Allaun regretfully notes, were never agreed by the NEC.[35]

Nevertheless, the group was able to contribute to *Labour's Programme 1982*, the party's 280-page blueprint of its policies, based on the work of the dozens of NEC sub-committees and study groups. The four-page section on the media was produced partly from existing policy statements, conference resolutions and advice from the media study group and contained the party's most substantial and left-wing *official* programme of media reform to date. The policy was premised on Benn's notion that the media were failing to live up to their democratic role and borrowed phrases directly from *The People and the Media*. It opens by claiming that 'although we are led to believe that we live in a free and open society, our [media] system is, in fact, remarkably closed'[36] and goes on to lament the absence of impartiality as 'the process of selection makes objectivity impossible.[37] The section is littered with radical critiques of the existing broadcasting system:

> We believe that separate radio and television corporations should replace the present very centralised structure of the BBC and Independent Broadcasting Authority … we also suggest that programme making itself should be carried out by a wide variety of dispersed programme units … We believe that it [advertising] should not be used for private profit, as now, but recycled within the system … We believe broadcasting needs a much more secure and diverse financial basis. It should be funded by a long-term grant awarded by parliament.[38]

There is, of course, an important difference between the party's *beliefs* and *suggestions* and its actual policies. Apart from a firm commitment to create an arts ministry and to phase out the licence fee in favour of an exchequer grant, the document contained few concrete promises about television and many vague hints about the future: legislation requiring broadcasting to honour diversity, an alteration of broadcasting's 'monolithic structures', increased public access to programme making, training programmes to challenge sexism and racism and a 'genuinely independent' complaints procedure.[39] These were, by now, relatively established themes of left thought concerning broadcasting but the section lacked any firm discussion as to how any of the above was to be achieved. For example, the detailed proposals contained in *TPATM* for a 'Communications Council' and a 'Public Broadcasting Commission' had disappeared as had any discussion as to the nature of the mechanism of recycling advertising revenue within the broadcasting system.

However loosely worded they may have been, the proposals contained in *Labour's Programme 1982* nevertheless bore the imprint of the left and demonstrated its continuing suspicion of the duopoly and its commitment to tackle British television's lack of impartiality. The few sentences that made it into Labour's election manifesto the following year were more obscure and contained 'strong generalities, but few specific plans'.[40] Gone were the promises to abolish the licence fee or to introduce an arts ministry, while references to broadcasting's 'monolithic structures' had been transformed into a commitment to make broadcasting 'more accountable and representative' and to 'promote a more wide-ranging and genuine pluralism in the media'.[41] By the time the NEC met in November of that year to reconsider the future of the party's policy formation, the media study group was described as non-essential and wound down. This time, unlike in 1974, there were no formal proposals and no published document for the leadership to marginalize.

The short section on cable and satellite in *Labour's Programme 1982* reflected the lack of attention inside the study group to new communication technologies. The document acknowledged the profound impact of the new technologies and made two important commitments: that Labour would place a national cable system under the control of British Telecom and regulate cable and satellite services in the interests of 'diversity and pluralism'. Closing the space which the previous Labour government's 1978 white paper had opened up for pay television, the document insisted that Labour was opposed to it because 'we believe that all citizens should receive an equal public service regardless of wealth and geographical location'.[42] The message seemed to be that while Labour intended to reform the existing duopoly for terrestrial television, it also wanted to bring new cable and satellite systems under the umbrella of precisely that duopoly, or at least the *principles* of that duopoly.

This brief response was hardly surprising. Both *TPATM* and the Annan Report had sidelined technological issues in the 1970s while Labour was now forced to react quickly to the activities of the Tories. From 1980 onwards, the government had initiated several reports and inquiries into the possible industrial benefits of satellite broadcasting and broadband cable networks and appeared enthusiastic to introduce commercial multi-channel television in the short term.[43] The response of some Labour policymakers was to cast doubts on the need for expanding broadcasting at all: 'There is no need or indeed demand for extra TV services', wrote Nicholas Garnham. As cable and satellite projects required huge investment, how could the drain on the public purse be justified, particularly during a recession?[44] However, Garnham also recognized that 'the chance to see a wide range of international programming in addition to our present services seems attractive and to resist such developments seems not only Luddite but also parochial and puritanical'.[45] This combination of opposing outright commercialization but also attempting not to appear hostile to all technological innovation proved to be a regular feature of Labour's approach to cable and satellite.

The different delivery systems raised different issues for Labour policymakers. While cable could be regulated on a national basis, satellite's supra-national footprints, according to Garnham, 'present an altogether more difficult problem and a real challenge to the internationalism of the British labour movement'.[46] Garnham therefore argued for a European solution including a strategy of convincing

Labour's fraternal parties on the continent to co-operate in the regulation of satellite systems in order to create some sort of pan-European public service 'cultural space'.⁴⁷ This was agreed at the media study group and incorporated into the proposals in *Labour's Programme 1982*. However, there was a clear gap between left and right over the issue. When William Whitelaw announced in March 1982 that the BBC was to be allowed to operate two satellite channels, the thought of a British-led satellite initiative with substantial industrial benefits appealed to several Labour MPs. Shirley Summerskill, replying on behalf of the Opposition to the home secretary's statement, welcomed the proposals 'because satellite broadcasting will allow the BBC further to inform, educate and entertain millions of viewers, and it will provide increased job opportunities in the television, aerospace and electronics industries'.⁴⁸ Former prime minister Harold Wilson was even more effusive and praised the statement 'as giving British satellite technology and programmes a great boost'⁴⁹ and complained only about the exclusion of ITV from the proposals.

Perhaps because of the sizeable delay before the start of any service together with the international dimension to the development, satellite television appeared to be a less urgent question and did not occupy the minds of Labour activists to any major extent. Cable was a different matter. In 1981, the government had created an information technology advisory panel to examine the possibilities of cable and IT while the following year it had set up a committee of inquiry, chaired by Lord Hunt, to investigate the prospects for cable broadcasting. Both reports recommended the immediate construction of privately financed broadband cable systems which would provide not only economic advantage to British industry but would also help to liberalize British broadcasting. Acting on this advice, the government initiated legislation and, before this was complete, awarded 11 franchises to the private sector at the end of 1983. Cable, therefore, appeared to present a much more short-term danger to Labour that required an urgent policy response.

Stuart Hood described this in the *New Socialist* as the 'most immediate threat to public service broadcasting'⁵⁰ while the ACTT's Alan Sapper warned the 1983 Labour conference that an unregulated cable system 'would undermine and destabilise the whole idea of public service broadcasting in this country'.⁵¹ According to the Labour MP and broadcaster Austin Mitchell, a Tory cable policy would mean 'wall-to-wall orgasm, constant pornography and potential trivialisa-tion'.⁵² The most immediate and detailed response, however, came not from the media study group but from the trade unions and Labour local authorities. In March 1982, the Hunt Committee invited submissions about the future of cable and received responses from a range of unions and political parties including the majority of the media unions, the Post Office Engineering Union (POEU), the TUC, the Liberal Party and the Scottish National Party. Despite an individual document from Garnham, there was no official submission from the Labour Party because the study group had not been able to produce one.

The submission from the POEU, the Labour-affiliated union that organized British Telecom (BT) engineers, welcomed the possibilities of cable but criticized the government's reliance on the private sector. This approach, it argued, 'would spread the provision of cable systems on a fitful and partial basis and the end result could be an unnecessary and wasteful duplication of broadcasting and telecommunications networks'.[53] The POEU's preferred option was to entrust the entire system to BT with its experience of running a national network and its knowledge of the most advanced fibre optic cable systems. Furthermore, programme provision should be kept wholly separate from the operation of the cable system itself.

These arguments were fed into both the media study group and the NEC's science and technology study group and certainly influenced the leadership's attitude towards cable. In the Commons debate on the Hunt Report, the shadow home secretary Roy Hattersley supported the idea of a properly regulated national cable system run by British Telecom. The problem was not the technology, he argued, but the policy:

> No one on the Opposition Benches has the slightest wish to stand in the path of history. The error of the Luddites was that they wished to smash the new machinery. We want to accept and welcome the existence of the new technology, but to make sure that it works on behalf of the community as a whole and not simply in the interests of a narrow group of speculators.[54]

The community referred to was most definitely the *British* community. Hattersley's attack was predicated not on hostility to private capital in general but to foreign capital in particular: it would be *foreign* technology that would undercut the prices of the British cable industry and *foreign* companies that would undermine the quality of British television. Echoing the anti-American comments of some Labour MPs during the passage of commercial television, Hattersley argued that a substantial quota of British programmes was needed because if we 'start off with cheap foreign rubbish we shall end up with it'.[55] But, apart from a demand for involvement of British Telecom and British content, Hattersley failed to elaborate on precisely how Labour would finance and operate a national cable network.

A more detailed vision of the democratic use of cable technology emerged out of Labour-controlled local authorities. Cable's potential to wire up *local* communities and to offer interactive services complemented the decentralizing and participatory models of municipal socialism. Several of the larger authorities like London, Sheffield and Manchester were attracted by the proposition of a democratically controlled local communications infrastructure. One report published in November 1982 by a new left-wing pressure group, the Campaign for Press and Broadcasting Freedom, advocated precisely such a strategy:

> Given that the State has abdicated responsibility at a national level, Labour-controlled local Authorities could take the initiative in formulating an oppositional communications policy, including proposals for democratic control at a regional level of the whole range of activities within the communications sector.[56]

The report suggested setting up 'industrial consortia' composed of local authorities (which had been excluded by government from cable systems) and private companies to bid for regional franchises to establish an 'alliance between capital and labour' that would represent the interest of non-commercial needs.[57] One of the key objectives of the left, claimed the report, should be to politicize the debate around cable and challenge the arguments of the free marketeers.

The GLC's Economic Policy Group published its report on *Cabling in London* the following month and repeated many of these arguments. It too recognized the democratic potential of cable if freed from the restrictions of private sector control, rejected the exclusion of local authorities and called for 'other interested parties to build a consortium of public sector and private sector interests to bid for a Londonwide franchise'.[58] The report identified the rise of an 'information economy' which might, if properly developed, provide real industrial benefits to Londoners. The best way to change the government's mind would be to convince it of the uneconomic nature of its proposals and to produce a more efficient financial model based on the public–private consortium. This was to be achieved through a further public inquiry into cable, the creation of a 'Communications Sub-committee' and a campaign against the private development of cable.[59]

In the end, little came of the debate. First, central government was not persuaded to change its mind on the involvement of local authorities; second, the amount of money which even the larger authorities could afford would have had little impact on constructing and maintaining broadband cable systems; finally, the government's own plans for cable were undermined by the failure of the initial broadband franchises.

Despite the contributions made by a range of Labour supporters, the official policy was all too often reduced to championing Labour's commitment to BT and repeating the threat that unregulated cable would present to public service television.[60] By the time that the 1984 broadcasting bill was read for the last time in Parliament, the Labour front bench had all but abandoned its opposition. Denis Howell, responding to the home secretary's introduction, could only retort that 'we welcome the Government's principal philosophy which is that we should provide the maximum choice for the people of this country'.[61] Despite the views of the left, the Labour Party had succumbed to the lure of new technologies and the soon-to-be irresistible lobby for consumer choice.

1983–87: LABOUR AND THE PEACOCK DEBATE

Labour's heavy defeat in the 1983 election both demoralized the Labour left and gave extra confidence to the rising generation of neo-liberal theorists. Free market think-tanks like the Adam Smith Institute and the Institute of Economic Affairs increasingly captured the attention of Downing Street while their leading lights scoured the British landscape for institutions and industries to privatize and liberalize. The television industry, it seemed, was a prime candidate. Dominated by a duopoly which had little incentive for competition, fiercely protected by a cumbersome regulatory regime and infested with trade union closed shops, the think-tanks gleefully produced a series of reports urging the radical restructuring of British broadcasting.[62] Documents like *Choice by Cable* (1983) and *The Omega File: Communications* (1984) argued that broadcasting needed to be treated like any other commodity, rather than being given special status because of its cultural importance. The reports called for free-market initiatives including the deregulation of broadcast television, the introduction of subscription television, the privatization of key units of broadcasting and the auctioning of ITV franchises. According to Peter Goodwin, 'Tory television policy radically but unacknowledgely shifted emphasis – away from new channels and new means of delivery, and towards an attempt to reform the established television system.'⁶³

Not surprisingly, the BBC was the focus of much of the neo-liberals' strategy, given its position as a publicly funded, non-commercial institution and its reputation among the right for being obsessively bureaucratic and biased in favour of the left. Prime minister Thatcher was particularly open to this view, harbouring a hostility towards the Corporation from its coverage of the 1982 Falklands War almost as great as Harold Wilson's had been in the 1960s. Alasdair Milne, the BBC's director general, described a meeting where Thatcher 'cheerfully accused us of insanity over our reporting of the disembarkation of troops from the QE2 in the Falklands, quoting as a parallel what she described as American television losing the Vietnam War'.⁶⁴ When the Corporation asked the government for a substantial increase in the licence fee at the end of 1984, it was received less than enthusiastically in Downing Street. In March 1985, the home secretary agreed to a partial increase in the licence fee but also set up a committee of inquiry, chaired by the free-market economist Sir Alan Peacock, to investigate alternatives to the licence fee, particularly advertising and subscription.

Labour's reaction took a number of forms. The first was a distinct ambivalence by those on the left to jump to the defence of the BBC and an inclination to support other types of broadcasting, notably Channel 4 and the model of independent production. James Curran, latterly the editor of the *New Socialist* and a figure associated with the Bennite left, recalls:

> The context of where we were at was that Channel Four had been a terrific success and Channel Four wasn't meant to be like Channel Four. Lord Tebbitt came out and said it was supposed to be about golf and yachting and gardening and not about gay and lesbian rights. That was how they conceived of it and their project was basically subverted. So flush with the new success of Channel Four, we were trying to think that the more you open new initiatives, [the better].⁶⁵

Geoff Mulgan and Ken Worpole from the GLC's Greater London Enterprise Board counterposed the creativity of the independent sector to the conservatism of the BBC:

> Many of the best and most innovative ideas have come from outside [the BBC]: from the illegal pirates, independents unable to survive the hierarchies of the BBC, from advertising and radical local groups. In the second half of the 1980s it is Channel 4,

ostensibly commercial and financed by advertising that is doing most to innovate with new forms of television and a new understanding of what public service can mean.[66]

In celebrating the cultural achievements of the new channel, left-wing supporters of Channel 4 had some unlikely allies. Writing in *The Times* in May 1985, Curran welcomed the Peacock inquiry as 'an opportunity for the left as well as the right to help reform British broadcasting', noted the similarities between the policies of both left and right for the BBC and supported the idea of an independent production quota 'which would breathe new life and diversity into the BBC'.[67] While distancing himself from free-market proposals to privatize the Corporation, Curran declared that he was not hostile to the introduction of limited advertising on the BBC if it did nothing to undermine the advertising revenue of Channel 4 and ITV. Noting later that 'very strange bedfellows got into bed over independent production', Curran explains:

> We'd been shat upon. We were the people who were the hard left, we were the people who were the Bennite bogeys, we were the people who were denied reasonable access ... We were deeply indignant at what we saw as the centrist arrogance of public service broadcasting and there were other people who were angry as well. It was as if the left and right were trying to attack the centre.[68]

Curran's support for the independent sector was echoed by the 25% Campaign, a small group of producers lobbying the government for a fixed quota of independently produced programmes. The group included David Graham, a friend of Peacock and a member of the free-market Institute of Economic Affairs, who arranged one meeting of the campaign at the Institute of Directors.[69] By mid-1986, the steering committee of the campaign included Phillip Whitehead, until recently a Labour MP, and was urgently lobbying ministers for a quota.[70] By November 1986, it had succeeded when, following the recommendation of the Peacock Committee, the government eventually conceded a quota of 25 per cent of independently produced material for all channels. According to Barnett and Curry, '[t]he Thatcherites had won an opportunistic victory with the help of allies among the growing band of independent producers who conveniently gave the attack cultural credibility'.[71]

Another Channel 4 supporter was Joe Ashton, Labour MP and *Daily Star* columnist, who declared to his readers that 'I think Channel 4 is great. I'm a compulsive viewer.' Anticipating some of the economic arguments of the free-market thinkers, although perhaps in a slightly more accessible manner, Ashton argued:

> Over the past 10 years, both BBC 1 and ITV have gradually turned television channels into supermarkets. Everything has been packaged into bland, soggy, cornflakes designed to offend nobody ... But because Channel 4 is a small delicatessen, it doesn't mean its goods are rubbish.[72]

Determined to demonstrate his support for commercial television, Ashton introduced a private members bill into the Commons in January 1985 arguing for the BBC to be allowed to take advertising. The bill coincided with the second of three high-profile editorials in *The Times* attacking the BBC's request for more money and demanding that the BBC must eventually take advertising.[73] Ashton argued that the licence fee was an unacceptable poll tax and also asserted that if left-wing newspapers took advertising, then why shouldn't broadcasting?[74] Although this was not a new position (Hugh Jenkins, the chair of Labour's communications group in the 1960s, had argued along the same lines in 1966), the idea of financing broadcasting in a similar way to the press was precisely one embraced by the Thatcherites in the mid-1980s. Despite the defeat of Ashton's bill (by only 159 to 118), the whole debate played into the hands of Tory reformers far more than it helped those determined to democratize broadcasting.

The second influence on Labour's approach to the television debate was that of the 'cultural industries' approach, pioneered by the Greater London Enterprise Board of the GLC. Inspired by the economic success of the Italian region of communist-controlled Emilio Romagna, based around networks of small co-operatives linking new technologies to older craft skills, GLEB developed its own Cultural Industries Unit. This was partly a reflection of the increasing grip of 'cultural politics' advocated in the pages of *Marxism Today*, but also a strategy to deal with the de-industrialization of major metropolitan areas, particularly London. According to Nicholas Garnham:

> The argument I put forward was that a major employer in London are media industries, they are growth industries. It's much better to focus on how you can maximize conditions of work employment there rather than trying to bring shipbuilding back or docks or empowering people through video cameras.[75]

The challenge was to devise strategies to direct investment towards socially relevant areas and to increase employment opportunities for the most disadvantaged groups in the hope that this would also allow previously marginalized voices to emerge. GLEB therefore supported a number of independent film and video production and distribution companies to take advantage of the space opened up by Channel 4. Similarly, a levy from the ITV companies allowed the ACTT union to collaborate with Channel 4 to franchise eight film workshops to produce material for the channel. A further levy from the film industry supported a substantial training programme for women and ethnic minorities in film production.

The cultural industries approach depended on working with the market to promote both diversity and jobs. Industry levies, grants, cross-subsidies and joint ventures were the preferred mechanisms of supporting innovative new projects. 'The market', according to Mulgan and Worpole, 'has never been separate from the state ... but there can be little doubt that it has provided many people with far more pleasures and entertainments than official, state-sponsored culture'.[76] Such a statement would have been a welcome tonic for a Labour leadership engaged in undermining the party's opposition to market forces. While the radical politics of some of the cultural industries' ventures may have worried Labour frontbenchers, the *principles* of public–private partnership and of the creativity of small co-ops was one that Neil Kinnock shared.

In the end, the cultural industries strategy was unable to buck either the market or the government. Before its abolition by the Conservatives, the GLC had managed to allocate a total of just under £1m to London's film and video sector over four years. Independent film and video workshops, which the GLC had been particularly keen to support, were given *at most* £50,000 each over that period.[77] Channel 4's budget for the ACTT-franchised workshops was cut from £875,000 in its first year to £500,000 in the following year. 'Things haven't quite worked out the way they might have', admitted Alan Fountain, the channel's commissioning editor for independent cinema and community programmes.[78]

Both the independent production and cultural industries approaches shared a hostility to large-scale state intervention into broadcasting and the paternalism of the BBC. Tom O'Malley of the Campaign for Press and Broadcasting Freedom believes that this 'anti-statist position' undermined the effectiveness of the left in opposing Tory attacks on public service broadcasting:

> In the 1980s, people who were around the Labour Party and sometimes in it had a very critical attitude towards the BBC and ITV at a time when they should have known better. Had they stopped and thought a little harder about the general political

context in which policy was developing after 1981, they would
have been more hesitant about developing an anti-statist position
… A lot of people in and around the Labour Party were
influenced by two sorts of shifts. One is the general shift to the
right in political elites; secondly, by the influence of *Marxism
Today* … which by the mid to late 1980s had accommodated itself
very rapidly with the priorities of new conservatism.[79]

While there was a need for a critique of the established broadcasters
and support for more grass-roots forms of communications, activists
could not afford to ignore the changing political context of the mid-
1980s where neo-liberal ideas were dominant.

In contrast to the anti-statist position, others in the labour
movement simply urged defence of the status quo. Gerald Kaufman,
the shadow home secretary, contrasted the shoddy state of Britain's
physical infrastructure with its reputation for producing high-quality
broadcasting. 'The race for commercials, and for ratings to attract the
commercials, would drive down the level of BBC programmes' which,
he argued, were 'still envied throughout the world'.[80] Alan Sapper,
general secretary of the ACTT, warned of the imminent 'breakdown of
Public Service Broadcasting. Thatcher is a privateer, hell-bent on
deregulation and she hates broadcasters.' Independent producers, he
argued, were 'the Trojan Horse of a deregulating government'[81] that
was determined to break union organization and destroy public
service principles. Responding to Curran's *Times* article, in which he
had posed the possibility of limited advertising on the BBC, Sapper
supported the present arrangements for regulating the BBC and ITV,
stating that '[i]t is essentially important for us to retain what we have
with as little interference as possible'.[82] Similarly, the TUC's
submission to the Peacock Committee opposed any talk of
sponsorship, subscription or advertising for the BBC and argued that
the government 'should be examining ways of entrenching the licence
fee as a consistent and equitable source of finance'.[83]

Labour's official evidence to the Peacock Committee was prepared
by Norman Buchan, the party's shadow arts minister. Buchan was
deeply committed to raising the profile of cultural politics and indeed
wrote the introduction to *Saturday Night or Sunday Morning*, the book
on cultural policy written by GLEB's Mulgan and Worpole. Now, he
had to accommodate those concerns about democratizing the media
with the powerful lobby in the party and the broadcasting unions to
preserve the status quo. The submission, prepared in the summer of
1985, ran to 22 typewritten pages and reflects the influence of both sets
of ideas.[84]

The submission opens with qualified support for the duopoly but makes it clear that 'the BBC has never been above reproach. It has often been paternalistic in its outlook and practices, and dominated by a small Oxbridge-educated elite based in London.'[85] Further on it states that 'the BBC has no monopoly on quality or diversity. Indeed the work of Channel 4 over the last 3 years has shown up just how unadventurous the BBC had become in its attitudes to many issues, often adopting an unjustifiably patronising and protective attitude to its public.'[86] Government initiatives in broadcasting, however, are not about any desire to challenge elitism as much as the wish 'to open up broadcasting as a source of profit for whoever is the highest bidder'.[87]

Moving on to an examination of the licence fee, the submission supports the *principles* of preserving the independence of the BBC from government interference and of treating broadcasting as a public good, but criticizes it for increasingly failing to do so *in practice*. The key argument against the licence fee, however, is that it is a 'highly regressive form of taxation ... from an age when television was considered a luxury service'.[88] The document then proposes to 'restructure', though not to abolish, the licence fee either by putting a levy on multi-set households and passing on the savings to the poor, or through a government grant. It recognizes that the latter idea might compromise the independence of the BBC but notes that 'the idea that the BBC is independent involves more than a little mythology' given the range of powers that the state already has in influencing the Corporation.[89] Distance from government might be maintained through a system of rolling finance, over three- or five-year periods, overseen by an independent review body.

The next, longer, section deals with the impact of advertising and quotes research demonstrating that advertising is a more expensive way of financing television than the licence fee. The report then works through the negative effects on other media sectors of the BBC taking advertising and suggests that 'it would be a salutary exercise for your committee and those submitting evidence to pose the question the other way round and to question whether advertising does not already play too large a role in our society'.[90] In a particularly teasing paragraph, the submission raises the point that

> if it is legitimate to question the licence fee should it not be equally legitimate to question the existing role of advertising as a means of financing broadcasting. For example, *if advertising was replaced by an expanded licence fee* (perhaps moderated by direct taxation) there would be a wide range of immediate benefits ... Financing television through advertising ... shifts the primary

economic relationship to that between advertisers and sellers of media space. Instead of providing programmes for viewers, the main function of broadcasters becomes the sale of an audience to advertisers. Replacing advertising by a more direct form of finance would open the way for new mechanisms of accountability and responsiveness.[91]

The absence of any other initiatives at the time to abolish television advertising suggests that this was a rather rhetorical proposal but it nevertheless indicates Buchan's desire to engage with more radical thinking on broadcasting. The suggestion itself has far more in common with the tone of 1970s discussions around *TPATM* than with the more cautious debates in Allaun's study group. The document then makes one final promise, repeatedly publicized by the press at the time: 'should advertising or sponsorship be introduced into the BBC, a future Labour government would remove it'.[92]

Buchan's submission was a thoughtful and challenging addition to the other pieces of evidence from the labour movement. It committed the party to doing very little but provided an articulate analysis of the economics of broadcasting and identified with both the creativity of the Channel 4 model and the responsibility of opposing the further commercialization of broadcasting. The firm pledge in *Labour's Programme 1982* to phase out the licence fee had now been superseded by a proposal to *either* extend the licence fee *or* to replace it with general taxation while advertising was now *either* to be abolished completely or to be kept at its present level.

The Peacock Committee's report was published in July 1986 and probably disappointed Thatcher more than Kinnock because it rejected the introduction of advertising on the BBC and the need for specific controls on content.[93] While recommending the auctioning of ITV franchises and subscription to replace part of the licence fee in the medium term, it argued that, in the present immature broadcasting market, scrapping the licence fee altogether would damage public service broadcasting, for which it envisaged a continuing role. One decision that might have pleased the Labour left as much as the radical right was the recommendation of a 40 per cent quota for independent production across all channels. Shadow home secretary Gerald Kaufman, however, was far from impressed. 'The report is a mess', he argued in Parliament when the report was released and stormed that 'the proper place for the report is not a pigeon hole, but a wastepaper basket'.[94] Kaufman rejected the committee's proposals one by one – except the plans for an increase in independent production – and accused the committee for going 'wildly beyond its terms of reference'[95] even though the official Labour Party submission had accused the original remit of being far too narrow.

The attack continued in the full parliamentary debate on the report later that year. Labour MPs, having decided that its immediate recommendations were not too threatening and that there was little they could do about them, concentrated on Peacock's 'intermediate proposals' and, not for the first time, on the dangers of Americanization. 'Commercial objectives would reign supreme over a variety of choice', warned Kaufman, 'and lead to a bland mash of quiz shows, chat shows and soap operas – the kind of thing which prevails in the United States.'[96] Buchan's contribution was a lengthy and impassioned attack on neo-liberal arguments, combining a critique of the 'philosophy of the Hayeks, Friedmans, Tebbits and Thatchers of this world'[97] with a first-hand account of the deregulated television system in Italy. The debate, he concluded, was about

> the type of civilisation that we wish to create. That cannot be left in the hands of the profit-makers, not only because that is the greater immorality, but because they have no vision or concept other than of profit. Indeed, they cannot, because by the nature of the beast, that is all it can do. Freedom will not remain if it is entrusted to the pockets and the purses of the Murdochs, Maxwells and Berlusconis. They will not preserve the quality of broadcasting, ensure the diversity of programmes nor will they seek to eliminate bias by extending genuine access.[98]

Peacock's recommendations might have opened some possibilities for an effective opposition to the commercialization of broadcasting as, according to Peter Goodwin, the committee's 'anti-censorious liberalism' and its rejection of Thatcher's desire to put advertising on the BBC 'threw Tory television policy into disarray'.[99] Labour's opposition to the Peacock Report, however, was blunted in two ways. First, Labour was not alone in defending public service principles – a substantial part of the Home Office, Tory 'wets', most of the other political parties and the vast majority of the broadcasting establishment were all committed to preserving the BBC in its current form. Second, Labour's attack on the consequences of commercial forces was undermined by the moves at the top of the party to seek some sort of accommodation with the market. A distinct political alternative to both the status quo and a market-led future was difficult to develop in the context of Labour's increasing revisionism.

Perhaps predictably then, Buchan's eloquent attack on the profit system and the motives of the media moguls only served to highlight the growing divide *inside* the Labour Party between left and right over the question of market forces and the party's commitment to tackle the growing conglomeration and concentration of the media. A month after Buchan made his speech in Parliament attacking the 'beast' of commercialism, he had been removed from his position as shadow arts spokesperson over a seemingly secondary issue. Buchan had long argued that a single arts ministry was necessary to co-ordinate the different branches of arts and cultural activities and that this ministry should have full responsibility for broadcasting. He was fully supported by the left and the media unions who saw it as a key demand for media reform[100] and as clear evidence, should it be implemented, of Labour's willingness to prioritize media issues. During discussions in January 1987 about the forthcoming election manifesto, Buchan once again raised the issue but was rebuffed by Neil Kinnock who, according to Tony Benn, told Buchan that 'I'll be in charge anyway, and the Home Office must be in control of broadcasting.'[101] Buchan refused to back down and was sacked.

Mark Fisher, who replaced Buchan as shadow arts spokesperson, provides one interpretation of events:

> 'Norrie' [Buchan] actually won the argument and convinced Neil Kinnock that this is what should happen and he convinced the shadow Cabinet. But, having been convinced in the second half of 1986, Kinnock said 'Right, I accept your case, but with an election likely to be some time in the next 12 months, I'm not going make this radical change now. We'll put it on the backburner' … Norrie unfortunately wouldn't accept that and, with a short temper, he put himself into a position where he felt, quite wrongly, that he had to resign … He should have, like a good trade union negotiator, taken the 70 per cent of the spoils that were on the table and come back for the other 30 per cent after the election.[102]

Others saw the whole event as a sign of Labour backing down from any programme of media reform and as an assertion of Kinnock stamping his authority on the party. Brian Sedgmore commented on the affair at the time:

> Policy on broadcasting is not apparently about art, entertainment and communication, but is to be treated on a par with regulations on the opening hours of pubs, parking restrictions and fines for dog shit … In other words Labour intends to maintain the status quo.[103]

Tom O'Malley's reading is that

> it was a re-establishment of control type move. One thing was
> that Norman's face didn't fit, too linked to a traditional cultural
> politics of the Labour movement. It was also a question of
> asserting control of that area – on the verge of Kinnock's move to
> modernization and following the expulsion of *Militant*. So their
> response to the politics of the period was to try and tighten
> control and they may have thought that this whole area was a
> mess, which of course it was.[104]

For Labour left-wingers Heffernan and Marqusee, the whole affair
suggested that Kinnock was desperate not to antagonize broadcasters
before an election. 'It was his [Kinnock's] own conviction that
anything that could be seen as a challenge to the status quo in media
control would provoke the wrath of the establishment.'[105]

The latter reading is borne out by the 1987 manifesto itself. While it
promised to introduce an arts ministry, it made it plain that the 'Home
Office will remain responsible for regulatory and statutory powers in
relation to broadcasting'.[106] The rest of the section simply reaffirmed
Labour's defence of the existing broadcasting structures in the light of
the Peacock proposals: 'We will protect the independence of the BBC
and the independent broadcasting organisations. We reject subscription television for the BBC and the auctioning of ITV franchises.'[107] The
Labour leadership had put aside all the left's comments on BBC bias,
media conglomeration, the distortions of advertising and the need for
reform and lined up firmly with the duopoly.

LABOUR AND THE 1990 BROADCASTING ACT

Neil Kinnock reacted to Labour's third consecutive election defeat by
stepping up the pace of the party's accommodation to market forces
with the launch of the policy review process. The Conservatives
celebrated their victory by turning their attention away from the BBC
and towards the restructuring of commercial television in particular.
In June 1988, a parliamentary select committee examining the future
of broadcasting published a report that broadly followed the spirit of
the Peacock Committee and proposed 'a tendering competition for
the [ITV] franchises based on the ability to meet programme
requirements and a bid based on a profit formula'.[108] While it was
hardly surprising that the Tories on the committee were in favour of

such a process, the agreement of the four Labour members on the committee was perhaps more unprecedented. For Shirley Littler, deputy director of the IBA, this cross-party consensus was particularly important. '[A]s far as I was concerned, the thing that absolutely ended the debate was that it was an All-Party report. And if the Labour Party is now saying they didn't like competitive tender, they jolly well went along with that … '.[109]

Labour activists, however, rejected this development. Anticipating the forthcoming white paper on broadcasting, the 1988 party conference passed a motion condemning the commercialization of broadcasting, the privatization of Channel 4 and, indeed, the auctioning of the ITV franchises. By this point, the idea that the independents were the cutting-edge of experimentation and innovation had been challenged by the support for an independent production quota at the top level of the Tories. Alan Sapper of the ACTT, proposing the motion, warned that such a quota was simply a cover for allowing foreign interests to take over: 'it really means that the megalith, multinational areas of America, Australia and Europe will move in under a British or European cover company and take over the job and products of our own people'.[110] This was a clear reference to Rupert Murdoch whose increasing domination of the British media and anti-union activities had earned him the accolade of being one of Labour's most hated figures. Hostility to Murdoch was a theme that was to be repeated frequently over the following years.

The white paper, *Broadcasting in the '90s: Competition, Choice and Quality*, was published by Douglas Hurd's department on 7 November 1988 and promised a commercial overhaul of substantial parts of British broadcasting with the auctioning of ITV franchises and the creation of a more 'light-touch' regulatory structure for commercial television.[111] The one area that departed significantly from Peacock's proposals was in the government's determination to highlight issues of taste and decency through the launch of the Broadcasting Standards Council on a statutory basis. Goodwin argues that there were two responses to the white paper – one 'general and apocalyptic', the other 'critical … of particular details of the proposals' – which together 'were to produce considerable modifications as the white paper blueprint was translated into statute in the 1990 Broadcasting Act'.[112] The question we wish to consider is the extent to which Labour contributed to this process.

Labour's parliamentary opposition veered between the 'general and apocalyptic' and the specific and tactical. What united it was the emphasis on protecting the high *standards* of British television. Roy

Hattersley, the shadow home secretary, wasted no time in attacking the document 'as a giant retreat from the concept of public service broadcasting. Its result will be less diversity and lower standards.'[113] Labour's amendment to the motion on the white paper argued that the document would 'discourage a wide variety of programme choice, and generally reduce the high standards and consistent quality of broadcasting in this country'.[114] The comments by broadcasting spokesperson Robin Corbett that the home secretary simply 'wants to do a demolition job' on public service broadcasting[115] emphasized Labour's belief that government plans were destroying everything that was good about British broadcasting and that Labour would rush to its defence.

Labour's opposition to the white paper focused on the vagueness of the proposals for the ITV franchise auctions, the dangers of conglomeration, the possibilities for foreign ownership of commercial television interests and the censorial power of the Broadcasting Standards Council. These disagreements coexisted with a recognition of the need for change, not on the basis of faults with the current television system but only because, 'thanks to technological advance, what we broadcast in the future can be better'.[116] Indeed, Labour had little desire to complain about the existing arrangements. According to Hattersley, ITV companies already existed 'as profit-making organisations. Therefore it is right and reasonable for those who run the programme companies to try to make a profit.'[117] ITV franchise renewals already involved scrutinizing standards, Channel Four was doing nothing wrong and should be left alone and, all in all, 'we believe that British broadcasting is among the best in the world'.[118] Labour, nevertheless, was to identify with the need for change because, as a leak of the party's response to the white paper put it, 'Labour must embrace the enthusiasm for expanding choice in broadcasting.'[119] The party's formal response was published in March 1989 and contained few surprises. Perhaps this was because, according to *Television Week*, '[s]ome Labour MPs have argued in private that large parts of the white paper are acceptable'.[120] It demanded a tightening of the 'standard threshold' for franchise applicants, stricter controls on cross-media ownership and the prevention of non-EU companies holding a franchise, the maintenance of Channel Four's funding structure and the abolition of the Broadcasting Standards Council.[121]

These debates were taking place in the final run-up to the publication of the party's two-year-old policy review, which appeared in May 1989 as *Meet the Challenge, Make the Change*.[122] The section on the media was part of the group examining 'Democracy for the Individual and the Community' and emphasized the importance of the question of media ownership in particular:

> Quality and integrity are determined by ownership. The ownership of independent television franchises therefore needs the most careful scrutiny. We are particularly concerned about the cross ownership of newspapers and television and will immediately refer this issue to our strengthened Monopolies and Mergers Commission ... We are not only concerned about the reduction in quality, diversity and standards throughout public and independent broadcasting system [sic]. We are equally determined to protect the standard of impartial and independent broadcasting of which we, as a country, are right to be proud.[123]

The target of the attack here was clearly not private ownership per se but the creation of new private monopolies that would undermine choice and restrict competitive behaviour. Hattersley stressed the real target of the policy when he introduced the 'Democracy' policy review proposals at that year's Labour conference:

> In a free society we need a diversity of media ownership. Without it, the whole industry will follow Rupert Murdoch nearer and nearer to the gutter, and will be characterised more and more by the concepts on which the Murdoch empire is built: profit, prejudice and prurience.[124]

Delegates may have been puzzled by his attack on one man's right to make profits but not that of the existing ITV companies. They may also have been surprised that, while Murdoch was being lambasted inside the conference hall, over at stands 50 and 51 just outside the hall, his satellite company Sky Television was inviting 'all conference delegates to stop by its exhibition stand to learn more about its unique range of broadcasting services'.[125]

Not all delegates were impressed with the leadership's policies. Tony Hearn, general secretary of the Broadcasting and Entertainment Tradrs Alliance (BETA),[126] the union representing BBC workers, criticized the 'lamentably too brief' media proposals in *Meet the Challenge*:

> It is alright as far as it goes, but, frankly, it does not go terribly far, and I question whether it fully highlights the crucial political issues of control and access to broadcasting that have got to be seized by this conference if a Labour government is going to be able effectively to implement its programme.[127]

BETA and its sister union, the ACTT, had already initiated a joint campaign in February 1989, the Public Service Broadcasting Campaign (PSBC) which was co-ordinated by Tom O'Malley of the Campaign for Press and Broadcasting Freedom. The campaign's aim was to raise broader political questions than those raised by Labour in Parliament, for example of workplace rights, continuity of employment, the role of advertising and sponsorship and general regulatory structures. 'What we did', according to O'Malley 'was to channel to a wider political audience within the labour and trade union movement the issues of accountability and quality that were being posed by the post-1986 situation.'[128]

However, the tone of the unions' campaign was far more defensive than their approach to media reform had been in the 1970s, reflecting the political climate and the impact of defeats for media workers at Wapping in 1986 and at TV-am in 1987. The PSBC's pamphlet, *Government Plans for Broadcasting in the 1990's*[129] was subtitled 'Campaign for Choice, Standards and Quality in Television and Radio', mirroring the concerns of the official Labour campaign. The focus was very much on lobbying MPs and writing in to local newspapers rather than attempting to organize industrial action among broadcasting workers in defence of their jobs and conditions. Instead, the campaign opted for an alliance with other progressive groups who wanted to defeat the government's plans. 'We reached out and were part of that general political noise that was created,' argues O'Malley, 'which involved the Church of England, Oxfam and the trade unions, which also sustained the culture of the Campaign for Quality Television [CQT]'.[130]

The CQT had a quite different background. Bankrolled by a £5,000 donation by David Plowright, the chair of Granada Television,[131] the campaign proved to be a highly effective front group for the ITV sector. It mobilized a range of high-profile television personalities, like Rowan Atkinson, Esther Rantzen and Michael Palin, together with politicians from both main parties, including shadow arts minister Mark Fisher, who were opposed to various aspects of the white paper.[132] In particular, it concentrated its efforts on resisting a blind auction process and negotiating a 'quality threshold' which ITV franchise applicants would have to meet. There is little doubt that the CQT's activities influenced Labour's broadcasting spokespeople more than the unions' campaign. Robin Corbett, the party's official broadcasting representative, recalls that he saw 'a lot of the ITV companies' during the passage of the bill: 'You're not against what they're doing because you've got a lot of constituents watching and liking what they're doing and that's the way I chose to do it.'[133] Fisher remembers taking advice at the time from 'loyal party members' like Plowright and Denis Forman (both senior executives at Granada TV) and Greg Dyke, chief executive of London Weekend Television, as well as Labour-supporting academics like James Curran and Jean Seaton.[134]

By September 1989, there was some discussion about the fragility of Labour's opposition to the white paper. Despite growing Tory backbench unease with the impact of government proposals on programme quality, left-wing MP Michael Meacher argued that 'we are in danger of becoming too reactive and too nervous in putting forward policy. There is a temptation to bend in the wind, to give a little ground in the hope of appeasing the critics. But however much ground you give it is never quite enough.'[135] Following an interview with Hattersley, one journalist described Labour's strategy as a 'timorous reaction to the present government's proposals. New and positive ideas which would set an alternative agenda for the media are absent.'[136] The one proposal that shook up the debate in the following few months was Labour's threat to reverse the auction of ITV licenses should the party win power before the process was complete. Should, however, the licences have already been awarded, Labour promised to honour the contracts fully.[137]

The bill was published in December 1989 and, by the time it received royal assent in November 1990, substantial changes had been made which blunted the most severe free-market proposals, most notably the concession of an 'exceptional circumstances' clause in the awarding of ITV franchises that would allow the regulator to reject the highest bidder because of the poor quality of its proposals. Labour MP Tony Banks commented at the time that 'I have done 14 or 15 bills at committee stage. This was the one in which most movement was achieved.'[138] To what extent can this be related to Labour's opposition?

Corbett argues that 'I think we did better than we could have hoped. We did end up laying down some quality requirements on both the national and regional news and very diminished but none-theless public service obligations [on ITV].'[139] In part, he attributes this to his very close working relationship with broadcasting minister David Mellor. 'I'm not saying that there was total agreement. Individually there probably was but he wasn't acting as an individual … I think that in the circumstances that we did quite well because she [Thatcher] would have tipped it all in the sea.'[140] Mark Fisher, however, remembers it quite differently:

> I think that is accepting at face value the line that David Mellor would take, that David would cast himself for a variety of

reasons as the defender of broadcasting against the government. I never believed that was the case and I think Mellor knew exactly what he was doing and that any victories won against the forces of Thatcher were actually victories that were going to be won anyway … Mellor was perfectly cordial but he did not attempt to create a joint front with the Opposition.[141]

O'Malley argues that the most effective opposition came not from Labour but from the CQT, the ITV companies and the IBA who were able to 'bend the ear' of Home Office ministers who had always been sympathetic to the arguments of the broadcasters.[142] Mellor himself argues that the CQT were particularly influential as 'they provided the pressure that gave me the ability to tell my elders and betters that change [to the legislation] had to be made'.[143]

Yet, whoever's voice was most influential during the passage of the bill, it remains the case that the government's main objective of further commercializing British broadcasting was intact. Labour may have provided the backbone of parliamentary opposition during the committee stage, but the agenda had already been set by a wide range of groups: backbench Tories, ITV executives, television personalities, broadcasting unions, church groups and perhaps even the broadcasting minister himself. Labour's weakness was that it had failed to articulate an imaginative and distinctive argument against the free-market vision of broadcasting together with a coherent plan of action for how to defeat it. As an editorial in *Broadcast* put it at the time, 'Labour's answer has been to argue for a status quo which, if only because of the changing economic and technological realities facing the industry, appears to be increasingly untenable.'[144]

Fisher now accepts this accusation but argues:

The reasons for it are not a lack of political nerve and will, but probably have more trivial roots in the realities of opposition. Whereas the government prepares for a broadcasting bill and has the resources of a small department and civil servants' time, the Opposition can't prepare in any detail until they see the bill and you're pretty much swept into it … You've got quite a narrow range of advice and you have to move quite quickly and you tend to react to what the government is saying rather than to set your own agenda and that is in the nature of scrutinizing legislation. The government proposes, all you can do is criticize. You have an opportunity to put down new clauses and have symbolic debates on different approaches but on the whole the agenda-setting is done by government.[145]

While this may be true about the complexities of responding to the details of legislation, Labour had no shortage of sympathetic academics, trade unionists, broadcasters and ordinary party members who were willing to give advice nor of policy documents in the party's recent past.[146]

A more persuasive argument is that the front bench had little inclination to tackle the broadcasting establishment and jeopardize its project of shedding a left-wing image in search of electoral respectability. While Kinnock was certainly bitter at the behaviour of the British press, he reserved no such venom for British television. Asked in 1993 about Labour's relationship with the media during his leadership, he replied:

> So far as the telly is concerned it is much healthier [than the press] because the television, both by charter and by culture, does accommodate the requirements of balance. There are some mistakes – but they are human institutions after all. Generally speaking, the mistakes go against us, but then I would say that, wouldn't I? *But it is not enough to be a real source of sustained complaint.*[147]

From 1982, when the party had criticized 'the closed and autocratic institutions' of broadcasting, Labour had shifted rapidly towards making peace with the broadcasting establishment. This was all the more important given the overwhelming hostility of sections of the press, most notably the Murdoch-owned newspapers, and the efforts of the shadow communications agency to improve the televisual nature of Labour's campaigning. Once again, Fisher attributes this to *realpolitik*:

> Did the party become more, I wouldn't say friendly, but more understanding of the existing realities? Instead of starting from a blank sheet and saying 'what sort of broadcasting policy ought an incoming socialist government to have?', we were asking that, given that we were coming into government and would inherit this configuration of broadcasting, how would we actually handle it?[148]

The task was left to Fisher himself to draw up a media policy that privileged short-term electoral considerations rather than issues of democracy and accountability in time for the 1992 election. In September 1991, he produced a 32-page document, *Arts and Media: Our Cultural Future*,[149] which presented a detailed series of commitments about the party's desire to take advantage of the growing economic importance of the 'cultural industries'. In terms of television, Labour promised to 'maintain the licence fee as the main source of the BBC's income for the forseeable future', to abolish the Broadcasting Standards Council, to continue with the present system of funding Channel 4 and to introduce a Freedom of Information Act to 'strengthen editorial independence'.[150] It repeated its commitment to a ministry for arts and media, although only with 'growing [i.e. not full regulatory] responsibilities for broadcasting'[151] and signalled its desire to tackle the issue of cross-media ownership. This latter point resurfaced in the party's 1992 manifesto which made no further comments on television policy but stated that it would 'establish an urgent enquiry by the Monopolies and Mergers Commission into the concentration of media ownership'.[152] This was to be a subject of great importance in the debates to take place later in the decade, but for now it looked like small consolation for the setbacks the party had suffered at the hands of the free marketeers during the 1980s.

What achievements could Labour point to in its opposition to government policies concerning television broadcasting during the 13-year period we have discussed? There was little real resistance to Whitelaw's plans for the fourth channel and the Labour left had been just as enthusiastic as the free-market right in celebrating the rise of the independent production sector. It had failed to dent the government's enthusiasm for the cable and satellite 'revolution', a phenomenon that was undermined far more by inconsistencies in the government's own approach than by a sustained or imaginative challenge from Labour. The party had countered the deregulatory ideas underpinning the launch of the Peacock Committee but were simply part of a broad alliance, including many Tories, who were uneasy about commercializing broadcasting. Indeed, O'Malley stresses the internal divisions in government as the key: 'Thatcher was not politically strong enough to force advertising on the BBC. She faced opposition from the Home Office and from her most senior Cabinet colleague, Whitelaw.'[153] Finally, while publicly criticizing the philosophy of the 1990 Broadcasting Act, Labour frontbenchers had privately conceded the need for some of the government reforms and had limited themselves to opposing specific details of the legislation. Labour, far from co-ordinating a distinct challenge to the bill was, once more, just part of the general 'noise' against the plans.

O'Malley argues that, given the general success of the Thatcher government in crushing all opposition, there were very limited possibilities of resisting market reform of broadcasting. 'The sheer weight of the economic and political forces behind the changes made opposition inside and outside the state very difficult.'[154] Yet, the debates over the 1988 white paper took place at precisely the same time as a successful series of strikes by BBC workers, while the passage of the 1990 Broadcasting Act coincided with the largest popular mobilization against the Conservatives in the shape of the anti-poll tax campaign. Indeed, Thatcher resigned as prime minister because of a lack of support from within her own party in exactly the same month as the bill became law. It was not that there was any lack of support for a coherent alternative to the free market from the left, but that the Labour leadership, engaged in a process of 'modernization', was reluctant to provide one. According to Labour activists Heffernan and Marqusee:

> Again and again, Labour conferences have demanded media reform, some minimal tilting of the balance away from the Conservative Party and the employers, but again and again Labour in Parliament has declined to pursue these demands, even when they were begging to be raised, as during the debates on the Broadcasting Bill in 1990.[155]

By 1992, Labour had published a substantial number of policy documents on the media while debates on press and broadcasting, Murdoch and monopolization were regular features of party conferences. It was not that Labour did not have a television policy but that its commitment to implement the policy, and increasingly the policy itself, was shaped by the party's acceptance of market forces and its desire not to alienate the broadcasting establishment. In the 1980s, the left continued to dominate the intellectual discussion within the labour movement concerning television policy, much as it had in the 1970s. The problem was that this took the form of ideas – such as the cultural industries approach and *Marxism Today*'s emphasis on consumerism and culture – which were either unable or unwilling to stop the party's march to the right.

What difference might Labour have made had it been in office in the 1980s? It would probably have set up an Open Broadcasting Authority to run the fourth channel but with a very similar remit to the one imposed on Channel 4 and with many of the financial problems predicted back in the original debates. British Telecom would have been entrusted with running a national broadband cable network, although there is no certainty that this would have avoided the problems experienced by the French socialist government's more innovative *Plan Cable* (see note 57 to this chapter). While Labour would have been far less influenced by radical right ideas of forcing the BBC to take advertising, such a proposition had already been contemplated by Labour ministers in the 1960s. Furthermore, it is unlikely that, given its past behaviour, Labour would have been any more generous with licence fee revenue or any less interventionist in its dealings with the BBC. Finally, while Labour would not have introduced the ITV auction, there is little reason to believe that it would not have pressed for a more commercially minded television system at the end of the decade to complement its wider political shift towards the market. Under pressure from neo-liberal arguments, the Labour leadership pursued a defensive strategy in the 1980s and by 1992 had aligned itself with the view that the commercialization of television was both desirable and inevitable.

NOTES

1. D. Kogan and M. Kogan, *The Battle for the Labour Party* (London: Kogan Page, 1982), p. 148.
2. See for example A. Thorpe, *A History of the British Labour Party* (London: Macmillan, 1997), p. 214
3. Quoted in A. J. Davies, *To Build a New Jerusalem* (London: Abacus, 1996), p. 389.
4. H. Pelling and A. Reid, *A Short History of the Labour Party*, 11th edn (London: Macmillan, 1996), p. 169.
5. E. Shaw, *The Labour Party since 1979: Crisis and Transformation* (London: Routledge, 1994), p. 13.
6. P. Seyd, *The Rise and Fall of the Labour Left* (London: Macmillan, 1987), p. 140.
7. Quoted in ibid., p. 153.
8. N. Kinnock, 'Reforming the Labour Party', *Contemporary Record*, 8, 3, Winter 1994, p. 547.
9. Quoted in E. Hobsbawm, 'The Face of Labour's Future', *Marxism Today*, October 1984, pp. 8–9.
10. E. Hobsbawm, 'The Forward March of Labour Halted', *Marxism Today*, September 1978.
11. Quoted in R. Heffernan and M. Marqusee, *Defeat from the Jaws of Victory* (London: Verso, 1992), p. 64.
12. Davies, *To Build a New Jerusalem*, pp. 409 and 411.
13. Ibid., pp. 417–18.
14. Labour Party, *Democratic Socialist Aims and Values* (London: Labour Party, 1988), p. 10.
15. Heffernan and Marqusee, *Defeat*, p. 323.
16. W. Whitelaw, speech to Royal Television Society convention, *Television*, 17, 12, November/December 1979, p. 25. For an in-depth discussion of the origins and early years of Channel 4, see P. Catterall (ed.), *The Making of Channel 4* (London: Frank Cass, 1999).
17. P. Goodwin, *Television under the Tories: Broadcasting Policy, 1979–1997* (London: BFI, 1998), p. 26.
18. S. Lambert, *Channel Four: Television with a Difference?* (London: BFI, 1982), p. 89.
19. GUMG, *Bad News* (London: Routledge & Kegan Paul, 1976) and *More Bad News* (London: Routledge & Kegan Paul, 1980).
20. TUC, *Behind the Headlines: TUC Discussion Document on the Media* (London: TUC, 1980), p. 4.
21. T. Benn, *Arguments for Democracy* (Harmondsworth: Penguin, 1981), pp. 102–20.
22. Labour Party, Media Study Group Programme of Work, RD: 409/May 1980, LA/BMC, p. 1.
23. J. Curran, interview with the author, 10 December 1999.
24. F. Allaun, letter to the author, received 11 November 1999.
25. See F. Allaun, *Spreading the News: A Guide to Media Reform* (Nottingham: Spokesman, 1988), pp. 87–9.

26.   Labour Party, NEC paper, Media Study Group, minutes (3), 27 October 1980, p. 2.
27.   Labour Party, *The People and the Media* (London: Labour Party, 1974), pp. 16–33.
28.   Labour Party, *Statement by the National Executive Committee, The Right to Reply* (London: Labour Party, 1982).
29.   Labour Party, Media Study Group, minutes (10), 22 June 1981, p. 2.
30.   The NCA would be responsible for the collection and distribution of income from a variety of sources, including advertising and government grants, while the NCC would co-ordinate media policy and act as a complaints body. Membership of the various bodies would be on the basis of direct elections. Allaun praises the plan as the most 'coherent' put forward to the study group but argues that they were 'so far-reaching that it is not surprising that not only did they attract opposition within the study group, but they also ran out of time'. See Allaun, *Spreading the News*, p. 90.
31.   Labour Party, Media Study Group, minutes (13), 16 November 1981, p. 1.
32.   Labour Party, Media Study Group, minutes (11), 16 September 1981, p. 1
33.   Labour Party, Media Study Group, minutes (13), p. 2.
34.   Labour Party, Media Study Group, minutes (16), 22 February 1982, p. 1.
35.   Allaun, *Spreading the News*, p. 89.
36.   Labour Party, *Labour's Programme 1982* (London: Labour Party, 1982), p. 211.
37.   Ibid., p. 213.
38.   Ibid., p. 213–14.
39.   Ibid., p. 213.
40.   Allaun, *Spreading the News*, p. 90.
41.   Quoted in F. Craig, *British General Election Manifestos 1959–1987* (Aldershot: Parliamentary Research Services, 1990), p. 381.
42.   Ibid., p. 214.
43.   For a full discussion of these developments, see Goodwin, *Television*, pp. 38–68.
44.   N. Garnham, 'Sky's the Limit', *New Socialist*, May/June 1982, p. 31.
45.   Ibid., p. 30.
46.   Ibid., p. 32.
47.   Ibid., p. 30.
48.   HoC Debates, 4 March 1982, col. 415.
49.   Ibid., col. 416.
50.   S. Hood, 'Up in the Air', *New Socialist*, November/December 1982, p. 21.
51.   A. Sapper, contribution to debate on the media, *Report of the 82nd Annual Conference of the Labour Party* (London: Labour Party, 1983), p. 208.
52.   HoC Debates, 2 December 1982, col. 477.
53.   POEU, *The Cabling of Britain* (London: POEU, 1982).
54.   HoC Debates, 2 December 1982, col. 426.
55.   HoC Debates, 30 June 1983, col. 735.
56.   CSE Communications Group, *Hunt on Cable TV: Chaos or Coherence?* (London: Campaign for Press and Broadcasting Freedom, 1982).
57.   Ibid., p. 65. This resembled the basis of the French Socialist government's 1982 *Plan Cable*, a giant public programme designed to wire up millions of French homes and provide them with a series of interactive applications. While the state-owned telecommunications operator provided the national infrastructure, public–private partnerships were required to operate local franchises. Ultimately, a combination of economic crisis and internal differences between the public and private sector forced the demise of the plan. See J.-M. Gueherno, 'France and the Electronic Media', in G. Ross, S. Hoffmann and S. Malzacher (eds), *The Mitterrand Experiment* (Cambridge: Polity, 1987), p. 283.
58.   GLC, *Cabling in London: Report by Economic Policy Group* (London: GLC, 1982), p. 77.
59.   Ibid., pp. 76–7.
60.   Labour's 1983 manifesto followed along precisely these lines: 'The high standards of British public service broadcasting are threatened by Tory plans to introduce cable TV on free-market lines … To avoid wasteful duplication, we will entrust the provision of the national cable system to British Telecom'. See Craig, *British General Election Manifestos*, p. 382.
61.   HoC Debates, 9 July 1984, col. 839.
62.   T. O'Malley, *Closedown? The BBC and Government Broadcasting Policy, 1979–1992* (London: Pluto, 1994), pp. 13–30 provides a thorough analysis of the output of the various think-tanks.
63.   Goodwin, *Television*, p. 69.

64. A. Milne, *DG: The Memoirs of a British Broadcaster* (London: Hodder & Stoughton, 1988), p. 123.
65. Curran, interview.
66. G. Mulgan and K. Worpole, *Saturday Night or Sunday Morning: From Arts to Industry – New Forms of Cultural Policy* (London: Comedia, 1986), p. 60.
67. J. Curran, 'Why the Left should Welcome Peacock', *The Times*, 6 May 1985.
68. Curran, interview.
69. S. Barnett and A. Curry, *The Battle for the BBC* (London: Aurum Press, 1994), p. 59.
70. Ibid., pp. 62–3
71. Ibid., p. 65.
72. J. Ashton, 'Channel 4 is such a Bobby Dazzler', *Daily Star*, 6 January 1983.
73. Goodwin, *Television*, pp. 74–5
74. J. Ashton, 'Advertising and the BBC', *Labour Weekly*, 11 January 1985.
75. N. Garnham, interview with the author, 27 February 1997.
76. G. Mulgan and K. Worpole, 'That's Entertainment: Inside the Cultural Economy', *New Socialist*, 41, September 1986, p. 22.
77. GLC Arts and Recreation Committee, *Campaign for a Popular Culture* (London: GLC, 1986), p. 88.
78. Quoted in B. Comely, 'Workshops: Persecuted Minorities?' *Broadcast*, 29 August 1983, p. 34.
79. T. O'Malley, interview with the author, 30 November 1999.
80. G. Kaufman, 'How to Protect British TV', *Observer*, 21 July 1985.
81. Quoted in M. Blakstad, 'Sapper Sounds Three-year Warning', *Broadcast*, 15 March 1985, p. 18.
82. A. Sapper, 'Independence of BBC', letter to *The Times*, 28 May 1985.
83. Quoted in *Financial Times*, 'TUC Urges Independent Funds Body', 29 May 1985.
84. Labour Party, Submission to Peacock Inquiry (London: Labour Party, 1985).
85. Ibid., p. 3.
86. Ibid., p. 18.
87. Ibid., p. 3.
88. Ibid., p. 6.
89. Ibid., p. 7.
90. Ibid., pp. 16–17.
91. Ibid., p. 17 – emphasis added.
92. Ibid., p. 22.
93. For a full analysis of the Peacock Report see Goodwin, *Television*, pp. 78–92 and O'Malley, *Closedown?*, pp. 106–17.
94. HoC Debates, 3 July 1986, col. 1179.
95. Ibid., col. 1178.
96. HoC Debates, 20 November 1986, cols 724–5.
97. Ibid., col. 760.
98. Ibid., col. 763.
99. Goodwin, *Television*, p. 85.
100. For example, see Meacher in Allaun, *Spreading the News*, p. 97, and Mulgan and Worpole, *Saturday Night or Sunday Morning*, p. 125.
101. Quoted in T. Benn, *The End of an Era: Diaries 1980–90* (London: Arrow, 1994), p. 488.
102. M. Fisher, interview with the author, 8 December 1999.
103. B. Sedgemore, 'The Art of Decline', *Marxism Today*, January 1987, pp. 39–40.
104. O'Malley, interview.
105. Heffernan and Marqusee, *Defeat*, pp. 123–4.
106. Quoted in Allaun, *Spreading the News*, p. 91.
107. Ibid.
108. Home Affairs Committee, *Third Report, The Future of Broadcasting*, vol. I, HC262-I (London: HMSO, 1988), para. 170.
109. Quoted in P. Bonner, *ITV and IBA, 1981–92: The Old Relationship Changes*: vol. V of *Independent Television in Britain* (London: Macmillan, 1998), p. 370.
110. A. Sapper, contribution to debate on the media, *Report of the 87th Annual Conference of the Labour Party* (London: Labour Party, 1988), p. 115.
111. Home Office, *Broadcasting in the '90s: Competition, Choice and Quality*, white paper, Cm 517 (London: HMSO, 1988). For details of and responses to the white paper, see Goodwin, *Television*, pp. 93–108.

112. Ibid., p. 100.
113. HoC Debates, 7 November 1988, col. 32.
114. HoC Debates, 8 February 1989, col. 1017.
115. Ibid., col. 1069.
116. Ibid., cols. 1017–18.
117. Ibid., cols. 1018–19.
118. Ibid., col. 1027.
119. Quoted in *Campaign*, 'Labour Plans Ballot to Elect TV Watchdogs', 3 February 1989, p. 21.
120. J. Lewis, 'Labour Fears Paper's Threat to Standards', *Television Week*, 16 March 1989, p. 2.
121. C. Hughes, 'Labour Calls for Strict Controls on Media Ownership', *Independent*, 13 March 1989, p. 4.
122. Labour Party, *Meet the Challenge, Make the Change: A New Agenda for Britain* (London: Labour Party, 1989).
123. Ibid., p. 9.
124. R. Hattersley, contribution to debate on 'Democracy for the Individual and the Community', *Report of the 88th Annual Conference of the Labour Party* (London: Labour Party, 1989), p. 121.
125. Labour Party, *Conference Guide*, Brighton (London: Labour Party, 1989), p. 8.
126. The ABS had merged with entertainment workers in the National Association of Theatrical, Television and Kine Employees (NATKE) to form BETA in 1984. BETA than merged with the ACTT in 1990 to form BECTU.
127. T. Hearn, contribution to debate on 'Rights in a Democracy', *Report of the 88th Annual Conference of the Labour Party*, p. 126.
128. O'Malley, interview.
129. ACTT/BETA, *Government Plans for Broadcasting in the 1990's* (London: ACTT/BETA, 1989/90).
130. O'Malley, interview.
131. Bonner, *Independent Television*, p. 389.
132. A. Davidson, *Under the Hammer: The ITV Franchise Battle* (London: Heinemann, 1992), pp. 17–26.
133. R. Corbett, interview with the author, 2 December 1999.
134. Fisher, interview.
135. M. Meacher, article on the media, *Tribune*, 29 September 1989, p. 9.
136. M. Wohrle, 'Business as Usual', *Guardian*, 2 October 1989, p. 21.
137. S. Mares, 'Labour Promises to Scrap Auction', *Broadcast*, 1 December 1989, p. 4.
138. Quoted in P. Goodwin, 'Broadcasting Bill: Where Are We Now?' *Broadcast*, 23 March 1990, p. 7.
139. Corbett, interview.
140. Ibid.
141. Fisher, interview.
142. O'Malley, interview.
143. Quoted in Bonner, *Independent Television*, p. 419.
144. *Broadcast*, 'Lost Opportunity', 23 March 1989, p. 6.
145. Fisher, interview.
146. J. Curran, J. Ecclestone, G. Oakley and A. Richardson (eds), *Bending Reality: The State of the Media* (London: Pluto, 1986), D. MacShane, 'Media Policy and the Left', in J. Seaton and B. Pimlott (eds), *The Media in British Politics* (Aldershot: Avebury, 1987), pp. 215–35) and Allaun, *Spreading the News* are just a few examples of discussions of television policy which were circulating in the labour movement at that time.
147. Kinnock, 'Reforming the Labour Party', p. 552 – emphasis added.
148. Fisher, interview.
149. Labour Party, *Arts and Media: Our Cultural Future* (London: Labour Party, 1991).
150. Ibid., pp. 31–2.
151. Ibid., p. 9.
152. Labour Party, *It's Time to Get Britain Working Again*, manifesto for the 1992 general election (London: Labour Party, 1992), p. 24.
153. O'Malley, *Closedown?*, pp. 115–16.
154. Ibid., p. 173.
155. Heffernan and Marqusee, *Defeat*, p. 206.

— 6 —

The Era of New Labour, 1992–2001

Appointed as Labour leader in July 1992, John Smith consolidated the party's attempt to relocate itself ideologically in the 'centre' and to reduce the influence of the union block vote by introducing 'one member, one vote' for the selection of parliamentary candidates. Yet Smith was reluctant to step up the pace of reform and was soon criticized by some shadow Cabinet members, like Tony Blair and Gordon Brown, who wanted to intensify the process of what they saw as 'modernization'. Wright and Carter note the 'rumblings of discontent'[1] that existed by 1993 over both Smith's consensual style of leadership and his gradualist attitude towards fundamental internal change. Tony Blair was then given the chance to implement his drive for root-and-branch reform of the party by John Smith's sudden death in May 1994. New Labour, as Blair's project came to be known at the end of 1994, could be characterized by its emphasis on three features: 'modernization' of party policies, ideologies and structures; the professionalization of the party's presentation and campaigning skills; and the neutralization of the influence of a traditionally anti-Labour mass media.

The call for modernization was a mantra for the leaders of New Labour. In practice, it resembled less Harold Wilson's tirade in the 1960s on the outdated mentality of those running British boardrooms than Neil Kinnock's attack on the left for being a barrier to electoral success. Indeed, Blair was particularly keen to be identified as a friend of business and to reposition Labour as the party of entrepreneurship and innovation. Blair and his shadow chancellor, Gordon Brown, toured the City convincing chief executives and managing directors that New Labour was no longer the party of high taxes and fiscal irresponsibility, but one that promised low inflation and low levels of public spending. The modernizers decided to prove this by tackling the sacred cow of the Labour left, Clause IV of the constitution that committed the party to 'common ownership of the means of production'. Blair launched a campaign to replace the clause with one in praise of wealth creation rather than distribution, which, in the context of an increasingly desperate mood for unity against the Conservatives, was easily passed at a special conference in April 1995.[2] The abolition of Clause IV was partly an example of political public relations but it also signified a genuine recognition that, as Peter Mandelson and Roger Liddle put it in an early clarification of what New Labour stood for, '[p]rofit was no longer a dirty word – profits are accepted as the motor of private enterprise'.[3]

It was in this context that New Labour's ideological framework developed, applying the Labour right's long-held belief in the notion of 'markets as tools of egalitarian choice'[4] to the new circumstances of the 1990s. New Labour leaders seized on market-led globalization as the key opportunity for business and consumers around the world. The speeches of Tony Blair and Gordon Brown were littered with references to the 'modern global economy where capital, raw materials and technology are internationally mobile and tradeable worldwide'.[5] For Blair, the 'driving force of economic change today is globalisation. Technology and capital are mobile. Industry is becoming fiercely competitive across national boundaries.'[6] Their definitions of globalization emphasized the triumph of free market flows and the mobility of capital: new centres of production were emerging outside established centres of manufacturing, imports and exports were now playing an increased role in the lives of national markets while economies and societies had become increasingly interdependent. Blair was particularly keen to conceptualize globalization in terms of developments concerning communications and culture:

> It is as if someone has pressed the fast-forward button on the video and there is no sign of it stopping. I also believe that the internationalisation of culture has played a significant part. In Tokyo and London, increasingly we are sharing the same rock music, the same designer clothes, the same films and surely, over time, the same attitude and tastes.[7]

The consequences of what New Labour saw as the relentless process of globalization were twofold. First, it meant that national governments were almost helpless against global market forces and multinational capital. Second, it increased the importance of New Labour's call for international competitiveness and for the application of techniques and disciplines that would increase efficiency on the global stage. One of New Labour's early economic documents argued that 'in an age of constant technological advance ... [t]he task is now to restore more industrial companies to the front rank of international innovation, productivity and profit'.[8]

Political reorientation was accompanied by the marginalization of annual conference, traditionally the bastion of Labour activism, the further centralization of candidate selection with the ability of the national party to impose candidates on local branches and the transformation of the role of the NEC to make it an 'auxiliary to the parliamentary party, rather than the other way round'.[9]

The second task central to the creation of New Labour was the improvement of the party's presentation and campaigning skills. According to Butler and Kavanagh, 'Tony Blair was impatient with talk of big ideas ... He thought the party had enough policies and should concentrate on projecting them.'[10] With this in mind, Blair resuscitated the communications infrastructure set up by Kinnock in the mid-1980s that John Smith had only recently dismantled. For New Labour, presentational and communication skills were to be not external to policy-making but at its very core. Blair therefore brought into his private office individuals – like Philip Gould, Peter Mandelson, Patricia Hewitt and Alastair Campbell – who were particularly versed in political communications and marketing, and sanctioned the creation of a purpose-built campaigns and media centre at Millbank. The effectiveness of Labour's communications and public relations strategy was seen as decisive, not simply in terms of electoral success, but in the actual creation and definition of New Labour.

One area in which Kinnock had failed, however, and in which Blair was determined to succeed, was to correct the party's poor relationship with the media and, in particular, with the tabloid newspapers which the previous leader had blamed for the 1992 defeat. Kinnock had claimed that the unrelenting hostility of papers like the *Sun* and the *Daily Mail* had made it virtually impossible for Labour to be electorally successful: 'I know people think it's weak to blame the media for everything, but they do determine the environment of politics.'[11] This argument was further put by the soon-to-be Labour MP Martin Linton in a report that provided statistical analysis of the impact of the tabloid press in turning voters away from Labour in 1992. Yet, while his argument concentrated on the role played by the tabloid press, Linton, partly influenced by media magnate Silvio

Berlusconi's control of Italian television, urged Labour not to take television for granted: 'Television is the most dangerous medium because it has semi-hypnotic qualities and is watched disproportionately by those with little education, low incomes and weak political commitment.'[12]

This uncritical conception of media influence was firmly adopted by New Labour who saw it as a priority to court journalists and broadcasters in order to undermine hostility towards Labour. In the words of Robin Corbett, the party's broadcasting spokesperson at the time, 'if you couldn't make friends, at least neutralize opposition'.[13] The principal object of Labour's new-found enthusiasm for media proprietors was Rupert Murdoch, owner of the most bitter anti-Labour newspapers in 1992 and key player in British Sky Broadcasting (BSkyB), the increasingly popular satellite television service. The first dinner between Blair and Murdoch took place in August 1994, a month after Blair's leadership victory, marking the start of articles attributed to Blair being published in the *Sun*.[14] Murdoch, however, was equally keen to impress Blair in order to soften Labour's 1992 manifesto commitment (clearly aimed at Murdoch) to launch a monopolies and mergers investigation into media concentration. Murdoch, furthermore, was disillusioned with John Major's administration and was seriously considering switching his support to New Labour.

In July 1995, Blair flew halfway across the world to address the annual conference of senior executives at Murdoch's News Corporation. Blair's speech combined an appeal to 'moral purpose' with a condemnation of the Conservatives' proposals for capping cross-media ownership that would prevent Murdoch from expanding in the UK.[15] New Labour's courtship of Murdoch paid off when, shortly before the 1997 election, both the *Sun* and the *News of the World* firmly endorsed Labour.

How important was New Labour's systematic and successful courtship of the media between 1994 and 1997? For Tony Blair himself, a positive relationship with editors, owners and broadcasters was both symptomatic of a 'modernized' party and essential for electoral success in what he described as a 'mass-multimedia society'.[16] Blair was so struck by the power of the tabloid press and so grateful for its backing in 1997 that, after the election, he sent a letter to *Sun* editor Stuart Higgins thanking him for the paper's 'magnificent' support. 'It really did make the difference', he wrote.[17] Other commentators were less convinced, arguing that there was little need for the Labour Party to appease media moguls because the latter group was lobbying what it already suspected would be the next government because of the enormous unpopularity of the Conservatives. 'Labour made a breakthrough in its methods of campaigning before and during the election. But the differences between the parties in using these skills and techniques did not decide the election' conclude Butler and Kavanagh,[18] insisting that economic and political factors in the preceding five years were far more decisive.

Labour did win the election in May 1997, capturing 43.2 per cent of the vote next to the Conservatives' 30.7 per cent, a New Labour landslide and a Conservative catastrophe. But how new *was* 'New Labour'? For Anderson and Mann, 'the making of New Labour has been going on a long time – and New Labour owes a lot more than it cares to admit to the old Labour right of the 1960s and 1970s'.[19] It is true that there has long been a revisionist current inside the party but there are some significant and distinctive features of New Labour. Its accommodation with media power, together with its obsession with political communication, its unapologetic embrace of profits and competition, its rejection of traditional Labourist policies and its centralization of party structures, suggest that a real transformation did occur between 1992 and 1997. To what extent was this mirrored in the party's media policies?

LABOUR'S TELEVISION POLICY, 1992–97

Shortly after his victory in the 1992 general election, John Major removed broadcasting from the Home Office and created a new Department of National Heritage (DNH) with full responsibilities for arts and media. Given that the Parliamentary Labour Party had had heated arguments about precisely this subject in the 1980s and that a commitment to move broadcasting to a new ministry was eventually left out of the 1992 manifesto, this gave Labour one less issue to argue about. The main focus concerning television policy for both main parties soon became clear as, after the drama of the 1990 Broadcasting Act and the ITV auctions, attention shifted back to the future of the BBC. With the Corporation's Charter due to expire in 1996, the government published a green paper in November 1992 and invited responses by April 1993. The green paper had a quite different stance to the antagonistic positions adopted by the Conservatives in the 1980s when Mrs Thatcher had raised privatization and advertising as possible scenarios for the BBC:

By 1992 the government seemed to have no intention of replacing
the licence fee as the major source of BBC funding, no intention
of getting the BBC to take advertising, no intention of cutting the
BBC's two television channels to one … or of breaking up the
Corporation.[20]

Goodwin argues that this change of approach was partially in
response to the unpopularity of the ITV auctions but also in response
to the BBC's own enthusiasm for efficiency savings and commercial
operations, particularly in its introduction in 1991 of an internal
market. Whatever the reason, the moderate tone of the green paper
provided Labour with an ideal opportunity to mount a stout defence
of the *principles* of public service broadcasting and to attack the
commercialization of British broadcasting.

The broadcasting brief in the shadow Cabinet was then held by
Ann Clwyd, a left-winger, who brought in Mike Jempson from the
Campaign for Press and Broadcasting Freedom to draft Labour's
response to the green paper. Jempson had helped to organize the
media unions' campaign during the 1990 Broadcasting Act (see
Chapter 5) and was a keen opponent of further commercialization.
Indeed, the submission, *Putting the Citizen at the Centre of British
Broadcasting*[21] pursued a vehemently anti-commercial line and
departed from the general enthusiasm for market principles held by
those at the top of the party. The document, published in April 1993,
condemned the 'damage of deregulation' and argued that
'deregulation stems from a political decision to stimulate market
forces, by commercialising every aspect of public life'.[22] Narrow
objectives of efficiency and lowering units costs were no guarantee of
increased diversity or programme quality and the document criticized
the view that 'broadcasting should be guided increasingly by the
demands of advertisers and sponsors, with audiences treated as
consumers, passive in all but their spending power'.[23] Instead, the
viewer ought to be seen as a citizen participating in the broadcasting
process and not simply a consumer with a wholly commercial outlook.

The document was unequivocal in its support for the licence fee
and attacked the Conservatives' squeeze on funding because they had
pegged the licence fee to the level of the Retail Price Index (RPI).
Labour's solution to growing political interference in the BBC's
finances was to suggest the creation of an independent review board
that would recommend suitable increases to the licence fee over a
sustained length of time to allow the BBC to plan ahead. The
document, however, was also critical of the BBC and recognized that
damage had been done to the BBC's public service structures under

the Conservatives, noting its poor accounting practices, the politicization of the appointments system and the unrepresentative nature of the governors. It therefore suggested a number of reforms to increase the institution's accountability. First, in lieu of the Charter, an Act of Parliament should formalize the BBC's position in law and should be backed up by a 'covenant' that set out the BBC's obligations to licence-fee payers. Second, the board of governors should be replaced by an independent set of trustees with responsibility not for management but for overseeing the BBC's remit. Third, the report called for the creation of a number of representative councils and panels to increase the transparency and accountability of the regulatory structures.

The tone of *Putting the Citizen at the Centre of Broadcasting* was a far cry from the wide-ranging and impassioned critiques of the duopoly and the BBC that Labour had produced in the 1970s and 1980s. It focused exclusively on the constitutional framework of the BBC and marginalized questions of bias and political diversity. However, the document was also a clear indication of a mood inside Labour to resist further commercialization and to halt the extension of the market to all areas of social life, indeed to treat people as 'citizens' and not as 'consumers'. Although Clwyd presented it to the shadow Cabinet and recalls that 'it was well received by the leadership',[24] the document was not circulated to the party conference as originally planned and its proposals were not developed before the government's white paper on the BBC appeared the following year.

In September 1993, Clwyd criticized the government's plans to relax the rules on ITV mergers and called for an extension of the existing moratorium on ITV takeovers. Hostile to any loosening of cross-media ownership rules, Clwyd, according to the *Guardian*, was determined to renew 'the party's attack on Rupert Murdoch, who "must and will be stopped"'.[25] Clwyd never got the chance because she was thrown off the shadow Cabinet the following month and replaced as shadow heritage secretary by the former shadow minister for citizen's rights and women's issues, Mo Mowlam. This was a key moment for Labour in the evolution of its market-led television policy and a new, relaxed attitude towards concentration of ownership. When the ITV moratorium ended in January 1994 with a flurry of takeovers[26] and the government announced a review of media ownership restrictions, Mowlam, 'who has been pressing for an inquiry into cross-media ownership, said she was pleased. "The emphasis must be on diversity and choice for the consumer."'[27] In July 1994, Labour supporter Lord Hollick, a key backer of Tony Blair and leading ITV business executive, attacked existing cross-media ownership controls, 'calling them confused, lacking in clarity and piecemeal' and calling for a redefinition of what constituted a monopoly.[28] The process of Labour 'removing the citizen from the centre of British broadcasting' was under way.

Tom O'Malley from the Campaign for Press and Broadcasting Freedom recalls that there was a shift in television policy from precisely this time:

> Mo Mowlam was a pivotal figure in that shift and she was clearly involved in courting, in a political sense, News International. I went to many a meeting where she had that man David Elstein, a lobbyist for Sky, and it was in that context that she organised the 21st Century Media conference.[29]

The conference, which took place even before Blair had won the leadership contest, was designed to familiarize media executives with Labour's plans for the industry and was the clearest sign yet of a repositioning away from traditional concerns about media concentration and long-established hostilities between Labour and the media industries. At £230 per head, it was attended by Labour's front bench and by top executives from the British media world, including ITV, BBC and News International, but not by consumer groups, trade unionists or ordinary party members. Peter Goodwin described the conference as

> a distinctly new-look Labour gathering. It is sponsored by the Cable Television Association – one of only two organisations which responded to the BBC Green Paper advocating the replacement of the licence fee by subscription. It is organised by Mike Craven – who doubles as paid lobbyist for the [British] Media Industry Group ... established last year to get the cross-media ownership rules relaxed.[30]

For Mike Jempson, who had recently drafted the party's policy on the BBC, the conference came as somewhat of a surprise:

> There was talk of a consultative conference to update Labour media policy, and we all rather assumed that conventional Labour allies would be involved, although Mo was making noises about potential sponsors from the commercial sector. Offers of joint sponsorship with the CPBF etc. were ignored. In the event ... we ended up with a razzamatazz event at the Queen Elizabeth Conference Centre, chaired by Mo, at which News International thanked a rather uncomfortable Margaret Beckett

for allowing them to contribute to Labour Party policy. There was no trade union involvement … The worm had turned, and most of us saw little point in being associated with policies that now apparently favoured greater deregulation especially re ownership and control measures, in order that UK media companies could compete freely in the global market. I have not been approached for advice on broadcasting policy since; I assume commercial lobbyists have literally plugged all the gaps.[31]

Labour's new-found enthusiasm for relaxing cross-media ownership rules was provided with a degree of intellectual rigour by the launch in early 1994 of a high-profile research project into media regulation at the Labour-supporting think-tank, the Institute of Public Policy Research (IPPR). The programme was backed by Patricia Hewitt, the deputy director of the IPPR, previously Neil Kinnock's press secretary and now part of the unofficial advisory circle around Tony Blair. It was funded by many of the companies who had attended the 21st Century Media conference and who represented the heavyweights of the UK communications sector: BT, the Cable Communication Association, LWT, Pearson, Mercury Communications and News International. In fact, according to one of the project's founders, Richard Collins, News International was the first company to commit to funding on condition that at least two others also backed the work.[32] The research aimed to provide a systematic and integrated approach to the communications industries at a time of convergence. For James Purnell, one of the IPPR researchers, later a policy adviser in Downing Street, the project was based on two key assumptions:

> Firstly, that markets weren't necessarily bad things, that there were some things that they were the best tool to deliver. Secondly, we had to adapt to the fact that technology was changing incredibly fast and that, whereas policy was based on the idea that you would have a very small number of channels and newspapers, those assumptions were being overturned.[33]

The research, eventually published as *New Media, New Policies*, strongly criticized the left's unerring hostility to market forces and called for a 'new, radical, synthesis'[34] of neo-liberal and old left approaches, a kind of broadcasting 'third way'.

The book examines a wide range of issues including the provision of universal service in telecommunications, the need for freedom of information, plans to disaggregate the BBC into semi-autonomous units and the reform of a regulatory structure defined by 'feudal muddle, patronage and preferment rather than what is appropriate to a modern state and to a vital sector of the UK economy'.[35] The spirit of the IPPR's call to modernization, however, is best exemplified by the book's discussion on ownership where it seeks to overturn another of the left's assumptions, that media concentration needs to be curbed. Collins and Murroni distinguish between *cross-ownership*, not in itself a problem, and the more undesirable *concentration of ownership*. They suggest, for example, that seven proprietors, each controlling about 15 per cent of the total media market, would seem to be 'a reasonable definition of a floor for ownership regulation'[36] and that the fewer *cross*-media interests a company has, the more share it can have of an individual media field.

By emphasizing the unstoppable process of convergence and the need to consider the total media market, the IPPR's research both implicitly sanctioned the existence of monopolies in specific media fields and explicitly welcomed the development of communications behemoths. 'Large, concentrated media organizations are not intrinsically undesirable', conclude Collins and Murroni. 'Large size tends to bring the resources required for comprehensive high quality reporting and the case of the BBC suggests that large organizations with a share of media markets can serve the public interest.'[37] This concession to the advantages of the centralization of production and distribution, rather than the Labour left's preferred route of decentralization, and the emphasis on the ability of large firms to deliver public service outcomes, perhaps explains why Richard Collins was so impressed by the behaviour of News International during the project. After all, how much did media moguls have to fear from the IPPR's proposals?

> It is striking that, given the reputation of News International in Labour Party circles, our experience was that they were very robust and fair in providing evidence. They never overstepped the line of legitimate influence, never attempted to improperly influence, never twisted our arms, never threatened.[38]

The party's shift on cross-media ownership did not please everyone in the labour movement. The 1994 TUC conference passed a motion opposing relaxation of ownership restrictions and calling for the rules to be extended to include satellite as well as terrestrial media. In moving the motion, the delegate from the print union, the GPMU, argued that 'it is extremely disconcerting to find the Labour Party's Marjorie Mowlam suggesting "That some loosening of cross-media restriction is inevitable". Any further loosening of cross-media restrictions would be disastrous.'[39] Labour's liberalization juggernaut continued, however, until the issue was highlighted once more with the publication of the government's white paper on media ownership in May 1995.[40] The Conservatives were by now anxious to win back ground from Labour on the subject of media ownership and proposed that newspaper groups controlling less than 20 per cent of total circulation would be able to buy into television companies, up to a limit of 15 per cent of the television market. For Goodwin, this was a technically ingenious as well as a politically pragmatic move because it allowed the owners of the *Financial Times, Guardian, Telegraph* and *Mail* newspapers to build up television interests, a demand for which they had been lobbying extensively during the previous year under the umbrella of the British Media Industry Group.[41] The losers were the Labour-supporting Mirror Group and, perhaps more surprising, Murdoch's News International, the backbone of Tory support until 1992, both of whose newspaper interests exceeded the 20 per cent limit.

What was New Labour's reaction to the possibility of some of the party's fiercest critics expanding their media interests? 'I welcome a broadened perspective for the media industry' commented broadcasting spokesperson Graham Allen, criticizing the proposals only for being too 'vague' and 'far too nebulous'.[42] When they were published in the broadcasting bill in December 1995, Labour's response was even more emphatic: the problem with the government's proposals on relaxing cross-media ownership rules was not that they went too far *but they did not go far enough.* The new team of shadow heritage secretary Jack Cunningham and his broadcasting spokesperson Lewis Moonie were anxious to make this clear:

> We will not go for the government's system, I can pretty much guarantee that. My own preference is for complete deregulation and allowing the Office of Fair Trading and the MMC [Monopolies and Mergers Commission] to sort things out. Cross-media ownership is a good thing. The whole point is to ensure the creation of bigger companies that can compete abroad.[43]

For New Labour, broadcasting diversity now referred not to a genuine cross-section of political viewpoints but to a plurality of ownership that could be policed by the competition authorities. Moonie clarified his position during the committee stage of the bill, arguing that the 20 per cent rule was deliberately discriminating against the Labour-supporting Mirror Group and not Murdoch because the latter was more interested in developing satellite rather than terrestrial interests. 'If the Government really believe in full and fair competition, they should accept that adequate rules and tests already exist and remove the 20 per cent rule altogether.'[44] Labour then joined with two right-wing Tory MPs in voting against the proposal to introduce the 20 per cent ceiling on newspaper circulation but was still defeated as the Liberal Democrats and Plaid Cymru MPs voted with the government.

Such a wholehearted passion for deregulation was bound to provoke a reaction from critics of New Labour. The heritage secretary Virginia Bottomley said that Labour had 'lurched from a paranoid terror of large media groups to a sycophantic devotion to them'.[45] The left-wing journalist Paul Foot attacked New Labour not only for betraying its principles but also for playing a dangerous game in accommodating to media moguls.

> The switching of Labour's policy, and the abandonment of long-established opposition to private monopolies in the media, not only stinks of the same back-scratching sleaze for which Labour are constantly and properly attacking the Tories. It is also counter-productive. It hands power, strength and confidence to unelected, irresponsible media oligarchies which, if their commercial interests are threatened for a single second, even by a Labour government, will turn on their former benefactors and tear them to pieces.[46]

Ownership was not the only issue related to television policy that the party leadership turned to in its attempt to consolidate and publicize the New Labour project. During the 1992 US elections, Bill Clinton and Al Gore had embraced the promise of the 'information superhighway' and the 'broadband revolution' as part of their own modernizing ambitions. The terminology and excitement soon followed across the Atlantic so that, by 1994, British politicians were queuing up to be associated with cutting-edge developments around multimedia and digital technologies. The Conservatives' response was a rather dry Trade and Industry Select Committee report urging the development of a privately built broadband infrastructure to take advantage of the likely economic benefits of optical fibre networks.[47] New Labour's initiative was much bolder and far more high profile.

Initially, Tony Blair set up a policy forum on the superhighway in November 1994, chaired by the new shadow heritage secretary Chris Smith, who had taken over from Mo Mowlam. With a membership of 32 people, drawn from all over the Labour Party, communications industries, academia and the unions, the policy group received over 200 written submissions and oral presentations from leading media and communications companies like News International, BT, Microsoft and the BBC. Its report, *Communicating Britain's Future* (*CBF*),[48] published in the summer of 1995,[49] was distributed on disk as well as hard copy and was breathless about digital developments:

> We stand on the threshold of a revolution as profound as that brought about by the invention of the printing press. New technologies, which enable rapid communication to take place in a myriad of different ways across the globe, and permit information to be provided, sought, and received on a scale so far unimaginable, will bring fundamental changes to all our lives.[50]

Yet, this communications network would be one developed only by private finance so that the government's role was essentially to create the appropriate competitive environment and to promote the use of the networks. Unlike Harold Wilson's invocation of the 'white heat of the technological revolution' to attempt to purposefully *plan* an industrial strategy, Blair's 'revolution' would have to be left to the mercy of market forces.

Blair used the rhetoric of the superhighway and broadband technology as the backdrop for his highly successful speech to the 1995 Labour conference. He triumphantly announced that he had concluded a deal with British Telecom in which, in return for BT being allowed to offer entertainment services down its phone lines,[51] it had agreed to connect every school, hospital, college and public library to the super-highway for free. It was a very rare example of communications policy, particularly Labour communications policy, hitting the headlines.[52]

The superhighway initiative impacted on television policy in a number of ways. First, it signalled Labour's acceptance of the inevitability of convergence and the need to adapt policy and regulation to meet the needs of converging media. This meant that New Labour saw less space for separate media policies and an urgent requirement to formulate a 'communications policy' in tune with the demands of a more competitive environment. Although *CBF* contained few references to television, it made a firm promise to combine the telecommunications regulator, Oftel, and the commercial television regulator, the Independent Television Commission (ITC), into a more streamlined structure, an 'OFCOM', that would 'regulate the whole communications infrastructure and ensure fair competition'.[53] In a clear hint at deregulation, a 'revamped' ITC would regulate content 'albeit with a lighter touch'.[54]

Second, *CBF* provided clear evidence of New Labour's willingness to consider broadcasting as part of industrial policy, which until that point had been more of a feature of the Tories' rather than Labour's approach. Although the brief was initially given to Chris Smith as shadow heritage secretary, Smith himself was aware that many of the issues were industrial ones 'about how you get the network in place and how you make sure you get as near to a nationwide network as you can. The issues that then follow on very rapidly are content issues.'[55] Lewis Moonie, shadow industry minister at the time, argues that Tony Blair was 'mistaken' in giving the brief to Smith and that there was tension between the shadow heritage and trade teams during the superhighway forum: 'I saw no very good reason from the point of view of that time for the heritage team to be having anything to do with it at all. Superhighways at present are largely a matter of creating infrastructure and that is entirely at present a matter for the DTI [Department of Trade and Industry].'[56] Ironically, in a further example of the overlap of the broadcasting and industry briefs, both Moonie and Jack Cunningham, the shadow trade secretary, were moved to heritage before the 1997 election while Smith was moved to health and the superhighway brief itself moved to industry.

The clearest sign that New Labour was preparing to approach broadcasting on the basis of industrial policy approaches was provided by its attitude to Rupert Murdoch's growing control of the pay-television market. In early December 1996, several of the broadsheet newspapers carried lengthy articles criticizing both Tories and Labour for doing nothing to wrest control of pay television away from Murdoch and for failing to enforce open standards for digital television. Moonie's response was to lambast the 'hysteria' of the press and to argue that Murdoch should be rewarded for his investment:

> I back having open systems and standards but I don't necessarily think that everybody should be able to have a free lunch. If they [the other broadcasters] want to use Murdoch's technology, then they're bloody well going to have to pay for it because that's what they would do in any other commercial field. No free lunches, a fair system and no unfair gatekeeping: that's what we're trying to achieve.[57]

New Labour's preferred way of ensuring free and fair competition, therefore, was to be through the use of the competition authorities and economic regulators and not the traditional broadcasting regulators whose remits are defined in terms of cultural as well as economic objectives.

New Labour's enthusiasm for the knobs and fibres of the superhighway and the broadband revolution was replicated in its support for the government's plans for digital terrestrial television

(DTT), embodied in the 1996 Broadcasting Act. Although expressing some reservations about the prospects for DTT in the light of strong competition from cable and satellite, Moonie spoke for the whole of the heritage team in wishing DTT well: 'We have no quarrel with the Government inasmuch as we want digital television to get going, as everyone else does.'[58] Labour's pre-election arts and media document, *Create the Future*, promised to 'promote the digital revolution'[59] and added that 'it is important that we maintain universal access to a wide range of television services in the digital age'.[60] If this meant guaranteeing the free-to-air broadcasters a place on the new digital channels, then Conservative legislation had already provided this assurance. More likely, it was a New Labour promise to ensure that no one should be denied access to the multi-channel revolution but with no further suggestion as to how to meet this pledge nor to provide public money to make it happen, Labour's approach was virtually identical to the Tories.

Create the Future made few new promises about television, repeating its support for a new regulator, OFCOM, pledging its support for the BBC 'as a flagship for British creativity and public service broadcasting'[61] and promising not to privatize Channel 4. The document emphasized the economic value of UK television and argued that there was no room for complacency in an internationally competitive market. However, 'the growing globalisation of media does not mean that we should be prepared to trade creativity or independence for a large-scale monoculture'.[62] New Labour's policy aims for television may be seen as reaching out to all constituencies, embracing tradition *and* innovation, creativity *and* diversity, public service *and* commercial success. These principles were then embodied in the party's manifesto, *New Labour: Because Britain Deserves Better*,[63] where the single paragraph on media and broadcasting – longer than the section on sport but shorter than the one on the national lottery – managed to include references to 'competition' or 'competitiveness' three times.[64]

How much of a change had there been since the last election manifesto? The shadow arts minister in 1997, Mark Fisher, blames the rapid turnover of broadcasting spokespeople for the lack of development of a coherent Labour television policy between 1992 and 1997: 'It wasn't so much that there was a philosophical turn [from the 1980s] but when you're playing pass-the-parcel with political responsibility as was the case in those five years, it's almost impossible to sustain either the contacts or the thinking.'[65] Yet New Labour's balancing act between the market and public service in the 1997 manifesto does little to obscure the fact that substantial changes *had* taken place between 1992 and 1997. In the five years since its last manifesto commitment to tackle media concentration, Labour had transformed itself into the party *of* media concentration; its pledge to curb the power of Rupert Murdoch and News International had been rethought as a campaign to *court* the power of Rupert Murdoch and News International. By 1997, New Labour had provided the clearest signal of any incoming Labour administration of its intentions for broadcasting once in office.

NEW LABOUR IN OFFICE

According to New Labour, the party's triumph in the polls in May 1997 was due to Blair's firm endorsement of an alternative to both traditional social democracy and the free market: the 'third way'. While Labour revisionists have long sought to tread a path between 'socialism' and 'capitalism', for Blair the 'third way' suggests a whole new sort of politics:

> My vision for the 21st century is of a popular politics reconciling themes which in the past have wrongly been regarded as antagonistic – patriotism *and* internationalism; rights *and* responsibilities; the promotion of enterprise *and* the attack on poverty and discrimination.[66]

Values of social justice, opportunity, responsibility and community are not antagonistic to market imperatives but indeed can only be delivered *through* market mechanisms. 'With the right policies, market mechanisms are critical to meeting social objectives, entrepreneurial zeal can promote social justice, and new technology represents an opportunity, not a threat.'[67]

Much of this is far from original and is, in reality, an invocation of capitalist competition, patriotism, welfare cuts and revisionist ideas about the disappearance of class antagonisms. Michael Freeden argues that Blair's 'third way' is simply the latest in a long line of middle ways between 'first' and 'second' ways of social democracy and neo-liberalism but with a new emphasis on community, responsibility and equality of opportunity.[68]

According to Blair, the first policy objective for 'third way' government is to create a 'dynamic knowledge-based economy founded on individual empowerment and opportunity'.[69] The key to success in this 'new economy' lies not so much with the provision of a physical infrastructure or the production of material goods but with the nurturing of a far less tangible commodity: creativity. Drawing on the ideas of Charles Leadbetter (which eventually ended up as the book *Living on Thin Air*),[70] Tony Blair claims that the 'new economy' is 'radically different. Services, knowledge, skills and small enterprises are its cornerstones. Most of its output cannot be weighed, touched or measured. Its most valuable assets are knowledge and creativity.'[71]

One major policy response to the recognition of the economic value of the commodification of knowledge lay in New Labour's vision of 'Creative Britain' or, as the press dubbed it, 'Cool Britannia'. This initiative sought to establish the UK as a cultural powerhouse whose television programmes, music, films, fashion and software programmes would triumphantly saturate world markets and make a significant impact on the UK's trade balance. One of the government's first actions was to launch the Creative Industries Taskforce in 1997 to examine ways of maximizing the value of a sector that contributes about £50 billion of activity to the UK economy.[72] For the incoming culture minister Chris Smith, these are the key industries of a knowledge economy, overshadowing traditional manufacturing and growing faster than any other sector: '[t]hey are where the wealth and the jobs of the future are going to be generated from'.[73]

New Labour's heady enthusiasm for market disciplines was reflected in the dominant theme of its first period in office: that the government would stick to the harsh limits on public spending laid down by the Conservatives so that there would be no additional public money to fund either basic services or the knowledge economy. While the government was reluctant to hand over money to cash-starved public services, it appeared to be eager to receive donations from millionaire businesspeople like David Sainsbury, Geoffrey Robinson and, most controversially of all, the boss of Formula One motor racing Bernie Ecclestone.[74] Accusations of 'sleaze' were followed by distinctly unmodernizing developments. A manifesto commitment to permit increased access to official information was compromised by the slow and rather reluctant passage of freedom of information legislation that was littered with exemptions protecting the government's right to secrecy until 2005. The government showed more enthusiasm in passing the Regulation of Investigatory Powers Act (2000), which sanctioned extensive and unprecedented surveillance of private electronic communication.

In June 2001, a population that was increasingly suspicious of government promises and Downing Street spin nevertheless re-elected Tony Blair for another term. The contrast with the atmosphere of the previous election was stark. According to *Observer* commentator Andrew Rawnsley, 'May Day 1997 was hailed as a dazzling new dawn for Britain; this was just another, slightly dreary day in the office. The people had not so much enthused as acquiesced in giving New Labour a second term.'⁷⁵ Had the government lived up to its promise to modernize British broadcasting and in what way had 'third way' politics influenced the four key areas of television policy emphasized by New Labour – regulation and ownership, the digital 'revolution', public service broadcasting and television exports?

Modernizing regulation and ownership

Tony Blair handed the heritage brief to Chris Smith immediately after the 1997 election. Two months later, the New Labour government scrapped the national heritage department and introduced a new Department of Culture, Media and Sport (DCMS), described by Smith as 'a department of the future. It is about creativity, innovation and excitement.'⁷⁶ Although New Labour came to power proclaiming the onset of a digital revolution and promised to shake up the existing regulatory system, the government proceeded cautiously to begin with. Uncertainty in the media industry led the government to postpone plans to introduce broadcasting legislation. According to the government's media policy adviser at the time:

> We thought it was the wrong time to do it because that was the time digital was being introduced and regulatory changes in the media are incredibly destabilizing. Sometimes change is good but, when people were taking very big risks in investing on new platforms, it was important to have regulatory stability.⁷⁷

This was an early sign that New Labour's media policy would do nothing to antagonize corporate interests in the media industry and that the immediate task for television policymakers was to protect the substantial investments that major British companies were making in new technologies.

The government's determination to maintain 'regulatory stability' was undermined by the publication of two reports within a year of taking office. First, in December 1997, the European Commission released a highly deregulatory green paper on the communications industries that called for the adoption of market mechanisms to embrace the possibilities of convergence and for the scrapping of any regulation that would act as a barrier to the creation of jobs and profits.[78] Next, in May 1998, the Culture, Media and Sport Select Committee published its report on *The Multi-media Revolution* attacking the plethora of regulatory agencies in the UK communications field as being 'more reminiscent of a feudal State than a regulatory structure for the multi-media age'.[79] The report called for the creation of a new 'Department of Communications' and for a 'Communications Regulation Commission', modelled on the American Federal Communications Commission (FCC), to replace the existing alphabet soup of regulators.[80]

While the government was sympathetic to the view expressed in both reports for increasing the use of competition law and reducing the scope of regulation, it concluded that there is 'sufficient flexibility within the current system of regulation to cope with developments over the next few years and the Government is actively encouraging co-ordination within the existing framework'.[81] Co-ordination took the form, not just of closer working relationships between the current regulators, the ITC, Oftel (for telecommunications) and the Office of Fair Trading (OFT), but also between the DCMS and the DTI. This was particularly ironic because, having spent over a decade arguing for a dedicated media ministry, as soon as Labour had set one up, it was forced to share responsibilities with a far more powerful department in Whitehall. On the other hand, this was simply evidence of the direction in which New Labour was headed – towards a conception of media policy as a branch of industrial policy – and therefore a very logical move.

The two departments published their joint green paper, *Regulating Communications*,[82] in July 1998. The document conceives of viewers purely as consumers – there are ten references to 'the consumer' in the executive summary alone – and sets out to find a balance between recognizing the needs of the 'providers' and protecting the interests of the 'consumers'. It is quite clear, however, that it will be market forces, wherever possible, that mediate this relationship: '[t]he government will seek to provide a structure which reflects market realities and will seek to distort them as little as possible'.[83] Having accepted convergence as inevitable, the government felt that it was time for traditional assumptions to be overturned: from now on, regulation should be the exception and not the rule. 'Regulation should be the minimum necesssary to achieve clearly defined policy objectives. The presumption that broadcasting and communications should be regulated should therefore in general be reversed.'[84] Furthermore, even the argument for any remaining regulation to be based on fixed principles was now too rigid:

The regulatory structure must also be sufficiently flexible to adapt to new developments in a fast-changing environment. We have to regulate for the reality of the market today and tomorrow, not for a snapshot of yesterday's market frozen in time, nor for a vision of the day after tomorrow which may never materialise in the form we anticipate.[85]

Regulating Communications was notable more for the way in which it shifted the agenda towards regulation only 'in the last instance' than for any specific policy proposals. The DCMS/DTI's *The Way Ahead*, published the following year, reaffirmed this stance of following market developments and pledged to 'continue with the evolutionary approach to adapting communications regulation set out in the Green Paper'.[86] It also stressed the importance of two new committees that had recently been set up to consider communications policy: the G3, comprised of members from the OFT, Oftel and the Independent Television Commission (ITC), and the G6, including officials from the DCMS and the communications policy and competition policy directorates of the DTI.[87] Both committees were clearly weighted towards the interests of economic regulators, deprioritizing the traditional concerns of broadcasting regulators. Indeed, although the report pledged the need for continuing content regulation of *generalist* television services 'to guard against misleading advertising and prevent viewers being shocked or harmed',[88] there should be as little interference as possible: 'It is important to consider whether regulatory objectives in communications can be achieved with a lighter touch and to ensure that the regulatory impositions on commercial broadcasters are no more than is necessary to protect the public interest.'[89]

This deregulatory approach was echoed in the eventual publication in December 2000 of the government's white paper, *A New Future for Communications*.[90] In attempting to 'make the UK home to the most dynamic and competitive communications and media market in the world',[91] the white paper proposed the creation of a single regulator for the whole communications industry, OFCOM, scrapped the rule preventing one ITV company from reaching more than 15 per cent of the total TV audience and allowed for the possibility of one company controlling ITV. The government's objective was perfectly clear: 'This lighter touch system of media and communications regulation reflects the Government's vision of industrial policy based on skills, innovation and enterprise.'[92] Although there was still a place for content regulation and public service obligations, the emphasis was very much on developing the appropriate market mechanisms to deliver competition, choice and quality. While the precise make-up of OFCOM is not yet clear, it is likely that it will be an enormously powerful regulator guided more by economic considerations than by cultural objectives. The left-wing critic John Pilger warned shortly after its publication that

> the white paper is a warning that for the first time since broadcasting began in Britain, legislation will take away a universal public service obligation, and commercialism will be unleashed. It will be a drip-drip process. Limp words about support for public service broadcasting are there to distract those co-opted by New Labour.[93]

The white paper avoided the issue of media ownership and, specifically, the thorny question of whether to relax existing cross-media ownership restrictions. This was partly because, in the months before the 2001 election, the government had no wish to upset those press proprietors like Rupert Murdoch who were anxious to extend into terrestrial television; it was also because the government was still unsure about its strategy concerning ownership and the need to develop 'national champions'. Blair's government had discussed this in its 1998 green paper where it argued that achieving international competitiveness is difficult but necessary:

> Since markets are increasingly global – particularly if they are mediated electronically across global networks – domestic firms increasingly must compete with strong players from abroad. It is clearly central to the health of the UK economy that UK firms are fully competitive in world markets, not only to defend the domestic position, but also to attract a share of global revenues and jobs to the UK.[94]

New Labour's preferred way of building up strong, domestic media firms to cope with foreign competition was to further review existing cross-media ownership rules and to continue the process it started while in opposition. In developing this strategy, the government was able to draw on the conclusions of a report, *The Multi-media Revolution*, produced by the influential Parliamentary Select Committee on Culture, Media and Sport. Chaired by the Labour MP Gerald Kaufman, a firm believer in the process of convergence and the need for liberalization, the committee insisted that *size matters*:

> excessive concern over ownership and size in a domestic context might create a market so fragmented that the United Kingdom lacks organisations with the range of skills and the investment capital to compete effectively in increasingly global markets. Dominant positions are often beneficial viewed in an

international context; they are also often a legitimate reward for risk and innovation. *The aim of regulation should be to reduce the possibilities for the abuse of a dominant position, not to reduce dominance.*[95]

Just as the IPPR's research had distinguished between the desirability of cross-ownership and the undesirability of media concentration, Kaufman's committee was keen to contrast the advantages of market domination with the abuses of that domination.

A single paragraph in *Regulating Communications* followed up this point and argued that '[s]ome concentration of ownership has been regarded as inevitable, and possibly desirable, since it confers advantage in terms of global competitiveness'.[96] However, the document also acknowledged the need for particular controls on media ownership that may be necessary to protect the aims of diversity and plurality of voice. The problem was that there was no firm indication about whether these rules were still necessary apart from a clear hint that 'the changes which are unfolding in broadcasting and telecommunications will call into question existing approaches to the achievement of those aims'.[97] This was a brief and ambivalent summary of the key areas of Labour's media policy up to the 1990s.

The government made its intentions even clearer with the publication of *The Way Ahead*. While its key policy aims were to 'foster competitive markets' and to 'ensure that the United Kingdom builds on its competitive strength',[98] there was no mention at all of the need for continuing with cross-media ownership restrictions. Instead, the document confirmed that more use should be made of the competition authorities and economic mechanisms rather than specific media regulation. General competition law, it suggested, would be enough to check any abuse of a dominant position while in no way discouraging the pursuit of dominance. Several months before *The Way Ahead*, the government had scrapped the Monopolies and Mergers Commission and introduced a Competition Commission that, together with the OFT, was given tough new powers to rule on anti-competitive behaviour without any political interference affecting key merger decisions. According to James Purnell at the Number 10 Policy Unit,

> our approach [to media ownership] will be very similar to what is now. Our primary tool is competition. As a government we're very keen on effective competition policy – we've replaced the Competition Act which is as tough as any in the world and we'll apply those principles to the media.[99]

The first example of this 'depoliticized' approach to media mergers happened in November 1999 when Stephen Byers, the trade and industry secretary, referred a merger between two cable companies, NTL and Cable & Wireless Communications, to the Competition Commission against the express advice of the OFT. The referral was inspired by government concerns not so much about the concentration of the cable television industry than by the threat that a powerful cable company might present to Murdoch's BSkyB. Byers' action, wrote the *Observer*, 'opened the way for criticism that the Government's relationship with Rupert Murdoch ... was more important than its aim of promoting competition'.[100] The decision of the New Labour competition minister, Kim Howells, to have lunch with the chief executive of BSkyB shortly afterwards did not help.[101]

In November 2001, four and a half years after originally winning office, the New Labour government finally published a consultation paper on Britain's media ownership rules. The thresholds, the document astutely argued, could be maintained, scrapped or raised. On the one hand, the government saw the need for continuing restrictions because existing competition law would not be able to 'provide the certainty we need that a significant number of different media voices will continue to be heard, or that prospective new entrants to the market will be able to add their voice'.[102] On the other hand, given the increasing choice of media outlets and the pace of digital convergence, 'we will be as deregulatory as possible, in the knowledge that new competition legislation should be more effective in preventing companies from abusing a dominant market position'.[103] Not surprisingly, given the document's adoption of two contradictory positions in quick succession, the government simply proposed a further consultation period before committing itself to making any concrete decisions that might open itself up to possible criticism from either Murdoch or non-Murdoch interests in the UK media.[104]

New Labour has vigorously embraced competition in the communications sector and has promoted the idea that the public interest – in television as in other areas – is best served not through regulation but through effective competition. The problem is, as yet, there are no obvious signs of effective competition in broadcasting. Indeed the fact that, in the UK, one company (BSkyB) dominates satellite television, two companies (Telewest and NTL) dominate cable and one company (most likely Granada) is set to dominate ITV, is hardly a ringing endorsement of vigorous competition and certainly not of diversity. The government's activity in this area increasingly points to a conception of broadcasting not as an area of cultural life with distinct needs and rules but as an industrial sector to be exploited using standard economic tools and arguments.

Promoting the digital revolution

Labour inherited the architecture of the 'digital revolution' from the previous Conservative government and, far from changing policy on the licensing of new services, immediately sought to step up the pace of digital take-up. Digital was high on Chris Smith's list of priorities when he first addressed the television industry in September 1997 as secretary of state, stressing the New Labour themes of access, competition and efficiency:

> I want digital services to develop on the basis of fair competition between providers to bring content to consumers – not as a war between different receiving equipment or delivery systems. I also want to ensure universal access to the current free-to-air public service channels and I want that access as soon as possible to be through digital services, so as to end the current wasteful use of valuable radio spectrum for analogue terrestrial broadcasting.[105]

These promises were scarcely controversial. The free-to-air channels had been guaranteed access to digital platforms under Conservative legislation and the policing of competition between different providers was to be done by the existing regulators and competition authorities, precisely as the Tories had envisaged. Furthermore, the switching-off of analogue spectrum, given its enormous market value, was a prize that every government was anxious to win. Smith repeated these pledges the following year when he argued that 'it is not a question of whether digital television will succeed, but only of how quickly it will win acceptance' and praised the digital providers for promising that 'their respective platforms will be interoperable'.[106]

His government's reliance on the market and competition authorities to stop a 'set-top box war' came unstuck fairly quickly. BSkyB launched its digital satellite service in October 1998, followed a month later by the digital terrestrial service, ONdigital (owned by ITV companies Carlton and Granada), both using distinct operating systems and separate boxes. The need for 'interoperability' was explained away by the fact that digital providers were giving away their boxes for free in order to increase consumer demand. Even if the end result of this for viewers wanting access to *all* channels was a substantial increase in subscription fees, the government could still claim that there was 'fair competition' for digital services. The *Observer* countered that the government had failed to use its power to enforce interoperability and that if 'the Government wants the consumer to come first it could do a lot worse than to start knocking a few heads together in the worlds of television and regulation'.[107] James Purnell, the media adviser at the Number 10 Policy Unit, defended New Labour's strategy and claimed that a key achievement of the government was in 'having an effective competition policy which has meant that digital has so far been introduced in a pro-competitive way. We're having a unique [market] subsidy of set-top boxes.'[108]

In September 1999, the government decided that, after observing digital television in the UK for nearly a full year, it was ready to announce its plans for the digital future. Analogue transmission would cease some time between 2006 and 2010 but only on the basis of two tests: availability and affordability. Digital signals would need to match the availability of current analogue ones, approximately 99.4 per cent of the UK population, while 95 per cent of consumers would have to have access to digital equipment in their homes before switchover was completed. The definition of affordability, however, was far less precise: '[i]t means prices which are within the reach of people on low and fixed incomes, particularly elderly people for many of whom television is the most important and reliable companion in their daily lives'.[109] Smith provided no clue as to what the government would do should prices not be within the reach of the poor or the elderly, apart from to rely on the charity of the digital providers because 'it will be in the interests of the television broadcasting industry to ensure that the final 5 per cent are helped directly to make the switch-over'.[110]

One solution that has definitely been discounted is the provision of public subsidies to encourage the take-up of digital services. According to the head of general broadcasting policy at the DCMS in 1997, Harry Reeves, it is

> highly unlikely that there will be crude subsidies, partly because of public finance considerations, partly because the government genuinely believes that this is something for the public to determine the pace and direction of development. I don't think there will be a subsidy, crude or sophisticated.[111]

If New Labour was serious about facilitating a digital revolution in which all citizens have a 'stake', it might well consider spending some of the billions it earned from the sale of radio spectrum to lower the cost of access to digital services.[112] This, however, would conflict with the government's determination to keep a tight rein on public spending and its reluctance to entertain any notion of subsidies, particularly in the provision of market goods. It would also conflict with its philosophy for digital, that new services will succeed or fail on the basis of consumer demand above all else.

The problem with this argument is that the government is clearly not just reacting to but attempting to stimulate consumer demand for digital in its ambitious timetable for switch-off. Not surprisingly, in his speech to the 1999 Labour conference, Smith failed to dwell on the part of the government's digital philosophy that dictated that a minority of households would have their television sets switched off should they be unable to afford to convert to digital. Instead he described the social implications of digital for the deaf, the housebound, flexible workers and the elderly and promised that 'we've told the broadcasters that the digital revolution in television must work for everyone'.[113] Once again, no mention was made of the penalties commercial broadcasters would incur should they fail to live up to this aim nor was there a clarification of the incentives for the industry to 'work for everyone', including the poorest households. New Labour's faith in the market allows them to articulate a vision of digital in which all groups would find a range of benefits but one where entry is guaranteed only to those who can afford to pay.

The government's digital strategy started to fall apart in 2001. In June, Charles Allen, the chief executive of Granada, wrote to Tony Blair pleading for the prime minister to introduce legislation allowing a merger between Granada and Carlton in order to rescue an ailing ONdigital. Frustrated by the government's indecision over the relaxation of cross-media ownership rules, Allen was convinced that a merger was necessary in order to maintain any degree of investor confidence in ONdigital. According to the *Guardian*, under the headline 'Is Digital a Dead Dog?', the letter

> conceded that ONdigital was in trouble, portraying the company as a business under siege both from foreign predators and its own investors … The threat to government was clear: 'Help us to get what we want or else your vision for a digital Britain could soon run out.'[114]

The 'pro-competitive' way in which the government had introduced digital television meant that the government was unwilling to intervene and rescue OnDigital for fear of showing that it favoured particular technologies or particular companies. Buffeted by increasing 'churn' and declining growth rates and undermined by a series of poor commercial decisions, most notably paying £315m for the rights to transmit non-Premier League soccer for three years, the newly rebranded ITV Digital stuttered along throughout 2001, eventually closing down at the end of April 2002.

The government, however, remains upbeat about the prospects for a digital future and boasts that the UK 'leads the world in digital television. Our broadcasters, manufacturers and retailers have put the UK at the forefront of this revolution. In just three years they have rolled out digital TV to one in three homes.'[115] The problem for the government is that there is no indication that this figure is going to increase enough to reach the levels necessary for switching off analogue broadcasts. Research commissioned by the DCMS in June 2001 showed that only 55 per cent of households would have digital television by 2006 and that a further 15 per cent indicated that they would never 'go digital'. This latter group, the report argued, was likely to be disproportionately composed of women, the elderly and the poor – precisely the groups that Smith argued would benefit from the digital revolution.[116] Furthermore, the remaining 30 per cent of the population were either unconvinced of the need for or put off by the cost of digital television and indicated that they were unlikely to get digital TV in the near future.[117] The government's reliance on market structures to develop digital platforms has led to massive uncertainty in the industry and resounding indifference in the majority of television households.

Defending public service broadcasting

In the light of a more commercial broadcasting environment, the role of public service broadcasting in providing an oasis of non-commercial aspirations would seem to be particularly important. New Labour's culture ministers have been enthusiastic supporters of this proposition. Attacking the notion that public service is dead, Chris Smith argued that it was more vital than ever: '[i]n an era of multiplying services and an ever tighter squeeze of budgets, quality is under unremitting pressure and it is part of the function of public service broadcasting to set and sustain benchmarks for quality'.[118] His successor, Tessa Jowell, appointed in a Cabinet reshuffle after the 2001 election, has promised to safeguard the licence fee for the immediate future, stating that '[i]t is our job to create the space in the digital environment for PSB and the BBC to continue to flourish, but to do so alongside a vibrant market'.[119] The government's aim, therefore, is vigorously to commercialize the broadcasting system at the same time as championing those institutions which are not solely driven by market considerations. One example of this broadcasting 'third way' is the government's reluctance, so far, to privatize the highly successful, advertising-funded Channel 4. Indeed, in 1998, Smith strengthened its public service remit and forced it to promise to commission more original programmes and to broadcast fewer repeats. Its licence was revised to clarify its public service status and to formalize its commitment to 'experiment, innovation, originality and diversity'.[120] For some, Channel 4 is a testament to the possibility of public service objectives being met through market mechanisms; for others, however, Channel 4 today is a testament only to consumerism and the power of marketing. Anthony Smith, one of its first board members, argues that the channel has lost its distinctive experimental vision and, in its obsession with youth-oriented programmes, 'doesn't seem to have a mission to be anything other than another television channel'.[121]

Of course, the key example of any government's support for public service broadcasting lies in its relationship to the BBC. While Gerald Kaufman, the Labour chair of the Heritage Select Committee, welcomed Labour's election victory as an opportunity to privatize the BBC,[122] the government has shown no such interest and has placed the future of the BBC at the heart of its broadcasting policy. This is not to say that the government's relationship with the Corporation has been particularly warm. In August 1997, Labour accused the editor of *The World at One*, Kevin Marsh, of waging a vendetta against the government for concentrating on Peter Mandelson's news management techniques. In December of that year the party's chief media spokesperson threatened to sever all contacts with the influential *Today* programme after a particularly bruising interview between one of its presenters and the social security minister.

However, just as Harold Wilson had regularly fallen out with the BBC in the 1960s before subsequently agreeing to licence fee increases, in October 1998 Chris Smith extended the licence fee until at least 2006 and set up a committee to examine the funding of the BBC until that time. The government was motivated by its determination to build up large multimedia companies to compete on the global stage and the BBC was the UK's best-known broadcasting 'brand'. With the Corporation demanding a substantial rise in its revenue to fund new digital channels, Smith turned to Gavyn Davies to head the committee. As a multimillionaire partner at the investment bank Goldman Sachs, Davies was perhaps not the most obvious choice to consider the future funding of a public service broadcaster. As a personal friend of both Tony Blair and Gordon Brown and a supporter of New Labour's economic policies, he was at least a reliable person to turn to.[123]

It soon became clear that the committee was considering the introduction of a supplementary licence fee for digital households, dubbed the 'digital levy', of between £30 and £40 a year,[124] to provide the BBC with the extra revenue it had requested. This suggestion was greeted with horror, largely by commercial broadcasters like BSkyB, Carlton and Granada who had already invested heavily in digital television. These broadcasters launched a vigorous lobbying campaign against the levy, claiming that it would deter the take-up of digital services and undermine the government's plans for analogue switch-off.

The committee's report was published in August 1999 and called for a lower than expected digital levy of £24 a year in order to placate the commercial lobby. It also proposed to maintain the existing index-linked licence fee and to privatize some of the Corporation's activities.[125] This was a neat package that fitted with New Labour ideology: support for a public service, a partial sell-off of public assets to demonstrate its commitment to efficiency, together with the shouldering of an extra burden by the minority of viewers who could afford to do so. The former minister Peter Mandelson supported the levy because it would mean that 'only those with digital televisions will pay for the costs of new digital services, rather than as now the poor subsidising the services received by those able to afford digital'.[126] Although this matched the language used by the Wilson government in arguing for a levy for colour television back in the 'white heat' of the 1960s[127] it was not enough to satisfy the commercial digital broadcasters who resumed their campaign to abolish the levy entirely. BSkyB, in particular, indicated that it would only drop its opposition if the government put pressure on the BBC to scrap its dedicated news channel, News 24, perceived as a rival to the Sky News channel.

By September, the *Financial Times* was able to reveal that Tony Blair was keen on the digital levy but concerned about the amount of opposition it had generated and was therefore considering alternatives including, according to one Whitehall adviser, advertising:

> Just raising the licence fee is less politically attractive even than the digital licence fee. If Number 10 decides that the digital licence fee is something the government shouldn't go for because of the impact on digital, it will have to look at alternatives, namely advertising on [the BBC's] digital channels or advertising on the main BBC channels.[128]

This marked a return of an old solution to an old problem. As with Tony Benn in the 1960s and with Margaret Thatcher in the 1980s, leading politicians were prepared to supplement the licence fee with a dose of advertising, partly because of an unwillingness to be seen as raising taxes. Indeed, even when Chris Smith suggested the compromise of a reduced digital levy combined with a small rise in the analogue licence fee, this was countered by Treasury officials 'wary of setting a precedent by reopening a five year settlement'.[129]

James Purnell, former media policy adviser at the Number 10 Policy Unit, insists that 'there wasn't actually a sort of pitched battle around the DTI and the DCMS and that all were agreed on the importance of the BBC's role in a multimedia future'.[130] This analysis appears to fly in the face of splits that had already developed. The prime minister initially supported the levy but was prepared to contemplate alternatives in order to pacify BSkyB and ITV; the Treasury was against the idea of any tax-raising schemes; the DTI was anxious not to undermine analogue switch-off; Smith at the DCMS was keen to keep all sides happy.

The tortuous negotiations were finally concluded in February 2000 when the government announced that there would be no digital levy but instead that the licence fee would increase by Retail Price Index (RPI) plus 1.5 per cent until 2006/07, giving the BBC an extra £200m a year to fund new digital television and radio channels. For the BBC, this generous deal came with a few strings attached: the government was to review the future of News 24, as BSkyB had demanded, while the Corporation would be expected to make over £1 billion in efficiency savings and to develop more public–private partnerships. The emphasis of this 'tough love' package was very much on efficiency savings, cutting red tape and increasing commercial competitiveness. According to a headline in the *Financial Times*, the 'Private Sector is a TV Winner in BBC Funding Deal'.[131] David Elstein, the chief executive of Channel 5, claimed that '[t]his is a big win for the commercial boys. There's no digital levy, limited BBC expansion, tighter control of BBC activities and no premium channels. It's a small win for the BBC. The only loser as usual is the poor, honest, single-set, non-digital licence payers.'[132] Given the government's vocal support for the BBC brand in the digital age, it would have been counter-productive to award anything other than a significant increase, but what appeared to be more important during the course of the negotiations was the government's desire to placate commercial interests in the broadcasting industry. 'This is a very political settlement', one broadcasting executive commented. 'It gives Sky and Rupert Murdoch what they wanted. It gives the BBC more money. And it tightens the screws on the BBC in terms of efficiency and transparency.'[133]

Ironically, the settlement initially satisfied neither the BBC (whose chair 'wore a brave face as he "welcomed" the government's statements on the corporation's future funding')[134] nor Rupert Murdoch. While praising the retreat from the digital levy, the *Sun* complained about the huge amounts of money being extorted by the BBC and that 'of course, it isn't the government's money to give away in the first place – it's YOURS'.[135] The fact is that the settlement amounted to an indirect tax rise which, given the regressive nature of the licence fee, would hit the poor the hardest. The government's commitment to a universal and inclusive public service broadcasting and its enthusiasm for the BBC to represent Britain in the digital revolution was therefore to be funded not by income tax receipts nor by the billions of pounds raised by the auction of radio spectrum, but from the pockets of those perhaps least able to afford it.

Promoting exports

One of the most consistent themes of ministers' statements on contemporary broadcasting concerns the need to take advantage of the popularity of the English language and to increase the exports of UK television output. This approach was first taken up in the early 1990s when Conservative government thinking 'had been stimulated by a sudden realisation that the country's pre-eminence in the cultural industries offered the UK tremendous export opportunities in a rapidly expanding international market'.[136] Michael Heseltine at the DTI and Peter Brooke at the DNH embraced the possibilities of an export-led strategy and incorporated this line of thinking into the government's 1994 white paper on the BBC, optimistically titled *Serving the Nation, Competing World-wide*.[137]

New Labour politicians followed up the vision of increased television exports with particular enthusiasm. In 1995, Tony Blair announced to Labour's conference that Britain has 'such huge advantages. Some of the finest telecommunications companies in the world. World leaders in broadcasting. The world's first language, English. Together, they could put us years ahead in education and technology and business.'[138] The following year, Peter Mandelson wrote that what he had learned from his visit to the Far East was that '[s]preading the word is Britain's secret weapon. Expanding the activities of the BBC and the British Council around the world … are essential economic policies for Britain.'[139] Globalization developments together with the increased saliency of television as a cultural force had moved broadcasting from the domestic to the international stage.

The most successful British exponent of global television at the time was long-standing Labour supporter and backer of Tony Blair, Greg Dyke, the then chief executive of Pearson TV and current director general of the BBC. According to Dyke, 'in every industry the globalisation concept is happening … The trick is can you globalise programming and make it local? You own a load of formats, you make them in different countries, you take them from one to another.'[140] The consequence of this conception of globalization was that Pearson owned three versions of *Family Feud* in Indonesia and controlled the rights to *Neighbours* across the world.

Once in office, Chris Smith and his civil servants at the DCMS eagerly adopted this approach and prioritized exports on the policy agenda. For Harry Reeves, the head of general broadcasting policy in 1997, there appeared to be no contradiction between the demands of the UK audience and the potential for increasing sales internationally.

> It [global television] is very high on the list of policy objectives. We're in one of those situations where it's move on or die … There is a widespread perception that there is a conflict between the cultural objectives and the economic objectives and to a degree there is. But I don't think that it has ever been demonstrated that the kind of [requirements for] quality and variety that is placed on broadcasters necessarily impairs their competitiveness in international markets.[141]

His colleague, Paul Heron, head of the DCMS' public service broadcasting branch, also saw no problem with the BBC following the guidelines laid down in *Serving the Nation, Competing World-wide*. 'There are great opportunities, great markets … extra revenue for the BBC which goes into quality public service broadcasting. The government would certainly not want to curtail the BBC's commercial activities … I don't see any contradiction [between public service and commercial activities].'[142] The government therefore encouraged the activities of the BBC's commercial arm, BBC Worldwide, and welcomed its commercial partnerships with companies like Flextech and the Discovery Channel, arguing that international sales could only benefit domestic viewers.

Smith at the time was relatively sanguine about the UK's position in the international market: 'Britain is the second biggest exporter of television programming in the world. We are ahead of the game in what is a rapidly growing market of great cultural and commercial significance.'[143] Other Labour supporters in the television industry were more impatient. The then independent producer Waheed Alli, recently made into a life peer by Tony Blair, argued that '[w]e focus on domestic market share when we should be focusing on global market share as a group of television companies'.[144] The DCMS therefore commissioned a piece of research to quantify the UK's share of the export market and to suggest if there was room for improvement. The report, *Building a Global Audience: British Television in Overseas Markets*, was co-written by David Graham, a former member of the free-market think-tank the Institute of Economic Affairs, and backed by the sales arms of some of the UK's leading broadcasters like Carlton, Pearson, Granada and the BBC.

The survey made for some grim reading. It found that British television was *not* perceived as the best in the world, that it had a relatively small share of the global export market and that the UK had a substantial trade deficit in television of some £272m in 1997.[145] This was partly because while UK programmes 'are praised by international executives for their high production values, quirky sense of humour, and high standards of acting … our drama is too dark; too slow; unattractive; too gritty or socio-political'.[146] The report also found that the length of programmes or series that were designed for the UK market was often too short for the international market and that the more popular genres abroad, like TV movies and the mini-series, were not ones produced in any quantity in the UK. The logic was that an emphasis on gritty dramas relevant to a UK audience should be replaced by output that is more internationally packageable: *Benny Hill, Mr Bean, Teletubbies, Thomas the Tank Engine, Survival* and *Don't Forget Your Toothbrush* were all mentioned as successful exports.

The recommendations of *Building a Global Audience* were particularly interesting and concentrated on one central issue: that the 'Government and regulators should consider whether domestic regulation hinders export performance'.[147] The report heartily suggested that any rights agreements with creative staff that might hinder the sale of programmes abroad should be renegotiated and that domestic scheduling patterns might be changed to suit international markets. The report was littered with hints that, despite the optimism of DCMS civil servants, 'excessive regulation can leave catalogues of material that are incompatible with overseas audiences'[148] and concluded that 'it is important to recognise that domestic regulation and export performance are in tension, if not in conflict … Another of our recommendations is that the Government and regulators consider this tension carefully. It may be constraining the UK's export potential.'[149]

This invitation to consider whether domestic regulation was under-mining international sales was eagerly received by a government engaged in its own discussions about whether to maintain the existing regulatory arrangements. Chris Smith immediately set up a creative industries taskforce panel to consider the recommendations made in *Building a Global Audience*. The panel comprised of representatives from the commercial broadcasting and independent production sectors as well as the ITC and the British Television Distributors Association. After only four months of discussion, the taskforce produced its own report that firmly rejected the line of thinking adopted by David Graham. Its key findings were that 'the UK is performing well in television exports' and that '[w]e are firmly in the number two position, as we would expect and hope'.[150] Just as pertinently, it rejected any idea that domestic regulation should be loosened to allow for increased sales abroad:

> Developing the international business is important for the industry, but serving the UK audience is essential. Dramatic modification to the style of UK programming is not, therefore, a realistic aim. It is not just the UK that prefers its own programmes – this is true across all territories. Local productions consistently attract the highest ratings.[151]

Indeed, according to panel member Sarah Thane of the ITC, the whole discussion of regulation as an impediment to exports 'was the dog that didn't bark. It basically became very clear to people on the taskforce that it was a non-issue.'[152] For the panel, the strength of UK television was precisely its orientation on domestic audiences and domestic issues and so it would simply not be possible to develop formats with a global appeal without undermining the domestic production base. Another non-issue was the notion, repeated by the government, that UK television was failing to take advantage of the popularity of the English language. Again, Thane disputes this:

> I felt quite strongly that we may use the same language but the *lingua franca* of television worldwide is American not English. All those cultural references, the language, the phraseology … is Disney English. We were kind of flagellating ourselves about not exploiting the English language fully when it's much more complex than that.[153]

To what extent is New Labour justified in its concentration on the economic importance of television exports given these criticisms from one of its own committees? First, the BBC's global strategy, backed by the government, has hardly transformed its financial base. Revenue from commercial activities outside Britain has risen from £44m in 1990 to £218m in 2001, up from 3 per cent of total revenue to 5.7 per cent today.[154] The remaining 94.3 per cent of income continues to derive either from the licence fee or commercial revenue *inside* Britain. The domestic audience is still the economic foundation of the BBC and an obsession with export sales is likely to compromise any remaining commitment to provide a diverse and relevant range of programming in the UK.[155] The initiative resembles elements of the 'Cool Britannia' strategy of rebranding the UK as a dynamic, cutting-edge creative economy more than an informed analysis of the complex nature of international broadcasting. According to Sarah Thane,

> I don't want to sound pejorative about people who are highly intelligent … But what I got a sense of was that there was a lot of activity going on in all sorts of government, particularly the DTI and the Treasury, showing Britain as a very entrepreneurial, forward-looking sort of place and that the DCMS wanted a slice of that. I take my hat off to Chris Smith and others for engendering a sense of the economic power and importance of the creative industries … But I'm saying that all he needed to do was just test whether our television industry was batting as effectively as it could do.[156]

New Labour's enthusiasm for the expansion of international trade in television appears, therefore, to be both undiminished and unwarranted.

A balance sheet

What achievements in television policy can New Labour point to since winning office? According to two *Guardian* journalists reflecting on the government's record on television in 2001, 'Labour had no general ideas worth the mention, more a set of *ad hoc* responses to rapidly changing circumstances.'[157] This underestimates the extent to which the government did, in fact, pursue a fairly consistent approach to policy-making. New Labour adopted the Conservatives' legislative approach to digital broadcasting and then proposed an ambitious timetable for analogue switch-off that was driven more by consideration of the prize to be gained for the Treasury than by the perceived needs or demands of viewers. It has maintained 'regulatory stability' but has shifted the balance of power towards the DTI and competition authorities and has marginalized traditional concerns about the dangers of media concentration. In championing the importance of public service broadcasting in the multi-channel age, the government has insisted any additional income must be matched by efficiency savings and commercial revenue and it has encouraged strategies for increasing television exports when the evidence points to the fact that this can only be done at the expense of the UK viewer.

In all of this, New Labour has followed the policy framework and ideological parameters of the previous government. The process of commercialization, developed under the Conservatives, has been consolidated and accelerated under the present administration so that commercial success and economic efficiency have become the 'benchmarks' of contemporary broadcasting, alongside which all other considerations are to be judged. A recent example of this industrial conception of broadcasting is the location in Labour's 2001 election manifesto of television policy in the section on productivity rather than in the section on culture.[158]

To what extent is New Labour's approach distinct from that of its Tory predecessors? For Sarah Thane of the commercial television regulator, the ITC, 'Labour governments [including the current one] tend to be more interventionist, tend to want to manage the process with regulators and with key players in a slightly greater way than Conservatives who will set a framework and broadly let you get on.'[159] The imprint of New Labour has found its way into a whole series of television-related issues that would ordinarily be the preserve of the regulators, from the scheduling of the former *News at Ten* to the government's plan for soap operas to be more 'on message'.[160] New Labour has also stressed the need for more transparency and accountability within public (though of course not private) broadcasting organizations and has advertised vacancies for BBC governors and ITC members. Indeed, the government has now appointed two black BBC governors and the average age of the board has fallen from 59 in 1995 to 55 today as part of New Labour's determination to embrace more representative institutions.[161]

Both examples, however, point to another development: the increased *politicization* of media policy. The 'modernization' of the appointments process has led to criticisms similar to those made against the Conservatives in the 1980s when Tory supporters were packed onto the BBC board. In 1998, the filmmaker Lord Puttnam was rejected by the selection panel in favour of the apparently more politically acceptable Baroness Young. The *Guardian* wondered 'whether the process is an improvement on the old one' and quoted a BBC insider asking whether the changes 'really made the system more open, or simply created a different sort of charmed circle'.[162] Accusations of political intervention are increasingly common. According to the Campaign for Press and Broadcasting Freedom, '[t]he Blair/Murdoch connection ensures that media policy is kept under careful scrutiny from Downing Street and it is rumoured that a section on cross media ownership was withdrawn from the Government's Green Paper on Convergence'.[163]

Whatever the truth of these accusations, there is a lingering perception that the government is beholden to its media allies, in particular to Rupert Murdoch, for their role in supporting the New Labour project. When Tony Blair intervened on behalf of Murdoch in 1998 and telephoned the Italian prime minister to recommend to him Murdoch's acquisition of an Italian television station, Downing Street justified this as Blair speaking up on behalf of British business. The *Financial Times* reported one Murdoch aide as saying that 'you'd have thought Blair would have wanted to avoid the faintest suggestion of cronyism. Fortunately for us it doesn't seem to bother him.'[164] Blair has certainly been loyal to his wealthy backers from the television industry, appointing Lord Hollick as a special adviser at the DTI and Granada TV's Gerry Robinson as chair of the Arts Council. The former head of Pearson Television, Greg Dyke, who described global television as a 'financial buy. You do it for money. This is a business not a cultural pursuit'[165] was asked to chair the NHS taskforce before being appointed as director general of the BBC in 1999.

Given all this activity, it is clear that New Labour has demonstrated its eagerness to develop close relations with corporate interests in the media. Leading figures in the television industry are no longer feared by the Labour Party but are embraced and nurtured. New Labour in government may have followed in the steps of the previous administration but it has demonstrated an 'activist' stance that suggests that Curran's formulation of the party's innately conservative approach to television policy may be obsolete. This should not, however, suggest that New Labour has produced any real innovations in the field but simply that television has moved closer to the core of Labour's policy agenda and that New Labour is determined to intensify the processes of deregulation and marketization launched by the Tories. As we enter the age of multi-channel television and digital convergence, New Labour's greatest achievement in the field of television may be that it is increasingly the home of media millionaires. MAI's Lord Hollick, Carlton's Lord Alli, the BBC's Greg Dyke and Granada's Gerry Robinson are all examples of the fact that there is no contradiction today – if there ever was one

– between being a millionaire television executive and being a Labour supporter.

NOTES

1. A. Wright and M. Carter, *The People's Party: The History of the Labour Party* (London: Thames & Hudson, 1997), p. 169.
2. The new statement of aims supported a 'dynamic economy, serving the public interest, in which the enterprise of the market and the rigour of competition are joined with the forces of partnership and co-operation, to produce the wealth the country needs'. See T. Jones, *Remaking the Labour Party: From Gaitskell to Blair* (London: Routledge, 1996), p. 144.
3. P. Mandelson and R. Liddle, *The Blair Revolution: Can Labour Deliver?* (London: Faber & Faber, 1996), p. 22.
4. M. Freeden, 'The Ideology of New Labour', *Political Quarterly*, 70, 1 (1999), p. 44.
5. G. Brown, *Fair Is Efficient: A Socialist Agenda for Fairness*, Fabian Pamphlet 563 (London: Fabian Society, 1994), p. 1.
6. T. Blair, *New Britain: My Vision of a Young Country* (London: Fourth Estate, 1996), p. 118.
7. Ibid., pp. 118–19.
8. Labour Party, *Making Britain's Future* (London: Labour Party, 1995), p. 3.
9. L. Panitch and C. Leys, *The End of Parliamentary Socialism: From New Left to New Labour* (London: Verso, 1997), p. 234.
10. D. Butler and D. Kavanagh, *The British General Election of 1997* (London: Macmillan, 1997), p. 62.
11. Quoted in M. Linton, *Was It The Sun Wot Won It?* (Oxford: Oxford University Press, 1995), p. 5.
12. Ibid., p. 38.
13. R. Corbett, interview with the author, 2 December 1999.
14. D. McKie, 'Swingers, Clingers, Waverers, Quaverers: The Tabloid Press in the 1997 General Election', in I. Crewe, B. Gosschalk and J. Bartle (eds), *Political Communication: Why Labour Won the General Election of 1997* (London: Frank Cass, 1998), p. 117.
15. Blair, *New Britain*, pp. 203–14.
16. Ibid., p. 205.
17. Quoted in D. Draper, *Blair's Hundred Days* (London: Faber & Faber, 1997), p. 129.
18. Butler and Kavanagh, *British General Election*, pp. 252–3
19. P. Anderson and N. Mann, *Safety First: The Making of New Labour* (London: Granta, 1997), p. 386.
20. P. Goodwin, *Television under the Tories: Broadcasting Policy, 1979–1997* (London: BFI, 1998), p. 124.
21. Labour Party, *Putting the Citizen at the Centre of British Broadcasting: A Labour Party Consultation Document* (London: Labour Party, 1993).
22. Ibid., p. 2.
23. Ibid., p. 9.
24. A. Clwyd, e-mail communication to the author, received 22 March 2000.
25. A. Culf, 'Clwyd Attacks Tory Line on Broadcasting', *Guardian*, 27 September 1993, p. 6.
26. Granada bought London Weekend Television for £600m while Carlton bought Central for £758m.
27. A. Culf, 'Limit on Press Stakes in ITV may be Lifted', *Guardian*, 4 January 1994, p. 4.
28. *Broadcast*, 'Hollick Attacks Media Controls, 1 July 1994, p. 5.
29. T. O'Malley, interview with the author, 30 November 1999.
30. P. Goodwin, 'Labouring under a Misapprehension', *Broadcast*, 8 July 1994, p. 18.
31. M. Jempson, e-mail communication to the author, received 23 March 2000.
32. R. Collins, interview with the author, 24 February 2000.
33. J. Purnell, interview with the author, 13 March 2000.
34. R. Collins and C. Murroni, *New Media: New Policies* (Cambridge: Polity, 1996), p. 1.

35. Ibid., p. 170.
36. Ibid., p. 70.
37. Ibid., p. 75.
38. Collins, interview.
39. T. Burke, contribution to debate on media ownership, *Report of the 126th Annual Trades Union Congress* (London: TUC, 1994), p. 390.
40. DNH, *Media Ownership: The Government's Proposals*, white paper, Cm 2872 (London: HMSO, 1995).
41. Goodwin, *Television*, pp. 147–8.
42. G. Allen, 'Labour: Fine Tuning will be Crucial', *Free Press*, 87, July–August 1995, p. 3.
43. Moonie, quoted in M. Prescott and N. Hellen, 'Blair to Oppose Tighter Rules on Media Ownership', *Sunday Times*, 7 April 1996, p. 2.
44. HoC Debates, 21 May, 1996, col. 412.
45. Quoted in R. Smithers, 'Labour's Media "U-turn" Mocked', *Guardian*, 17 April 1996.
46. P. Foot, 'Sour Note, Moonie Tune', *Guardian*, 15 April 1996.
47. See Goodwin, *Television*, pp. 141–3.
48. Labour Party, *Communicating Britain's Future* (*CBF*) (London: Labour Party, 1995).
49. *CBF* was launched at the second 21st Century Communications conference with very much the same corporate audience as the previous year's event. According to the Campaign for Press and Broadcasting Freedom, the conference 'was a sort of meeting for the faithful. The CPBF and the media unions received no publicity about the event and had to make a direct approach to attend and have a stall'. See T. O'Malley, 'Market Farces', *Free Press*, 88, September/October 1995, p. 3.
50. Labour Party, *CBF*, p. 3.
51. In 1994, the Conservative government had prevented BT from offering broadcast entertainment services on its network in order to maintain competition in the communications infrastructure and to protect the investment of the cable companies.
52. Headlines about the superhighway have long been superseded by concerns about the slow rate of broadband take-up in the UK. As of February 2002, 46 per cent of the UK's 24 million homes were connected to the Internet while broadband (by the end of June 2002) had a total 709,000 end users, including the public and private sector as well as private individuals. See Oftel, *Internet and Broadband Brief*, July 2002, available at http://www.oftel.org.uk/publications/internet/internet_brief/broad0702.htm (accessed 14 July 2002).
53. Labour Party, *CBF*, p. 8.
54. Ibid., p. 9.
55. C. Smith, interview with the author, 13 December 1996.
56. L. Moonie, interview with the author, 13 December 1996.
57. Ibid.
58. HoC Debates, 16 April 1996, col. 605.
59. Labour Party, *Create the Future: A Strategy for Cultural Policy, Arts and the Creative Economy* (London: Labour Party, 1997), p. 8.
60. Ibid., p. 11.
61. Ibid., p. 8.
62. Ibid., p. 11.
63. Labour Party, *New Labour: Because Britain Deserves Better*, election manifesto (London: Labour Party, 1997).
64. The full paragraph reads as follows: 'Labour aims for a thriving, diverse media industry, combining commercial success and public service. We will ensure that the BBC continues to be a flagship for British creativity and public service broadcasting, but we believe that the combination of public and private sectors in competition is a key spur to innovation and high standards. The regulatory framework for media and broadcasting should reflect the realities of a far more open and competitive economy, and enormous technological advance, for example with digital television. Labour will balance sensible rules, fair regulation and international competition, so maintaining quality and diversity for the benefit of viewers.' Ibid., p. 31.
65. M. Fisher, interview with the author, 8 December 1999.
66. T. Blair, *The Third Way: New Politics for the New Century*, Fabian Pamphlet 588 (London: Fabian Society, 1998), p. 1.
67. Ibid., p. 4. Perhaps the clearest exposition of 'third way' politics is A. Giddens, *The Third*

Way (Cambridge, Polity, 1998) critiqued by A. Callinicos, *Against the Third Way* (Cambridge: Polity, 2001).

68. Freeden, 'The Ideology of New Labour'.
69. Blair, *The Third Way*, p. 7.
70. C. Leadbetter, *Living on Thin Air* (London: Viking, 1999).
71. Blair, *The Third Way*, p. 8. For a critique of these notions of the 'weightless', 'new' and 'knowledge' economies, see U. Huws, 'Material World: The Myth of the Weightless Economy', in L. Panitch and C. Leys (eds), *The Socialist Register 1999* (Rendlesham: Merlin Press, 1999), pp. 29–55.
72. C. Smith, *Creative Britain* (London: Faber & Faber, 1998), p. 31.
73. Ibid.
74. See A. Rawnsley, *Servants of the People: The Inside Story of New Labour* (London: Penguin, 2001), pp. 89–105 for details of the Ecclestone affair and P. Toynbee and D. Walker, *Did Things Get Better? An Audit of Labour's Successes and Failures* (London: Penguin, 2001) for an overall analysis of New Labour's first period in office.
75. Rawnsley, *Servants*, p. 506.
76. Quoted in A. Thorncroft, 'Old Heritage Ministry Sports Cultured Name', *Financial Times*, 15 July 1997.
77. Purnell, interview.
78. European Commission, *Green Paper on the Convergence of the Telecommunications, Media and Information Technology Sectors, and the Implications for Regulation: Towards an Information Society Approach*, Com (97) 623 (Brussels: European Commission, 1997).
79. House of Commons Select Committee on Culture, Media and Sport, 4th report, *The Multi-Media Revolution*, HC 520-I (London: House of Commons, 1998), para. 157.
80. Ibid., para. 158.
81. DCMS/DTI, *Government Response to 'The Multimedia Revolution'*, available at http://www.culture.gov.uk/MEDREV.HTM (London: DCMS/DTI, 1998) (accessed 8 February 2000), para. xx.
82. DCMS/DTI, Regulating *Communications: Approaching Convergence in the Information Age*, green paper, CM4022 (London: DCMS/DTI, 1998).
83. Ibid, p. 10.
84. Ibid., p. 23.
85. Ibid., p. 24.
86. DCMS/DTI, *Regulating Communications: The Way Ahead. Results of the Consultation on the Convergence Green Paper* (London: DCMS/DTI, 1999), para. 1.19.
87. Ibid., para. 2.2.
88. Ibid., para. 3.12.
89. Ibid., para. 3.10.
90. DCMS/DTI, *A New Future for Communications*, white paper (London: DCMS/DTI, 2000).
91. Ibid., p. 10.
92. Trade secretary Stephen Byers, DTI press release. 'Government Gives Green Light to Communications Revolution', P/2000/836, 12 December 2000.
93. J. Pilger, 'Speak Up!', *Free Press*, 121, March–April 2001, p. 4.
94. DCMS/DTI, *Regulating Communications*, 1998, p. 14.
95. House of Commons Select Committee on Culture, Media and Sport, 4th report, *The Multi-Media Revolution*, para. 81 – emphasis added.
96. DCMS/DTI, *Regulating Communications*, 1998, p. 16.
97. Ibid., p. 18.
98. DCMS/DTI, *Regulating Communications*, 1999, para 1.1.
99. Purnell, interview.
100. O. Morgan, 'Did Blair Order Byers' Block?' *Observer*, 21 November 1999.
101. See D. Wighton, 'Minister Rekindles Row over Television Mergers', *Financial Times*, 17 November 1999.
102. DCMS, *Consultation on Media Ownership Rules* (London: DCMS, 2001), p. 10.
103. Ibid., p. 11.
104. The situation has been further clarified with the publication in May 2002 of a heavily deregulatory draft communications bill (http://www.communicationsbill.gov.uk). While promising to maintain the '20% rule' (that prevents the largest newspaper groups from buying into ITV), the bill also allows for the creation of a single ITV, abolishes restrictions

on foreign ownership of commercial television in the UK and, most controversially, sanctions the possibility of Murdoch's BSkyB buying the terrestrial service Channel 5. According to *Guardian* commentator Steven Barnett:

> Rupert will have his slice of British terrestrial television after all – and at the invitation of a Labour government. Either the prime minister is more desperate than we thought to win his referendum on the euro, or Number 10 simply doesn't grasp the inevitable consequence of its proposed relaxation of ownership laws (or maybe it no longer cares). The government's position is not only illogical but leaves in tatters its proclaimed commitment to pluralism.

S. Barnett, 'One Man, One Media?', 8 May 2002, available at http://media.guardian.co.uk/whitepaper/story/0,7521,711822,00.html (accessed 8 July 2002).

105. C. Smith, 'Beyond 2000: Out of Control?', a speech to the 1997 Royal Television Society convention, *Television*, October 1997, p. 10.
106. C. Smith, speech to the 1998 Royal Television Society convention, 14 October 1998, available at http://www.culture.gov.uk/BROAD.htm (accessed 8 February 2000).
107. E. Bell, 'So You Didn't See the Footie or the Golf. Blame this Man … ', *Observer*, 3 October 1999.
108. Purnell, interview.
109. C. Smith, 'The Big Switch', speech to the 1999 Royal Television Society convention, *Television*, October 1999, p. 9.
110. HoC Debates, 29 October 1999, col. 1210.
111. H. Reeves, interview with the author, 17 December 1997.
112. The government earned £22.48 billion in April 2000 from the auction of third-generation (3G) mobile phone licences.
113. C. Smith, speech to 1999 Labour conference, 1 October 1999.
114. M. Wells and D. Teather, 'Is Digital a Dead Dog?', *Guardian*, 2 July 2001, Media section, p. 2.
115. DCMS/DTI, 'Digital Television Action Plan: The Government's Vision', available at http://www.digitaltelevision.gov.uk/ministers_fwd.html (accessed 9 July 2002).
116. MORI, *Digital Television 2001*, Research Study Conducted for the Department for Culture, Media and Sport (London: DCMS, 2001), p. 3.
117. Ibid.
118. Smith, *Creative Britain*, p. 8.
119. T. Jowell, 'Public Service Broadcasting in the Digital Age and the New BBC Services', speech to the Royal Television Society convention, 13 September 2001.
120. ITC, 'Public Consultation Launched on Revision to Channel 4 Licence', press release 85/97, 23 October 1997.
121. Quoted in A. Beckett, 'Growing Pains', *Guardian*, 23 March 2000.
122. G. Kaufman, 'Now it's Time to Privatise the BBC', *Daily Mail*, 8 May 1997.
123. See B. Laurance, 'Sachs 'n' Bucks 'n' Quiet Control', *Observer*, 21 March 1999, p. 27.
124. See W. Hutton, 'Money, or the Lack of it, is the Root of All the BBC's Evils', *Observer*, 21 March 1999, p. 30.
125. G. Davies (chair), *The Future Funding of the BBC*, Report of the Independent Review Panel (London: DCMS, 1999).
126. Quoted in BBC, 'Mandelson Backs Digital TV Licence', 26 July 1999, available at http://news.bbc.co.uk/hi/english/uk_politics/newsid_404000/404524.stm (accessed 16 February 2000).
127. 'It is the Government's view that the cost of colour programmes, which are likely at the outset to be available only to a small minority of viewers because of the cost of receivers, should not fall upon viewers in general. Accordingly a supplementary licence of £5 [a 100 per cent increase] will be required from those equipped to receive colour programmes.' See white paper, *Broadcasting*, Cmnd. 3169 (London: HMSO, 1966), p. 6.
128. Quoted in C. Newman, 'Blair May Revive BBC Adverts Plan', *Financial Times*, 24 September 1999.
129. C. Newman, 'Government Considers Two-tier TV Licence Fee', *Financial Times*, 6 January 2000, p. 2.
130. Purnell, interview.
131. J. Harding, 'Private Sector is a TV Winner in BBC Funding Deal', *Financial Times*, 22 February 2000, p. 3.
132. Quoted in 'Upping the Auntie', *Broadcast*, 25 February 2000, p. 5.

133. Quoted in Harding, 'Private Sector is a TV Winner'.
134. J. Gibson, 'Blow for BBC Means Dyke Must Get Tough', *Guardian*, 22 February 2000, p. 6.
135. *Sun*, 'Price too High for the BBC-fee', 22 February 2000, p. 8.
136. S. Barnett and A. Curry, *The Battle for the BBC* (London: Aurum Press, 1994), p. 221.
137. DNH, *The Future of the BBC: Serving the Nation, Competing World-wide*, white paper, Cm. 2621 (London: HMSO, 1994).
138. T. Blair, speech to Labour conference, 3 October 1995.
139. P. Mandelson, 'Lessons for Labour from Asia', *Financial Times*, 22 April 1996.
140. Quoted in M. Baker, 'Dyke: A Long-Running TV Drama', *Broadcast*, 21 November 1997, p. 16.
141. Reeves, interview.
142. P. Heron, interview with the author, 17 December 1997.
143. Smith, *Creative Britain*, p. 101.
144. Quoted in 'We Can't Wait Any Longer to Map the Digital Landscape', media policy roundtable, *New Statesman*, 3 April 1998, p. 42.
145. D. Graham and Associates, *Building a Global Audience: British Television in Overseas Markets* (London: DCMS, 1999), p. 8.
146. Ibid., p. 24.
147. Ibid., p. 11.
148. Ibid., p. 32.
149. Ibid., p. 40.
150. DCMS, *UK Television Exports Inquiry: The Report of the Creative Industries Task Force Inquiry into Television Exports* (London: DCMS, 1999), p. 40.
151. Ibid., p. 47.
152. S. Thane, interview with the author, 14 March 2000.
153. Ibid.
154. See BBC, *Annual Report and Accounts* (London: BBC, 1990 and 2001).
155. See D. Freedman, 'The Politics of Television Exports', *Information, Communication and Society*, 2003, forthcoming.
156. Thane, interview.
157. Toynbee and Walker, *Did Things Get Better?*, p. 70.
158. Under the heading of 'Digital nation', the manifesto boasts that '[w]e have the best TV in the world', publicizes the government's commitment to digital TV, supports a publicly owned Channel 4 and promises to launch Ofcom in the near future. See Labour Party, *Ambitions for Britain, Labour's Manifesto 2001* (London: Labour Party, 2001), p. 11.
159. Thane, interview.
160. See A. McSmith, 'Spin Doctors Peddle New Twists to Soap Opera Plots', *Observer*, 30 January 2000.
161. On the other hand, recent research by the IPPR into the make-up of appointees to media regulatory bodies has found that little has changed under Labour rule. 'Clearly five years of Labour government have done little to loosen the grip of the traditional Oxbridge male elders' concludes the report's author Damien Tambini, quoted in K. Ahmed, 'Wanted: Artbiters of Taste. Only Oxbridge White Males Need Apply', *Observer*, 14 April 2002, p. 12.
162. M. Brown, 'Blairite "Charmed Circle" Gets Grip on BBC', *Guardian*, 11 July 1998.
163. Campaign for Press and Broadcasting Freedom, 'Labour and the Media: The Mid-term Report', document presented to CPBF annual conference, 15 May 1999.
164. Quoted in R. Preston and J. Blitz, 'Treading the Line Between Politics and "Cronyism"', *Financial Times*, 25 March 1998.
165. Quoted in Baker, *Dyke*, p. 16.

Conclusion: Labour and Reform

This book opened with the proposition that the Labour Party has traditionally adopted a conservative and reactive stance towards broadcasting developments and that the party's lack of policies concerning television stems from its ambivalence to questions of culture and communications. The rest of the book has, I hope, illustrated that the real picture is more complicated. Labour has not only had extensive discussions about the role and the structures of British television but both right and left have turned to the subject of television as part of a wider political argument about the direction of the party as a whole. Revisionists in the 1950s referred to the popularity of ITV and advertising as justification for dropping policies on public ownership in favour of attempts to identify the party with consumerism and choice. Harold Wilson then used developments in communications as part of his attempt in the following decade to paint Labour as the party of science, technology and progress. More recent Labour leaders like Neil Kinnock and Tony Blair have used the alleged power of the media as a reason for shedding left-wing policies and embracing the market. The Labour left, on the other hand, has been deeply involved in discussions concerning television reform and, in the 1970s and early 1980s, prioritized this area as an important part of its struggle for industrial democracy and grass-roots involvement in politics and the community.

Party members and committees have made positive and innovative contributions to all the main debates about television since 1951. Anticipating contemporary discussions about the need for local television and regional identity, Labour MPs like George Darling and Tony Benn and publications like *Tribune* and the *New Statesman* proposed plans for the decentralization and regionalization of broadcasting back in the early 1950s. Over 20 years before Channel 4 was launched, Labour had already decided that it was in favour of a new corporation independent of the BBC and ITV while a key figure like Anthony Crosland was publicly committed to a new channel for minority and experimental programmes in the early 1960s. Similarly, well before Margaret Thatcher pressed for the introduction of advertising on BBC services in the mid-1980s, Tony Benn and Hugh Jenkins had already argued that advertising finance might be used to supplement the licence fee and improve the quality of public service broadcasting. Also in the 1960s, Labour ministers had pondered the industrial benefits of broadcasting, discussed the advantages and disadvantages of pay television and even proposed a public–private partnership for a new fourth television channel.

The issue, therefore, is not that the party leadership has been lacking in proposals for television reform but that it has shown a weak commitment to implement them, leaving the initiative for television development to the Conservatives. This is partly because the Tories have been in office for longer and have been able to benefit from policy initiatives developed under Labour governments. For example, the initiative to set up Channel 4 lay with the Annan Committee instigated by Labour although it was the Conservatives that eventually took the credit for launching the new network. A more important reason, however, for Labour's thin record in television policy derives from divisions within the party itself. Conflict between left and right has repeatedly prevented Labour from developing a policy on which all sides could agree. In the 1970s, the party had several television policies running concurrently: the one developed in *The People and the Media*, the one contained in the party manifestos and the one discussed at Cabinet level. Furthermore, there has also been a concern on the right of the party that radical proposals for television, such as the left's opposition to commercial television in the 1950s, would be electorally damaging.

These battles between right and left over television policy have led to the establishment of compromise positions that fall back time and again on the broadcasting status quo, inviting accusations that the party has no firm proposals for television. This is a mistaken view because the party's apparent conservatism regarding television policy is the consequence not of indifference but of profound disagreements concerning the issue of television reform. The party leadership's formal opposition to commercial television in the 1950s, to a fourth channel in the 1960s or to the marketization of broadcasting in the 1980s was not the result of an instinctive desire to block broadcasting developments. Rather, this opposition masked a variety of positions that were argued out at different levels of the party, including suggestions for radical reform as well as a defence of the broadcasting establishment.

Labour's television policy has been developed through the input of a range of competing groups and constituencies. Forums like the NEC and annual conference, which were dominated by the left from the late 1960s to the early 1980s, regularly expressed their desire for democratization and their disdain for the commercialization of television. Left activists were the most vocal opponents inside the Labour Party of the duopoly and pressed hard for new voices to be heard and new structures to be established. Socialist arguments for television reform, culminating in the publication of *TPATM* in 1974 and *Labour's Progamme* in 1982, were favourably received in the party at a time when the left had won control of key sections of the party. The left dominated discussion of broadcasting reform throughout the 1970s but socialists influenced the terms of the debate from much earlier, particularly with the rise of a New Left that articulated a 'cultural politics' in the early 1960s. Indeed, all sides of the party purported to agree with left-wing arguments against media concentration and it was not until the 1990s that these arguments were systematically challenged with the emergence of New Labour.

Labour's parliamentary leadership has approached television policy with rather different concerns in mind. First, it has aimed to reach out to, or at least not to alienate, floating voters. Both Gaitskell and Crosland considered media policy in the second half of the 1950s as an opportunity to relate to the aspirations of the growing television audience and sought to distance the party from threats to scrap ITV. Second, the leadership has pursued policies designed not to antagonize media owners and television executives. While this is clearly the case with New Labour's behaviour in recent years, it also characterizes Harold Wilson's close relationship with the ITV companies in the 1960s and the influence of business people such as Sidney Bernstein and Cecil King in the 1950s. New Labour can now count on the backing of an unprecedented number of media moguls but it was not New Labour that initiated the link in the first place.

In an effort to placate these two crucial electoral constituencies – floating voters and corporate interests – the leadership has attempted to marginalize the party's more left-wing media proposals in several different ways. When Labour's annual conference voted for the restructuring of ITV in 1962, the leadership simply ignored the resolution and went on to be a firm supporter of commercial television. In the 1970s, the Labour government dealt with the pressure for radical media reform expressed in *TPATM* and at TUC conferences by setting up the Annan Committee and therefore postponing difficult decisions for a substantial period of time.

The media unions have also played an ambiguous role in policy-making because of both political and organizational reasons. First, for most of the period covered in this book, the vast majority of television technicians were organized in different unions – ITV workers in the ACTT and BBC staff in the ABS – undermining the possibility of a united lobby on behalf of workers employed in television. While the ACTT was affiliated to the Labour Party, the ABS (until its merger with NATKE in 1984 to form BETA) was not. BBC staff, therefore, did not have the formal representation in Labour policy-making circles that ITV workers were always entitled to. While BETA and ACTT did work together in the Public Service Broadcasting Campaign in the run-up to the 1990 Broadcasting Act and eventually merged to form BECTU in 1990, this distinction may partially explain Labour's particular identification with commercial television interests.

Second, the ACTT has on many occasions separated its often politically radical proposals for the industry as a whole from its more conservative approach to changes affecting the pay and conditions of its members. Despite opposing the introduction of commercial television in the early 1950s, the union reserved the right to change its position and recruit ITV members to the union. Despite its criticisms of ITV's excess profits in the early 1960s, it sought to amend Labour and TUC motions supporting the Pilkington Committee's proposals to reform ITV for fear that they would undermine the economic viability of the commercial companies. Despite calling for the social ownership of mass communications in the 1970s, the ACTT backed the call for an 'ITV-2' instead of an 'Open Broadcasting Authority'. Representatives of the media unions have played an important role in the party's various study groups and sub-committees on broadcasting but have consistently placed the sectional interests of their members above the movements to democratize television structures. This sectionalism has reinforced the more conservative approach towards television policy-making of the party leadership and stands in stark contrast to the activities of media workers, especially those in the Free Communications Group, who have sought to connect questions of pay and conditions to broader issues of media content and accountability.

Influenced by these different constituencies, the Labour Party has regularly divided along the lines of a 'democratizing left' versus a 'conservative right' in debates over television policy, although that division is by no means comprehensive. There are, for example, those on the left who want to increase social ownership of the media *and* those who favour public service objectives in a mixed economy. *The People and the Media*, for example, was the product of debates between different sections of the left, with some arguing for nationalization and others for reforms within the existing structures of television. There are also divisions on the right of the party between those who want to embrace market structures and those who contend that broadcasting has a moral and cultural responsibility that requires strong guidance from the state. The market-led conception of broadcasting advocated by the IPPR in 1994 is distinct from the then shadow home secretary Roy Hattersley's defence of public service broadcasting following the 1988 white paper. Indeed, the model of a 'radical' left and a 'conservative' right does not necessarily reflect the debates in broadcasting policy in the party. In the 1950s it was mainly the revisionists on the right of the party who took up the issue of television in order to shift attention from questions of production to consumption while the Bevanite left largely ignored it. Similarly, in recent years, it has been New Labour that has sought to reform television along market lines while the left has attempted to defend the party's traditional positions against the 'new revisionists'. In these situations, we may instead talk of a split between a 'radical' right and a 'conservative' left.

This echoes James Curran's argument that 'the simple dichotomy of left and right does not adequately describe the politics of the media'.[1] His point that tensions in the Conservative Party are similar to those in the Labour Party is supported by the example of how parts of the 'libertarian' Labour left shared the radical right's desire for independent production in the 1980s. Critical of the narrow consensus of the duopoly, left-wing Labour supporters were prepared to join with free-market theorists in the Conservatives in pressing for an independent production quota which both groups thought would help to open up broadcasting to new voices.

Nevertheless, disagreements between the Labour left and the parliamentary leadership have regularly surfaced throughout the periods of government *and* opposition covered in this study and have been crucial in determining the eventual outcome of television policy. In practice, the shadow Cabinet did not share the enthusiasm for a new television corporation in 1958 and attempted to distance itself from the party conference's firm support for the Pilkington Report's attack on ITV in 1962. The majority of the Cabinet did not share the NEC's criticisms of advertising in the 1960s and profoundly disagreed with *TPATM*'s proposals for abolishing the BBC, ITV and the licence fee. Kinnock refused to act on the left's demand for an arts ministry with Cabinet status while Blair totally ignored the criticisms from union and grass-roots activists over his plan to relax cross-media ownership restrictions in the mid-1990s. However, unlike other areas of policy (for example over public spending cuts and incomes policy), where there has been particularly vocal opposition to the leadership, television policy has rarely resulted in public displays of dissension. With the exception of the resistance to the proposals in the draft white paper in 1978 to hand over the fourth channel to the IBA, there were no high-profile backbench revolts against Wilson's attacks on the BBC nor against Callaghan's accommodation to cable interests.

This is a reflection of the fact that, up until the emergence of New Labour, television policy was simply not a key issue for the party leadership. In opposition and government, the leadership was always far more interested in the use of television to project a modern image and to publicize personalities and policies. To the extent that it did consider policy, television was used as a means of identifying Labour with key themes: the consumer revolution in the 1950s, technological developments in the 1960s, questions of accountability and democracy in the 1970s and with issues of quality and standards in the 1980s. From its very inception, however, New Labour focused on broadcasting as a vital part of 'rebranding' the party as modern and dynamic *and* as an important area of policy in the 'knowledge economy'. Although New Labour's television policy has involved some dramatic changes to the party's traditional views on media concentration and the role of the market, there are nevertheless examples of commercial interests driving television policy in previous discussions within the party. Both the revisionists in the 1950s and Neil Kinnock in the late 1980s emphasized the need for Labour to accommodate to the growing consumerist instincts of the population while Harold Wilson was loath to tame the profit-making instincts of the commercial television companies in the 1960s. It would, therefore, be too simplistic to suggest that New Labour has transformed what was previously a monolithic policy on the media into a more relevant and multidimensional one given that there are strong *continuities* in the evolution of Labour's television policies.

For example, Labour's relationship with the BBC has followed a predictable pattern characterized by both loyalty and criticism. Whenever the Conservatives have attacked the BBC because of its status as a public body with non-commercial principles, the Labour leadership has tended to jump to the Corporation's defence. This was the case particularly in the early 1950s and 1980s when Labour was in opposition and prepared to champion the cause of public service broadcasting as a necessary corrective to the market. However, when Labour has been in government, it has been just as ready as the Tories to withhold or minimize licence fee increases either because of difficult economic conditions or because of hostility to what it perceives as anti-Labour coverage. This was especially true for Harold Wilson who continually threatened to starve the BBC of funds in the 1960s and then agreed to licence fee increases because of the lack of suitable alternatives. It is also broadly similar to New Labour's attitude towards the BBC that combines hearty praise for the Corporation's high-quality brand name with warnings that it must improve its efficiency and temper its attacks on government. Labour, therefore, has been simultaneously supportive of the BBC's public service mission, reluctant to fully fund that mission and hostile to its occasionally critical political interventions.

The BBC has also always faced dissenting voices from within the Labour Party. One strand in the centre has accused the Corporation of being too bureaucratic and stuffy and has argued that its monopoly status has resulted in complacency rather than innovation. George Darling's attack on the BBC monopoly in his submission to the Beveridge Report in 1950 and, more recently, the IPPR's proposals to restructure the BBC along federal lines typify this approach. The call to privatize the BBC by Labour MP Gerald Kaufman, the chair of the Select Committee on Media, Culture and Sport, is an example of hostility to the BBC from the right of the party. There has also been a long tradition of criticism by left-wingers of the Corporation's paternalistic, establishment-minded and anti-labour outlook, exemplified by the arguments in *TPATM*. These critics have issued a series of proposals to either abolish or to radically restructure the BBC and to replace the licence fee with a more egalitarian revenue source. Yet, some of the most staunch defenders of the BBC and the licence fee against these proposals have been Labour leaders, including Attlee, Callaghan and Kinnock. When Tony Benn pressed for advertising to be introduced on the BBC in the mid-1960s to compensate for the declining amount of licence fee revenue, even Harold Wilson, despite his personal battles with senior BBC figures, was not able to bring himself to agree with the plan.

The Labour leadership's relationship to commercial television has been rather less ambiguous. Time and again, conference delegates, trade unionists and party committees have demanded that ITV's profits be curbed while the Labour front bench, mindful of the popularity of commercial television with its supporters, has refused to accede to these requests. At the height of the controversy over excess profits in 1960, Labour's sub-committee on television suggested a far less drastic tax on profits than the one eventually introduced by a Conservative PMG. It was a Labour government that raised the levy later in the decade but then, concerned about the impact of the rise in the run-up to the 1970 election, lowered it again. The leadership has always had a far more comfortable relationship with ITV than with the BBC, from Wilson's warm friendship with the ITA's Charles Hill in the 1960s to the Labour front bench's close ties with the ITV companies during the 1990 Broadcasting Act. While the NEC and the Labour left have, at different times, called for alternatives to advertising on ITV or at least for the centralized collection of advertising revenue, Labour leaders have consistently rejected these arguments. Ironically, given Labour's status for many years as a party committed to social ownership, it has been the Conservatives who have introduced the measures that have been least popular with the ITV companies: the introduction of the levy in 1964 and the auction of ITV franchises in the 1990 Broadcasting Act.

While the struggle for television reform cannot, however, simply be reduced to a clash between Labour's grass roots and the leadership or between left and right, the parliamentary leadership always has the controlling power. There appears to be, therefore, an impasse between the demands of left-wing reformers, determined to open up television to new voices and to restrict the activities of both state and the market, and those who are keen to maintain the existing framework and priorities of broadcasting. As long as Labour remains above all a parliamentary machine, with an eye on opinion polls and a nervous approach to left-wing innovations in policy, this impasse will always be resolved in favour of the status quo.

This perhaps explains the consensus between Labour and Conservative leaderships over television policy. Once again this is partly because television policy has generally been of secondary importance to both parties and is unlikely to be the site of inter-party struggle. But it is also the case that, while in office, Labour has never attempted to change the framework of broadcasting that it inherited from the Conservatives. In opposition, Labour committees have challenged Tory priorities for television and suggested a wide range of alternative structures, but in government Labour has endorsed all the broadcasting developments initiated by the Conservatives. Labour governments have made no attempt to restructure the ITV network nor the BBC, while New Labour has accepted the framework for Channels 4 and 5 and has clung to the vision of digital television first developed by the Conservatives. The one major Labour innovation, the Open University, has in practice had far more of an impact on educational structures than it has had on broadcasting. Furthermore, where Labour *has* departed from the consensus, for example with New Labour's vigorous attempt to loosen cross-media ownership restrictions ahead of the Tories, this has been done on the basis of market, rather than traditional socialist, principles.

Labour's inconsistent approach to democratizing television in the UK is not a question of individual betrayals, indifference to the area, nor of ignorance of the issues themselves. A whole host of imaginative and creative policies have been proposed at virtually all levels of the party, many of which were innovative responses to problems posed at the time about the lack of accountability or lack of diversity of British broadcasting. There has been no shortage of enthusiasm in party sub-committees and conference discussions and among intellectuals and Labour-supporting publications for proposals to open up television in ways that would reflect the principles of Labourism.

The problem is a structural one. Socialists who oppose the commercialization of broadcasting find themselves in a party with people who have gained from commercialization; reformers who wish to see an independent and critical television system are confronted by parliamentary leaders who have no such desire; activists who want to curb the power of millionaire television executives are rebuffed by senior Labour figures who want to court the influence of media entrepreneurs. Left-wing demands for more accountability and diversity have been articulated throughout the last 50 years inside the party and then cast aside by a leadership with little inclination to act on these demands. By repeatedly emphasizing electoral respectability and sound economic government, the party has in practice consistently shied away from challenging the status quo and alienating those in positions of power in the media.

The many demands for television reform expressed inside the Labour Party have fallen victim to the contradictions of a party that seeks to contain and minimize movements for radical change. The party's poor record in democratizing British television reflects its position as a political organization that is more accountable and responsive to the system it aims to manage than to those constituents on whose behalf it claims to govern. Under 'Old Labour' there were many conference resolutions protesting against media monopolies, many sub-committees considering how to make television more representative of the majority of the population and many party statements promising to increase diversity and plurality. However, as long as the party remained firmly committed to the political establishment, there could be no challenges to the institutions and individuals that dominated the television industry. Under New Labour, there are now policy commissions, think-tanks and civil service departments determined to *increase* the liberalization and corporate control of British television. The gap between those who wish to see broadcasting serving the needs of the public and Labour leaders who see communications as, above all, serving the needs of business and government is growing ever wider.

NOTES

1.   J. Curran and J. Seaton, *Power Without Responsibility* (London: Routledge, 1997), p. 353.

Bibliography

PRIMARY SOURCES

Labour Party sources

National Executive Committee (NEC) minutes and papers.
Parliamentary Labour Party (PLP) minutes.
Annual conference reports.
General election manifestos.
General secretary's file on broadcasting (GS/BCST), National Museum of Labour History.

Labour Party published documents

Not Fit For Children, Labour Party leaflet against commercial television, 1953.
'Labour Says NO to Sponsored TV', *Let's Have the Truth*, 3, 1953.
Signposts for the Sixties: A Statement of Labour Party Home Policy Submitted by the NEC to the 60th Annual Conference, 1961.
Labour's Social Strategy, 1969.
Advertising, green paper, 1972.
Labour's Programme 1973, 1973.
The People and the Media, 1974.
Statement by the National Executive Committee, The Right to Reply, 1982.
Labour's Programme 1982, 1982.
Submission to Peacock Inquiry, 1985.
Democratic Socialist Aims and Values, 1988.
Meet the Challenge, Make the Change: A New Agenda for Britain, 1989.
Arts and Media: Our Cultural Future, 1991.
Putting the Citizen at the Centre of British Broadcasting: A Labour Party Consultation Document, 1993.

Making Britain's Future, 1995.
Communicating Britain's Future, 1995.
Create the Future: A Strategy for Cultural Policy, Arts and the Creative Economy, 1997.

Trade union sources

TUC annual conference reports.
ACT and ACTT annual conference reports.

Trade union published documents

ACTT, *A Report on the Allocation of the 4th Channel*, ACTT Television Commission (London: ACTT, 1971).
ACTT/BETA, *Government Plans for Broadcasting in the 1990's* (London: ACT/BETA, 1989/90).
POEU (Post Office Engineering Union), *The Cabling of Britain* (London: POEU, 1982).
TUC, *Behind the Headlines: TUC Discussion Document on the Media* (London: TUC, 1980).

Official sources (Public Record Office)

Cabinet records, CAB 128: Minutes (CM and CC Series), 1945–1974.
Prime Minister's Office, PREM 13: Correspondence and Papers 1964–1970.

BBC sources (BBC written archives, Caversham)

Director general's file, R78.

Official documents

Hansard, *House of Commons Debates*.

Government publications

Annan, Lord (chair), *Report of the Committee on the Future of Broadcasting*, Cmnd. 6753 (London: HMSO, 1977).
Davies, G. (chair), *The Future Funding of the BBC*, Report of the Independent Review Panel (London: DCMS, 1999).
Department for Culture, Media and Sport, *UK Television Exports Inquiry: The Report of the Creative Industries Task Force Inquiry into Television Exports* (London: DCMS, 1999.
DCMS, *Consultation on Media Ownership Rules* (London: DCMS, 2001.

DCMS/DTI, *Regulating Communications: Approaching Convergence in the Information Age*, green paper, CM4022 (London: DCMS/DTI, 1998).

DCMS/DTI, *Government Response to 'The Multimedia Revolution'*, available at http://www.culture.gov.uk/MEDREV.HTM (london: DCMS/DTI, 1998).

DCMS/DTI, *Regulating Communications: The Way Ahead. Results of the Consultation on the Convergence Green Paper* (London: DCMS/DTI, 1999).

DCMS/DTI, *A New Future for Communications*, white paper (London: DCMS/DTI, 2000).

DCMS/DTI Draft Communications Bill, May 2002, available at http://www.communicationsbill.gov.uk/.

Department for National Heritage, *The Future of the BBC: Serving the Nation, Competing World-wide*, white paper, Cm. 2621 (London: HMSO, 1994).

DNH, *Media Ownership: The Government's Proposals*, white paper, Cm 2872 (London: HMSO, 1995).

Graham, D. and Associates, *Building a Global Audience: British Television in Overseas Markets* (London: DCMS, 1999).

Home Affairs Committee, *Third Report, The Future of Broadcasting*, vol. i, HC262-I (London: HMSO, 1988).

Home Office, *Broadcasting*, white paper, Cmnd. 7294 (London: HMSO, 1978).

Home Office, *Broadcasting in the '90s: Competition, Choice and Quality*, white paper, Cm 517 (London: HMSO, 1988).

House of Commons Second Report from the Select Committee on Nationalized Industries, Session 1971–72, *Independent Broadcasting Authority* (London: HMSO, 1972).

House of Commons Select Committee on Culture, Media and Sport, 4th report, *The Multi-Media Revolution*, HC 520-I (London: HMSO, 1998).

MORI, *Digital Television 2001*, Research Study Conducted for the Department for Culture, Media and Sport (London: DCMS, 2001).

Pilkington, Sir H. (chair), *Report of the Committee on Broadcasting*, Cmnd. 1753 (London: HMSO, 1962).

White paper, *Broadcasting*, Cmnd. 3169 (London: HMSO, 1966).

Interviews and correspondence

Allaun, F., letter to the author, received 11 November 1999.
Annan, Lord, interview with the author, 29 April 1999.
Benn, T., interview with the author, 19 February 1997.
Clwyd, A., e-mail communication to the author, received 22 March 2000.
Collins, R., interview with the author, 24 February 2000.
Corbett, R., interview with the author, 2 December 1999.
Curran, J., interview with the author, 17 February 1997.
Curran, J., interview with the author, 10 December 1999.
Dawes, C., interview with the author, 2 March 2000.
Fisher, M., interview with the author, 8 December 1999.

Garnham, N., interview with the author, 27 February 1997.
Heron, P., interview with the author, 17 December 1997.
Hoggart, R., letter to the author, 21 April 1998.
Jempson, M., e-mail communication to the author, received 23 March 2000.
Moonie, L., interview with the author, 13 December 1996.
O'Malley, T., interview with the author, 30 November 1999.
Purnell, J., interview with the author, 13 March 2000.
Reeves, H., interview with the author, 17 December 1997.
Short, E., interview with the author, 21 April 1998.
Smith, A., interview with the author, 6 May 1999.
Smith, C., interview with the author, 13 December 1996.
Thane, S., interview with the author, 14 March 2000.
Whitehead, P., interview with the author, 22 April 1999.

Newspapers and periodicals

ABS Bulletin, Broadcast, Campaign, Contemporary British History, Contemporary Record, Daily Star, International Socialism, The Economist, Film and Television Technician, Financial Times, Free Press, Guardian, Independent, Labour Weekly, Listener, Marxism Today, New Left Review, New Socialist, New Statesman, Observer, Open Secret, Private Eye, Socialist Commentary, Political Quarterly, Sunday Express, Sunday Times, Television, Television Today, Television Week, The Times, Tribune, Variety.

SECONDARY SOURCES

Abrams, M. and Rose, R., *Must Labour Lose?* (Harmondsworth: Penguin, 1960).
Adams, J., *Tony Benn: A Biography* (London: Macmillan, 1992).
Allaun, F., *Spreading the News: A Guide to Media Reform* (Nottingham: Spokesman, 1988).
Anderson, P. and Mann, N., *Safety First: The Making of New Labour* (London: Granta, 1997).
Annan, Lord, 'The Politics of Broadcasting', Encyclopaedia Britannica Lecture, Edinburgh University, 7 November 1977.
Annan, Lord, 'The Politics of a Broadcasting Enquiry', 1981 Ulster Television Lecture, 29 May 1981.
Barnett, S. and Curry, A., *The Battle for the BBC* (London: Aurum Press, 1994).
Barnett, S. and Gaber, I., *Westminster Tales: The Twenty-first-century Crisis in Political Journalism* (London: Continuum, 2001)
Beckerman, W. (ed.), *The Labour Government's Economic Record, 1964–1970* (London: Duckworth, 1970).

Benn, T., *Arguments for Democracy* (Harmondsworth: Penguin, 1981).

Benn, T., *Out of the Wilderness: Diaries 1963–67* (London: Arrow, 1988).

Benn, T., *Office without Power: Diaries 1968–72* (London: Hutchinson, 1988).

Benn, T., *Against the Tide: Diaries 1973–76* (London: Arrow, 1990).

Benn, T., *Conflicts of Interest: Diaries 1977–80* (London: Hutchinson, 1990).

Benn, T., *Years of Hope: Diaries, Letters and Papers 1940–1962* (London: Hutchinson, 1994).

Benn, T., *The End of an Era: Diaries 1980–90* (London: Arrow, 1994).

Blair, T., *New Britain: My Vision of a Young Country* (London: Fourth Estate, 1996).

Blair, T., *The Third Way: New Politics for the New Century*, Fabian Pamphlet 588 (London: Fabian Society, 1998).

Bogdanor, V., 'The Labour Party in Opposition, 1951–1964', in V. Bogdanor and R. Skidelsky (eds), *The Age of Affluence, 1951–1964* (London: Macmillan, 1970), pp. 78–116.

Bonner, P., *ITV and IBA, 1981–92: The Old Relationship Changes*: vol. V of *Independent Television in Britain* (London: Macmillan, 1998).

Booker, C., *The Neophiliacs: The Revolution in English Life in the Fifties and Sixties*, 2nd edn (London: Pimlico, 1992).

Briggs, A., *Sound and Vision*: vol. IV of *The History of Broadcasting in the United Kingdom* (Oxford: Oxford University Press, 1979).

Briggs, A., *Competition, 1955–1974*: zol. V of *The History of Broadcasting in the United Kingdom* (Oxford: Oxford University Press, 1995).

Brown, G., *Fair Is Efficient: A Socialist Agenda for Fairness*, Fabian Pamphlet 563 (London: Fabian Society, 1994).

Butler, D. and Kavanagh, D., *The British General Election of 1997* (London: Macmillan, 1997).

Callinicos, A., *Against the Third Way* (Cambridge: Polity, 2001).

Campbell, J., *Nye Bevan and the Mirage of British Socialism* (London: Weidenfeld & Nicolson, 1987).

Catterall, P. (ed.), *The Making of Channel 4* (London: Frank Cass, 1999).

Cliff, T. and Gluckstein, D., *The Labour Party: A Marxist History* (London: Bookmarks, 1988).

Coates. K. and Topham, T., *The New Unionism: The Case for Workers' Control* (London: Peter Owen, 1972).

Cockerell, M., *Live from Number 10: The Inside Story of Prime Ministers and Television* (London: Faber & Faber, 1989).

Collins, R. and Murroni, C., *New Media, New Policies* (Cambridge: Polity, 1996).

Craig, F., *British General Election Manifestos 1900–1974* (London: Macmillan, 1975).

Craig, F., *British General Election Manifestos 1959–1987* (Aldershot: Parliamentary Research Services, 1990).

Crisell, A., *An Introductory History of British Broadcasting* (London: Routledge, 1997)

Cronin, J., *Labour and Society in Britain, 1918–1979* (London: Batsford Academic, 1984).

Crosland, A., 'The Transition from Capitalism', in R. H. S. Crossman (ed.), *New Fabian Essays* (London: Turnstile Press, 1952), pp. 33–68.

Crosland, A., *The Future of Socialism* (London: Jonathan Cape, 1980).

Crossman, R., *The Diaries of a Cabinet Minister*, 3 vols (London: Hamish Hamilton and Jonathan Cape, 1975/76/77).

Crossman, R., *The Backbench Diaries of Richard Crossman* (London: Hamish Hamilton and Jonathan Cape, 1981).

Curran, J., Ecclestone, J., Oakley, G. and Richardson, A. (eds), *Bending Reality: The State of the Media* (London: Pluto Press, 1986).

Curran, J. and Seaton, J., *Power Without Responsibility*, 5th edn (London: Routledge, 1997).

Davidson, A., *Under the Hammer: The ITV Franchise Battle* (London Heinemann, 1992).

Davies, A. J., *To Build a New Jerusalem* (London: Abacus, 1996).

Donoghue, B., *Prime Minister* (London: Cape, 1987).

Draper, D., *Blair's Hundred Days* (London: Faber & Faber, 1997).

Dunkley, C., *Television Today and Tomorrow: Wall-to-Wall Dallas?* (Harmondsworth: Penguin, 1985).

Dworkin, D., *Cultural Marxism in Postwar Britain* (London: Duke University Press, 1997).

Fletcher, E., *Random Reminiscences of Lord Fletcher of Islington* (London: Bishopsgate Press, 1986).

Foot, M., *Aneurin Bevan: A Biography, Volume Two: 1945–1960* (London: Davis-Poynter, 1973).

Foot, P., *The Politics of Harold Wilson* (Harmondsworth: Penguin, 1968).

Foote, G., *The Labour Party's Political Thought: A History*, 3rd edn (New York: St Martin's Press, 1997).

Freeden, M., 'The Ideology of New Labour', *Political Quarterly*, 70, 1 (1999), pp. 42–51.

Freedman, D., 'The Politics of Television Exports', *Information, Communication and Society*, 6, 1 (2003).

Garnham, N., *Structures of Television* (London: BFI, 1980).

Giddens, A., *The Third Way* (Cambridge: Polity, 1998).

Glasgow University Media Group, *Bad News* (London: Routledge & Kegan Paul, 1976).

Glasgow University Media Group, *More Bad News* (London: Routledge & Kegan Paul, 1980).

Goldie, G. W., *Facing the Nation: Television and Politics 1936–1976* (London: Bodley Head, 1977).

Goodwin, P., *Television under the Tories: Broadcasting Policy, 1979–1997* (London: BFI, 1998).

Gould, P., *The Unfinished Revolution: How the Modernisers Saved the Labour*

Party (London: Little, Brown, 1998).

Harris, K., *Attlee* (London: Weidenfeld & Nicolson, 1982).

Harrison, R., 'Introduction', in R. Harrison (ed.), *The Independent Collier* (Hassocks: Harvester Press, 1978), pp. 1–16.

Haseler, S., *The Gaitskellites* (London: Macmillan, 1969).

Hatfield, M., *The House the Left Built: Inside Labour Policy Making 1970–1975* (London: Victor Gollancz, 1978).

Heffernan, R. and Marqusee, M., *Defeat from the Jaws of Victory* (London: Verso, 1992).

Hennessy, P., Walker, D. and Cockerell, M., *Sources Close to the Prime Minister* (London: Macmillan, 1985).

Hewison, R., *Too Much: Art and Society in the Sixties: 1960–1975* (London: Macmillan, 1988).

Hill, Lord, *Behind the Screen: The Broadcasting Memoirs of Lord Hill of Luton* (London: Sidgwick & Jackson, 1974).

Hodgson, G., *Labour at the Crossroads* (Oxford: Martin Robertson, 1981).

Hoggart, R., *The Uses of Literacy* (Harmondsworth: Penguin, 1960).

Holland, S., *The Socialist Challenge* (London: Quartet, 1975).

Holmes, M., *The Labour Government: 1974–79: Political Aims and Economic Reality* (London: Macmillan, 1985).

Hood, S., *On Television* (London: Pluto, 1987).

Hughes, C. and Wintour, P., *Labour Rebuilt: The New Model Party* (London: Fourth Estate, 1990).

Isaacs, J., *Storm Over 4: A Personal Account* (London: Weidenfeld & Nicolson, 1989).

Jenkins, M., *Bevanism: Labour's High Tide* (Nottingham: Spokesman, 1979).

Jenkins, R., *Tony Benn: A Political Biography* (London: Writers & Readers, 1980).

Jenkins, R., *A Life at the Centre* (London: Macmillan, 1991).

Jones, T., 'Neil Kinnock's Socialist Journey: From Clause Four to the Policy Review', *Contemporary Record*, 8, 3 (1994), pp. 567–88.

Jones, T., *Remaking the Labour Party: From Gaitskell to Blair* (London: Routledge, 1996).

Kinnock, N., 'Reforming the Labour Party', *Contemporary Record*, 8, 3 (1994), pp. 535–54.

Kogan, D. and Kogan, M., *The Battle for the Labour Party* (London: Kogan Page, 1982).

Lambert, S., *Channel Four: Television with a Difference?* (London: BFI, 1982).

Leadbetter, C., *Living on Thin Air* (London: Viking, 1999).

MacShane, D., 'Media Policy and the Left', in J. Seaton and B. Pimlott (eds), *The Media in British Politics* (Aldershot: Avebury, 1987), pp. 215–35.

Mandelson, P. and Liddle, R., *The Blair Revolution: Can New Labour Deliver?* (London: Faber & Faber, 1996).

Mayhew, C., *Dear Viewer* (London: Lincolns Praeger, 1953).

Mayhew, C., *Commercial Television: What is to be Done?* (London: Fabian Society, 1959).

Mikardo, I., *Back-Bencher* (London: Weidenfeld & Nicolson, 1988).

Miliband, R., *Parliamentary Socialism: A Study in the Politics of Labour* (London: George Allen & Unwin, 1961).

Milne, A., *DG: The Memoirs of a British Broadcaster* (London: Hodder & Stoughton, 1988).

Minkin, L., *The Labour Party Conference* (Manchester: Manchester University Press, 1980).

Moorhead, C., *Sidney Bernstein: A Biography* (London: Jonathan Cape, 1984).

Morgan, A., *Harold Wilson* (London: Pluto, 1992).

Mulgan, G. and Worpole, K., *Saturday Night or Sunday Morning: From Arts to Industry – New Forms of Cultural Policy* (London: Comedia, 1986).

National Television Council, *Britain Unites against Commercial TV* (London: NTC, 1953).

O'Malley, T., *Closedown? The BBC and Government Broadcasting Policy, 1979–92* (London: Pluto, 1994).

O'Malley, T., 'Labour and the 1947–9 Royal Commission on the Press', in M. Bromley and T. O'Malley (eds), *A Journalism Reader* (London: Routledge, 1997), pp. 126–58.

Panitch, L. and Leys, C., *The End of Parliamentary Socialism: From New Left to New Labour* (London: Verso, 1997).

Pelling, H. and Reid, A., *A Short History of the Labour Party*, 11th edn (London: Macmillan, 1996).

Pimlott, B., 'The Labour Left', in C. Cook and I. Taylor (eds), *The Labour Party* (London: Longman, 1980), pp. 163–88.

Pimlott, B., *Harold Wilson* (London: Harper Collins, 1993).

Ponting, C., *Breach of Promise: Labour in Power 1964–1970* (London: Hamish Hamilton, 1989).

Potter, J., *Politics and Control, 1968–80* (vol. III of *Independent Television in Britain*) (London: Macmillan, 1989).

Rawnsley, A., *Servants of the People: The Inside Story of New Labour* (London: Penguin, 2001).

Robinson, D., *Contrast on Pilkington* (London: BFI, 1962).

Sendall, B., *Origin and Foundation, 1946–62*: vol. I of *Independent Television in Britain* (London: Macmillan, 1982).

Sendall, B., *Expansion and Change, 1958–68*: vol. II of *Independent Television in Britain* (London: Macmillan, 1983).

Seyd, P., *The Rise and Fall of the Labour Left* (London: Macmillan, 1987).

Shaw, E., *Discipline and Discord in the Labour Party* (Manchester: Manchester University Press, 1988).

Shaw, E., *The Labour Party since 1979: Crisis and Transformation* (London: Routledge, 1994).

Shonfield, A., *Modern Capitalism: The Changing Balance of Public and Private*

Power (New York: Oxford University Press, 1969).

Shulman, M., *The Least Worst Television in the World* (London: Barrie & Jenkins, 1973).

Smith, A. (ed.), *British Broadcasting* (Newton Abbot: David & Charles, 1974).

Smith, A., *The Shadow in the Cave* (London: Quartet, 1976).

Smith, C., *Creative Britain* (London: Faber & Faber, 1998).

Thompson, E. P., 'The New Left', *The New Reasoner*, Summer 1959, pp. 1–17.

Thompson, E. P., *Customs in Common* (Harmondsworth: Penguin, 1993).

Thorpe, A., *A History of the British Labour Party* (London: Macmillan, 1997).

Toynbee, P. and Walker, D., *Did Things Get Better: An Audit of Labour's Successes and Failures* (London: Penguin, 2001).

Warde, A., *Consensus and Beyond: The Development of Labour Party Strategy since the Second World War* (Manchester: Manchester University Press, 1982).

Whale, J., *The Politics of the Media* (London: Fontana, 1977).

Whitehead, P., *The Writing on the Wall: Britain in the Seventies* (London: Michael Joseph, 1985).

Whitehead, P., 'The Labour Governments: 1974–1979', in P. Hennessy and A. Seldon (eds), *Ruling Performance: British Governments from Attlee to Thatcher* (Oxford: Basil Blackwell, 1989), pp. 241–73.

Williams, P., *Hugh Gaitskell: A Political Biography* (London: Jonathan Cape, 1979).

Williams, R., *The Long Revolution* (London: Chatto & Windus, 1961).

Williams, R., *The Existing Alternatives in Comunications* (London: Fabian Society, 1963).

Wilson, H., *The Labour Government 1964–70* (Harmondsworth: Pelican, 1974).

Wilson, H. H., *Pressure Group: The Campaign for Commercial Television* (London: Secker & Warburg, 1961).

Wright, A. and Carter, M., *The People's Party: The History of the Labour Party* (London: Thames & Hudson, 1997).

Ziegler, P., *Wilson: The Authorised Life* (London: Weidenfeld & Nicolson, 1993).

Index

DISCARDED
CONCORDIA UNIV. LIBRARY
CONCORDIA UNIVERSITY LIBRARIES
GEORGES P. VANIER LIBRARY LOYOLA CAMPUS